Erol Gelenbe · Paolo Campegiani
Tadeusz Czachórski · Sokratis K. Katsikas
Ioannis Komnios · Luigi Romano
Dimitrios Tzovaras (Eds.)

Security in Computer and Information Sciences

First International ISCIS Security Workshop 2018
Euro-CYBERSEC 2018
London, UK, February 26–27, 2018
Revised Selected Papers

Editors
Erol Gelenbe
Imperial College
London, UK

Paolo Campegiani
bit4id
Napoli, Italy

Tadeusz Czachórski
Institute of Theoretical and Applied Informatics
Polish Academy of Sciences
Gliwice, Poland

Sokratis K. Katsikas
Norwegian University of Science and Technology
Gjovik, Norway

Ioannis Komnios
EXUS SOFTWARE
London, UK

Luigi Romano
University of Naples Parthenope
Naples, Italy

Dimitrios Tzovaras
CERTH/Informatics and Telematics Institute
Thessaloniki, Greece

https://doi.org/10.1007/978-3-319-95189-8

Preface

The International Symposia on Computer and Information Sciences (ISCIS) were launched in Ankara, Turkey, in 1986 and the 31st event took place in Krakow, Poland, in 2016. Recent ISCIS symposia, centered broadly on computer science and engineering, have been published by Springer and have attracted hundreds of thousands of paper downloads over the years [1–7]. In 2018, both the present ISCIS 2018 Workshop on Cybersecurity, and the regular ISCIS 2018 Symposium took place.

Cybersecurity is at the forefront of our concerns for information technology across the world. Thus the number of research projects funded by the European Commission in this field has significantly increased, and these proceedings present some of the current trends and outcomes of this research.

I am particularly grateful to my co-editors, P. Campegiani, T. Czachórski, S. Katsikas, I. Komnios, L. Romano, and D. Tzovaras, for their active participation in refereeing and improving the papers. I am also grateful to all those who submitted papers; unfortunately we were unable to include into these proceedings all the papers that were submitted.

The proceedings start with an overview of the contents of this volume, providing insight into how some of these contributions are interconnected and linking them to prior ideas and work. It then follows with a series of research papers on cybersecurity research in Europe that covers five projects funded by the European Commission:

- KONFIDO on the security of communications and data transfers for interconnected European national or regional health services
- GHOST regarding the security of IoT systems for the home and the design of secure IoT home gateways
- SerIoT on the cybersecurity of IoT systems in general with a range of applications in supply chains, smart cities, and other areas
- NEMESYS, a now completed research project on the security of mobile networks
- SDK4ED, a new project that addresses security only incidentally but that focuses of broader issues of computation time, energy consumption, and reliability of software

The overview is followed by three papers included from the KONFIDO project concerning the security of trans-European data transfers.

They are followed by papers concerning security of the IoT starting with work that discusses the creation of a market for IoT Security. The following three papers from the GHOST project are directly related to IoT security. They are followed by a paper that describes the European Commission-funded SerIoT project that started in 2018.

Mobile phones can connect opportunistically to ambient wireless networks, resulting in some malware being installed on the devices; this issue is discussed in the next paper in which machine-learning techniques are used to detect malware attacks. On a related but distinct matter, a paper from the NEMESYS Project [9] presents research on attacks to the signalling and control plane of mobile networks, and shows how such attacks may be detected and mitigated.

The final paper addresses a problem that is common to all of the projects and papers in this volume, namely, how to check the security of the software that is used in all of our systems. Thus this last paper proposes a static analysis approach to test and verify the security of software, and emanates from the SDK4ED project funded by the European Commission.

June 2018 Erol Gelenbe

References

1. Gelenbe, E., Lent, R., Sakellari, G., Sacan, A., Toroslu, I. H., Yazici, A. (eds.): Computer and Information Sciences - Proceedings of the 25th International Symposium on Computer and Information Sciences, London, UK, September 22–24, 2010, Lecture Notes in Electrical Engineering, vol. 62. Springer (2010), https://doi.org/10.1007/978-90-481-9794-1
2. Gelenbe, E., Lent, R., Sakellari, G. (eds.): Computer and Information Sciences II - 26th International Symposium on Computer and Information Sciences, London, UK, 26–28 September 2011. Springer (2011), https://doi.org/10.1007/978-1-4471-2155-8
3. Gelenbe, E., Lent, R. (eds.): Computer and Information Sciences III - 27th International Symposium on Computer and Information Sciences, Paris, France, October 3-4, 2012. Springer (2013), https://doi.org/10.1007/978-1-4471-4594-3
4. Gelenbe, E., Lent, R. (eds.): Information Sciences and Systems 2013 - Proceedings of the 28th International Symposium on Computer and Information Sciences, ISCIS 2013, Paris, France, October 28–29, 2013, Lecture Notes in Electrical Engineering, vol. 264. Springer (2013), https://doi.org/10.1007/978-3-319-01604-7
5. Czachórski, T., Gelenbe, E., Lent, R. (eds.): Information Sciences and Systems 2014 - Proceedings of the 29th International Symposium on Computer and Information Sciences, ISCIS 2014, Krakow, Poland, October 27–28, 2014. Springer (2014), https://doi.org/10.1007/978-3-319-09465-6
6. Abdelrahman, O. H., Gelenbe, E., Görbil, G., Lent, R. (eds.): Information Sciences and Systems 2015 - 30th International Symposium on Computer and Information Sciences, ISCIS 2015, London, UK, 21–24 September 2015, Lecture Notes in Electrical Engineering, vol. 363. Springer (2016), https://doi.org/10.1007/978-3-319-22635-4
7. Czachórski, T., Gelenbe, E., Grochla, K., Lent, R. (eds.): Computer and Information Sciences - 31st International Symposium, ISCIS 2016, Kraków, Poland, October 27–28, 2016, Proceedings, Communications in Computer and Information Science, vol. 659 (2016), https://doi.org/10.1007/978-3-319-47217-1

8. Gorbil, G., Gelenbe, E.: Opportunistic communications for emergency support systems. Procedia Computer Science 5, 39–47 (2011)
9. Gelenbe, E., Gorbil, G., Tzovaras, D., Liebergeld, S., Garcia, D., Baltatu, M., Lyberopoulos, G.: Security for smart mobile networks: The NEMESYS approach. In: Privacy and Security in Mobile Systems (PRISMS), 2013 International Conference on. pp. 1–8. IEEE (2013)

Organization

The 32nd International Symposium on Computer and Information Sciences was held at Imperial College London on February 26 2018.

Symposium Chair and Organizer

Erol Gelenbe	Imperial College London, UK

Program Committee

Erol Gelenbe	Imperial College London, UK
Paolo Campegiani	Bit4id, Naples, Italy
Tadeusz Czachòrski	IITIS-PAN, Gliwice, Poland
Ioannis Komnios	EXUS, London, UK
Sokratis Katsikas	NTNU, Gjøvik, Norway
Luigi Romano	Università Parthenope, Naples, Italy
Dimitrios Tzovaras	ITI-CERTH, Thessaloniki, Greece

Contents

Some Current Cybersecurity Research in Europe

Mehmet Ufuk Çağlayan(✉)

Department of Computer Engineering, Yaşar University, Izmir, Turkey
ufuk.caglayan@yasar.edu.tr

Abstract. We present a brief summary of the papers that were presented at the Security Workshop 2018 of the International Symposium on Computer and Information Sciences (ISCIS) that was held on February 26, 2018 at Imperial College, London. These papers are primarily based on several research projects funded by the European Commission. The subjects that are covered include the cybersecurity of the Internet of Things (IoT), the security of networked health systems that are used to provide health services, the security of mobile telephony, and the security of software itself. The papers include overall presentations project objectives, plans and achievements, and their specific research findings.

Keywords: Cybersecurity · European Commission · E-health User requirements · Cryptography · IoT · Network attacks Attack detection · Random Neural Network · System reliability Cognitive Packet Routing · Block-chains

1 Introduction

The International Symposia on Computer and Information Sciences (ISCIS) were started by Erol Gelenbe in 1986 in Turkey, and over the years they have been held in Turkey, France, the USA, the UK, and Poland. Examples of ISCIS proceedings [3,13,14,40,41,44,45], include research on a wide range of topics in Computer Science and Engineering, and have typically been published by Springer Verlag in recent years. This first ISCIS 2018 Symposium breaks the tradition and for the first time specializes on Cybersecurity, which has been my own major area of research for many years [5,18,69].

Cybersecurity has now come to the forefront of our interests and concern in Computer Science and Engineering, and in 2017 the European Union published its recommendation for security and privacy. In addition, both the lack of security and the techniques used to defend networks increase the energy consumption in computer systems and networks [34], resulting in an increase of their CO^2 impact and of their operating costs [20,34,67]. Thus the number of research projects funded by the European Commission in this field has significantly increased, and these Proceedings [23] present some of the current trends and outcomes of this research.

E. Gelenbe et al. (Eds.): Euro-CYBERSEC 2018, CCIS 821, pp. 1–10, 2018.
https://doi.org/10.1007/978-3-319-95189-8_1

These Proceedings contain a series of papers regarding research undertaken throughout Europe on Cybersecurity, including five recent projects funded by the European Commission:

- KONFIDO on the security of communications and data transfers for interconnected European national or regional health services,
- GHOST regarding the security of IoT systems for the home, and the design of secure IoT home gateways,
- SerIoT on the Cybersecurity of IoT systems in general with a range of applications in supply chains, smart cities, and other areas,
- NEMESYS concerning the security of mobile networks, and
- SDK4ED concerning the optimisation of software for energy consumption, security and computation time.

It also includes research results from the previous NEMESYS project [4,36,37] and the new SDK4ED project of the European Commission. This symposium's main organiser developed early work on Distributed Denial of Service (DDoS) Attacks [51] and proposed to use the Cognitive Packet Network routing protocol (CPN) [43] as a way to detect DDoS, counter-attack by tracing the attacking traffic upstream, and to use CPN's ACK packets to give "drop orders" to upstream routers that convey the attack [51,73]. This approach was evaluated to detect worm attacks and to forward the users' traffic on routes avoiding infected nodes [77,78], and continued with the study of software viruses [28], the security of cyber-physical systems [1,6,15,29,31,60], the management of cryptographic keys [83,84], and also on control plane attacks on mobile networks [2,65].

2 Security of the Trans-European Health Informatics Network

The first set of papers in this volume emanate from the KONFIDO project which addresses the important issue of providing a secure support to European health systems.

Indeed, large numbers of travellers from one European country to another sometimes need to access health services in the country they are visiting. These health services are typically based on a national model, or a regional model inside a given country such as Italy.

The corresponding informatics systems, with their patient data bases are also nationally or regionally based, so that when the medical practitioner in one country or region is required to diagnose and treat a visitor from some other region or country, she/he will need to access the patient's data remotely. KONFIDO's aim is to improve the cybersecurity of such systems, while improving also their inter-operability across countries and regions in Europe.

Thus the work in [80] presents an overall view and challenges of the project, while in [71] the authors present an analysis of the corresponding user requirements. Such systems have obvious ethics and privacy constraints which are discussed in [19].

A specific physics based technique for generating unique keys for the encryption needs for such systems is discussed in [7]. Keeping track of the transactions in such a system through blockchains is suggested in [10].

3 Contributions to the Security of the IoT

The first paper in the second group of papers concerning the IoT, examines the creation of markets which can exploit the value that the IoT generated provides [66]. Obviously, this will require the protection of privacy and will need that the data be rendered strongly anonymous. It will also require specific security not just for the IoT devices and networks, but also for the IoT data repositories in the Cloud and their access networks.

The second paper [11] is an overview of the principles and current achievements of the GHOST project which started in May of 2017 and which runs for three years. The project addresses safe-guarding home IoT environments through appropriate software that can be installed on home IoT gateways, and it also creates a prototype and test-bed using specific equipment from the TELEVES company that is coordinating the project.

Related to this project, another paper uses machine learning methods for the detection of network attacks on IoT gateways [9] based on Deep Learning [61] with the Random Neural Network [12,25,26]. Related to the GHOST project, other recent work published elsewhere, discusses the effect and mitigation of attacks on the batteries which supply the power of many light-weight IoT network nodes [38].

The following paper, also emanating from the GHOST project, discusses the use of novel blockchain techniques to enhance the security of IoT systems [68].

The final paper in this section is a description of the new SerIoT project that was started in 2018 [17]. Further details regarding this project can be found in a forthcoming paper [35]. Among its technical objectives is the design of Ser-CPN [16], a specific network for managing geographically distributed IoT devices using the principles of the Cognitive Packet Network (CPN) and using Software Defined Neyworks that has been tested in several experiments [42,43,46,47,49]. CPN uses "Smart" Packets (SPs) to search [1] for paths and measure QoS while the network is in operation, via Reinforcement Learning using a Random Neural Network [24], and based on the QoS Goal pursued by the end user. When an SP reaches its destination, its measurements are returned by an ACK packet to the intermediate nodes of the path that was identified by the SP, and to the end user, providing the QoS offered by the path that the SP travelled. The end user, which may be a source node or a decision making software package for a QoS Class, receives many such ACKs and takes the decision to switch to the one offering the best security or quality of service, or to stay with the current path [30,39,48]. An extension using genetic algorithms [27,50] was implemented [70], a version for overlay networks [8] and a related system for Cloud computing [81,82] were also tested.

An interesting development in SerIoT will combine energy aware routing [52,53] and security in a Software Defined Network (SDN) approach [21,22,32].

It could also address admission control [58] as a means to improve security. Adaptive techniques for the management of wireless IoT device traffic to achieve better QoS will also be used by SerIoT [54–56,72].

4 Improving the Security of Mobile Telephony

The final two papers in this volume address the cybersecurity of mobile telephony. Many mobile phones also offer opportunistic connections [64] to WIFI and other wireless networks. This creates vulnerabilities that need to be constantly monitored on the mobile device itself, which is the motivations for the work in [62] which investigates machine learning techniques to this effect.

On the other hand, the work described in [74] is a comprehensive review of the work of the author and of his colleagues [63], regarding attacks on the signalling plane of the core network of the mobile network operator, and especially the mitigation of such attacks. This work was conducted in the context of the European Commission funded project NEMESYS [75,76] and makes extensive use of methods from the theory of Queueing Networks [57].

5 Conclusions

The reality of diverse, numerous and powerful cyber attacks has allowed the field of Cybersecurity to transition from an area concerned primarily with cryptography and the management of cryptographic keys, to a far broader field concerned with all forms of attacks on our cyber-infrastructure. These developments are illustrated by the diversity of the research and contributions presented in this volume. Subtending all these issues is the security of the software modules that we use in all the systems we develop and use. Thus the final paper in this volume relates to a static analysis approach to test and verify the security of software [79] which emanates from the European Commission's funded SDK4ED research project. An important area that is left out of this volume concerns the integrated security of physical and cyber systems [33,59].

We believe that the field has entered a new phase of substantial activity, and its support through funding from the European Commission illustrates the importance and vigour of European Research in Cybersecurity.

References

1. Abdelrahman, O.H., Gelenbe, E.: Time and energy in team-based search. Phys. Rev. E **87**(3), 032125 (2013)
2. Abdelrahman, O.H., Gelenbe, E.: Signalling storms in 3G mobile networks. In: IEEE International Conference on Communications, ICC 2014, Sydney, Australia, 10–14 June 2014, pp. 1017–1022. IEEE (2014). https://doi.org/10.1109/ICC.2014.6883453

3. Abdelrahman, O.H., Gelenbe, E., Görbil, G., Lent, R. (eds.): Information Sciences and Systems 2015. LNEE, vol. 363. Springer, Heidelberg (2016). https://doi.org/10.1007/978-3-319-22635-4
4. Abdelrahman, O.H., Gelenbe, E., Görbil, G., Oklander, B.: Mobile network anomaly detection and mitigation: the NEMESYS approach. In: Gelenbe, E., Lent, R. (eds.) Information Sciences and Systems 2013. LNEE, vol. 264, pp. 429–438. Springer, Cham (2013). https://doi.org/10.1007/978-3-319-01604-7_42
5. Akgün, M., Çaglayan, M.U.: Towards scalable identification in RFID systems. Wirel. Pers. Commun. **86**(2), 403–421 (2016). https://doi.org/10.1007/s11277-015-2936-7
6. Akinwande, O.J., Bi, H., Gelenbe, E.: Managing crowds in hazards with dynamic grouping. IEEE Access **3**, 1060–1070 (2015)
7. Akriotou, M., et al.: Random number generation from a secure photonic physical unclonable hardware module. In: Gelenbe, E., et al. (eds.) Euro-CYBERSEC 2018. CCIS, vol. 821, pp. 28–37. Springer, Heidelberg (2018)
8. Brun, O., Wang, L., Gelenbe, E.: Big data for autonomic intercontinental communications. IEEE Trans. Sel. Areas Commun. **34**(3), 575–583 (2016)
9. Brun, O., et al.: Deep learning with dense random neural networks for detecting attacks against IoT-connected home environments. In: Gelenbe, E., et al. (eds.) Euro-CYBERSEC 2018. CCIS, vol. 821, pp. 79–89. Springer, Heidelberg (2018)
10. Castaldo, L., Cinque, V.: Blockchain based logging for the cross-border exchange of eHealth data in Europe. In: Gelenbe, E., et al. (eds.) Euro-CYBERSEC 2018. CCIS, vol. 821, pp. 46–56. Springer, Heidelberg (2018)
11. Collen, A., et al.: Ghost - safe-guarding home IoT environments with personalised real-time risk control. In: Gelenbe, E., et al. (eds.) Euro-CYBERSEC 2018. CCIS, vol. 821, pp. 68–78. Springer, Heidelberg (2018)
12. Cramer, C.E., Gelenbe, E.: Video quality and traffic QoS in learning-based subsampled and receiver-interpolated video sequences. IEEE J. Sel. Areas Commun. **18**(2), 150–167 (2000)
13. Czachórski, T., Gelenbe, E., Grochla, K., Lent, R. (eds.): Computer and Information Sciences. CCIS, vol. 659. Springer, Cham (2016). https://doi.org/10.1007/978-3-319-47217-1
14. Czachórski, T., Gelenbe, E., Lent, R. (eds.): Information Sciences and Systems 2014. Springer, Cham (2014). https://doi.org/10.1007/978-3-319-09465-6
15. Desmet, A., Gelenbe, E.: Graph and analytical models for emergency evacuation. In: 2013 IEEE International Conference on Pervasive Computing and Communications Workshops, PERCOM 2013 Workshops, San Diego, CA, USA, March 18–22, 2013, pp. 523–527 (2013). https://doi.org/10.1109/PerComW.2013.6529552
16. Domanska, J., Czachòrski, T., Nowak, M., Nowak, S., Gelenbe, E.: Sercpn: smart software defined network for IoT (2018, to appear)
17. Domanska, J., Gelenbe, E., Czachorski, T., Drosou, A., Tzovaras, D.: Research and innovation action for the security of the Internet of Things: the SerIoT project. In: Gelenbe, E., et al. (eds.) Euro-CYBERSEC 2018. CCIS, vol. 821, pp. 101–118. Springer, Heidelberg (2018)
18. Ermis, O., Bahtiyar, S., Anarim, E., Çaglayan, M.U.: A key agreement protocol with partial backward confidentiality. Comput. Netw. **129**, 159–177 (2017). https://doi.org/10.1016/j.comnet.2017.09.008
19. Faiella, G., et al.: Building an ethical framework for cross-border applications: the KONFIDO project. In: Gelenbe, E., et al. (eds.) Euro-CYBERSEC 2018. CCIS, vol. 821, pp. 38–45. Springer, Heidelberg (2018)

20. François, F., Abdelrahman, O.H., Gelenbe, E.: Impact of signaling storms on energy consumption and latency of LTE user equipment. In: 17th IEEE International Conference on High Performance Computing and Communications, HPCC 2015, 7th IEEE International Symposium on Cyberspace Safety and Security, CSS 2015, and 12th IEEE International Conference on Embedded Software and Systems, ICESS 2015, New York, NY, USA, 24–26 August 2015, pp. 1248–1255 (2015). https://doi.org/10.1109/HPCC-CSS-ICESS.2015.84
21. François, F., Gelenbe, E.: Optimizing secure SDN-enabled inter-data centre overlay networks through cognitive routing. In: 24th IEEE International Symposium on Modeling, Analysis and Simulation of Computer and Telecommunication Systems, MASCOTS 2016, London, United Kingdom, 19–21 September 2016, pp. 283–288 (2016). https://doi.org/10.1109/MASCOTS.2016.26
22. François, F., Gelenbe, E.: Towards a cognitive routing engine for software defined networks. In: 2016 IEEE International Conference on Communications, ICC 2016, Kuala Lumpur, Malaysia, 22–27 May 2016, pp. 1–6 (2016). https://doi.org/10.1109/ICC.2016.7511138
23. Gelenbe, E., Campegiani, P., Czachorski, T., Katsikas, S., Komnios, I., Romano, L., Tzovaras, D. (eds.): Proceedings of the Security Workshop: Recent Cybersecurity Research in Europe. Lecture Notes CCIS. Springer, Berlin (2018)
24. Gelenbe, E.: Random neural networks with negative and positive signals and product form solution. Neural Comput. **1**(4), 502–510 (1989)
25. Gelenbe, E.: Réseaux neuronaux aléatoires stables. Comptes Rendus de l'Académie des sciences. Série 2 **310**(3), 177–180 (1990)
26. Gelenbe, E.: Learning in the recurrent random neural network. Neural Comput. **5**(1), 154–164 (1993)
27. Gelenbe, E.: Genetic algorithms with analytical solution. In: Proceedings of the 1st Annual Conference on Genetic Programming, pp. 437–443. MIT Press (1996)
28. Gelenbe, E.: Dealing with software viruses: a biological paradigm. Inf. Secur. Techn. Rep. **12**(4), 242–250 (2007)
29. Gelenbe, E.: Steady-state solution of probabilistic gene regulatory networks. Phys. Rev. E **76**(1), 031903 (2007)
30. Gelenbe, E.: Steps toward self-aware networks. Commun. ACM **52**(7), 66–75 (2009)
31. Gelenbe, E.: Search in unknown random environments. Phys. Rev. E **82**(6), 061112 (2010)
32. Gelenbe, E.: A software defined self-aware network: the cognitive packet network. In: IEEE 3rd Symposium on Network Cloud Computing and Applications, NCCA 2014, Rome, Italy, 5–7 February 2014, pp. 9–14 (2014). https://doi.org/10.1109/NCCA.2014.9
33. Gelenbe, E., Bi, H.: Emergency navigation without an infrastructure. Sensors **14**(8), 15142–15162 (2014)
34. Gelenbe, E., Caseau, Y.: The impact of information technology on energy consumption and carbon emissions. Ubiquity **2015**(June), 1 (2015)
35. Gelenbe, E., Domanska, J., Czachorski, T., Drosou, A., Tzovaras, D.: Security for internet of things: the SerIoT project. In: Proceedings of the International Symposium on Networks, Computers and Communications. IEEE, June 2018
36. Gelenbe, E., Görbil, G., Tzovaras, D., Liebergeld, S., Garcia, D., Baltatu, M., Lyberopoulos, G.: NEMESYS: enhanced network security for seamless service provisioning in the smart mobile ecosystem. In: Gelenbe, E., Lent, R. (eds.) Information Sciences and Systems 2013. LNEE, pp. 369–378. Springer, Cham (2013). https://doi.org/10.1007/978-3-319-01604-7_36

37. Gelenbe, E., Gorbil, G., Tzovaras, D., Liebergeld, S., Garcia, D., Baltatu, M., Lyberopoulos, G.: Security for smart mobile networks: the NEMESYS approach. In: 2013 International Conference on Privacy and Security in Mobile Systems (PRISMS), pp. 1–8. IEEE (2013)
38. Gelenbe, E., Kadioglu, Y.M.: Energy life-time of wireless nodes with network attacks and mitigation. In: Proceedings of W04: IEEE Workshop on Energy Harvesting Wireless Communications. ICC 2018, 20–24 May 2018. IEEE (2018)
39. Gelenbe, E., Lent, R.: Power-aware ad hoc cognitive packet networks. Ad Hoc Netw. **2**(3), 205–216 (2004)
40. Gelenbe, E., Lent, R. (eds.): Computer and Information Sciences III. Springer, Cham (2013). https://doi.org/10.1007/978-1-4471-4594-3
41. Gelenbe, E., Lent, R. (eds.): Information Sciences and Systems 2013, vol. 264. Springer, Cham (2013). https://doi.org/10.1007/978-1-4471-4594-3
42. Gelenbe, E., Lent, R., Montuori, A., Xu, Z.: Cognitive packet networks: QoS and performance. In: Proceedings of 10th IEEE International Symposium on Modeling, Analysis and Simulation of Computer and Telecommunications Systems, MASCOTS 2002, pp. 3–9. IEEE (2002)
43. Gelenbe, E., Lent, R., Nunez, A.: Self-aware networks and QoS. Proc. IEEE **92**(9), 1478–1489 (2004)
44. Gelenbe, E., Lent, R., Sakellari, G. (eds.): Computer and Information Sciences II. Springer, Cham (2011). https://doi.org/10.1007/978-1-4471-2155-8
45. Gelenbe, E., Lent, R., Sakellari, G., Sacan, A., Toroslu, I.H., Yazici, A. (eds.): Computer and Information Sciences. LNEE, vol. 62. Springer, Cham (2010). https://doi.org/10.1007/978-90-481-9794-1
46. Gelenbe, E., Lent, R., Xu, Z.: Design and performance of cognitive packet networks. Perform. Evol. **46**(2), 155–176 (2001)
47. Gelenbe, E., Lent, R., Xu, Z.: Measurement and performance of a cognitive packet network. Comput. Netw. **37**(6), 691–701 (2001)
48. Gelenbe, E., Lent, R., Xu, Z.: Towards networks with cognitive packets. In: Goto, K., Hasegawa, T., Takagi, H., Takahashi, Y. (eds.) Performance and QoS of next generation networking, pp. 3–17. Springer, Heidelberg (2001). https://doi.org/10.1007/978-1-4471-0705-7_1
49. Gelenbe, E., Liu, P.: Qos and routing in the cognitive packet network. In: Sixth IEEE International Symposium on World of Wireless Mobile and Multimedia Networks, WoWMoM 2005, pp. 517–521. IEEE (2005)
50. Gelenbe, E., Liu, P., Laine, J.: Genetic algorithms for route discovery. IEEE Trans. Syst. Man Cybern. Part B (Cybern.) **36**(6), 1247–1254 (2006)
51. Gelenbe, E., Loukas, G.: A self-aware approach to denial of service defence. Comput. Netw. **51**(5), 1299–1314 (2007)
52. Gelenbe, E., Mahmoodi, T.: Energy-aware routing in the cognitive packet network. In: ENERGY, pp. 7–12 (2011)
53. Gelenbe, E., Mahmoodi, T.: Distributed energy-aware routing protocol. In: Gelenbe, E., Lent, R., Sakellari, G. (eds.) Computer and Information Sciences II, pp. 149–154. Springer, London (2011). https://doi.org/10.1007/978-1-4471-2155-8_18
54. Gelenbe, E., Ngai, E.C.H.: Adaptive QoS routing for significant events in wireless sensor networks. In: 5th IEEE International Conference on Mobile Ad Hoc and Sensor Systems, MASS 2008, pp. 410–415. IEEE (2008)
55. Gelenbe, E., Ngai, E.C.: Adaptive random re-routing in sensor networks. In: Proceedings of the Annual Conference of ITA (ACITA08), 16–18 September 2008, pp. 348–349 (2008)

56. Gelenbe, E., Ngai, E.C., Yadav, P.: Routing of high-priority packets in wireless sensor networks. IEEE Second International Conference on Computer and Network Technology. IEEE (2010)
57. Gelenbe, E., Pujolle, G.: Introduction aux réseaux de files d'attente. Edition Hommes et Techniques et Techniques, Eyrolles (1982)
58. Gelenbe, E., Sakellari, G., D'arienzo, M.: Admission of QoS aware users in a smart network. ACM Trans. Auton. Adapt. Syst. **3**(1), 4 (2008)
59. Gelenbe, E., Wu, F.J.: Large scale simulation for human evacuation and rescue. Comput. Math. Appl. **64**(12), 3869–3880 (2012)
60. Gelenbe, E., Wu, F.J.: Future research on cyber-physical emergency management systems. Future Internet **5**(3), 336–354 (2013)
61. Gelenbe, E., Yin, Y.: Deep learning with random neural networks. In: Bi, Y., Kapoor, S., Bhatia, R. (eds.) IntelliSys 2016. LNNS, vol. 16, pp. 450–462. Springer, Cham (2018). https://doi.org/10.1007/978-3-319-56991-8_34
62. Geneiatakis, D., Baldini, G., Fovino, I.N., Vakalis, I.: Towards a mobile malware detection framework with the support of machine learning. In: Gelenbe, E., et al. (eds.) Euro-CYBERSEC 2018. CCIS, vol. 821, pp. 119–129. Springer, Heidelberg (2018)
63. Gorbil, G., Abdelrahman, A.H., Pavloski, M., Gelenbe, E.: Modeling and analysis of RRC-based signaling storms in 3G networks. IEEE Trans. Emerg. Topics Comput. 4, 113–127 (2016)
64. Gorbil, G., Gelenbe, E.: Opportunistic communications for emergency support systems. Procedia Comput. Sci. **5**, 39–47 (2011)
65. Görbil, G., Abdelrahman, O.H., Gelenbe, E.: Storms in mobile networks. In: Mueller, P., Foschini, L., Yu, R. (eds.) Q2SWinet'14, Proceedings of the 10th ACM Symposium on QoS and Security for Wireless and Mobile Networks, Montreal, QC, Canada, September 21–22, 2014, pp. 119–126. ACM (2014). https://doi.org/10.1145/2642687.2642688
66. Horváth, M., Buttyán, L.: Problem domain analysis of IoT-driven secure data markets. In: Gelenbe, E., et al. (eds.) Euro-CYBERSEC 2018. CCIS, vol. 821, pp. 57–67. Springer, Heidelberg (2018)
67. Jiang, H., Liu, F., Thulasiram, R.K., Gelenbe, E.: Guest editorial: special issue on green pervasive and ubiquitous systems. IEEE Syst. J. **11**(2), 806–812 (2017). https://doi.org/10.1109/JSYST.2017.2673218
68. Kouzinopoulos, C.S., et al.: Using blockchains to strengthen the security of internet of things. In: Gelenbe, E., et al. (eds.) Euro-CYBERSEC 2018. CCIS, vol. 821, pp. 90–100. Springer, Heidelberg (2018)
69. Levi, A., Çaglayan, M.U., Koç, Ç.K.: Use of nested certificates for efficient, dynamic, and trust preserving public key infrastructure. ACM Trans. Inf. Syst. Secur. **7**(1), 21–59 (2004). https://doi.org/10.1145/984334.984336
70. Liu, P., Gelenbe, E.: Recursive routing in the cognitive packet network. In: TridentCom 2007 3rd International Conference on Testbeds and Research Infrastructure for the Development of Networks and Communities, pp. 1–6. IEEE (2007)
71. Natsiavas, P., et al.: User requirements elicitation for secure and interoperable health data exchange. In: Gelenbe, E., et al. (eds.) Recent Cybersecurity Research in Europe. CCIS, vol. 821. Springer, Berlin (2018)
72. Ngai, E.C., Gelenbe, E., Humber, G.: Information-aware traffic reduction for wireless sensor networks. In: IEEE 34th Conference on Local Computer Networks LCN 2009, pp. 451–458. IEEE (2009)

73. Oke, G., Loukas, G., Gelenbe, E.: Detecting denial of service attacks with Bayesian classifiers and the random neural network. In: IEEE International Conference on Fuzzy Systems Conference, FUZZ-IEEE 2007, pp. 1–6. IEEE (2007)
74. Pavloski, M.: Signalling attacks in mobile telephony. In: Gelenbe, E., et al. (eds.) Euro-CYBERSEC 2018. CCIS, vol. 821, pp. 130–141. Springer, Heidelberg (2018)
75. Pavloski, M., Gelenbe, E.: Mitigating for signalling attacks in UMTS networks. In: Czachórski, T., Gelenbe, E., Lent, R. (eds.) Information Sciences and Systems 2014, pp. 159–165. Springer, Cham (2014). https://doi.org/10.1007/978-3-319-09465-6_17
76. Pavloski, M., Gelenbe, E.: Signaling attacks in mobile telephony. In: SECRYPT 2014 - Proceedings of the 11th International Conference on Security and Cryptography, Vienna, Austria, 28–30 August 2014, pp. 206–212 (2014). https://doi.org/10.5220/0005019802060212
77. Sakellari, G., Gelenbe, E.: Adaptive resilience of the cognitive packet network in the presence of network worms. In: Proceedings of the NATO Symposium on C3I for Crisis, Emergency and Consequence Management, pp. 11–12 (2009)
78. Sakellari, G., Hey, L., Gelenbe, E.: Adaptability and failure resilience of the cognitive packet network. DemoSession of the 27th IEEE Conference on Computer Communications (INFOCOM2008), Phoenix, Arizona, USA (2008)
79. Siavvas, M., Gelenbe, E., Kehagias, D., Tzovaras, D.: Static analysis-based approaches for secure software development. In: Gelenbe, E., et al. (eds.) Euro-CYBERSEC 2018. CCIS, vol. 821, pp. 142–157. Springer, Heidelberg (2018)
80. Staffa, M., et al.: Konfido: An openncp-based secure ehealth data exchange system. In: Gelenbe, E., et al. (eds.) Euro-CYBERSEC 2018. CCIS, vol. 821, pp. 11–27. Springer, Heidelberg (2018)
81. Wang, L., Brun, O., Gelenbe, E.: Adaptive workload distribution for local and remote clouds. In: 2016 IEEE International Conference on Systems, Man, and Cybernetics (SMC), pp. 003984–003988. IEEE (2016)
82. Wang, L., Gelenbe, E.: Adaptive dispatching of tasks in the cloud. IEEE Trans. Cloud Comput. **6**(1), 33–45 (2018)
83. Yu, C., Ni, G., Chen, I., Gelenbe, E., Kuo, S.: Top-k query result completeness verification in tiered sensor networks. IEEE Trans. Inf. Forensics Secur. **9**(1), 109–124 (2014). https://doi.org/10.1109/TIFS.2013.2291326
84. Yu, C.M., Ni, G.K., Chen, Y., Gelenbe, E., Kuo, S.Y.: Top-k query result completeness verification in sensor networks. In: 2013 IEEE International Conference on Communications Workshops (ICC), pp. 1026–1030. IEEE (2013)

KONFIDO: An OpenNCP-Based Secure eHealth Data Exchange System

Mariacarla Staffa[1(✉)], Luigi Coppolino[2], Luigi Sgaglione[2], Erol Gelenbe[3], Ioannis Komnios[4], Evangelos Grivas[5], Oana Stan[6], and Luigi Castaldo[7]

[1] Department of Physics, University of Naples Federico II, Naples, Italy
mariacarla.staffa@unina.it
[2] Department of Engineering, University of Naples Parthenope, Naples, Italy
[3] Department of Electrical and Electronic Engineering, Imperial College, London, UK
[4] EXUS Software LTD, London, UK
[5] Eulambia Advanced Technologies LTD, Athens, Greece
[6] CEA, LIST, Point Courrier 172, 91191 Gif-sur-Yvette Cedex, France
[7] Bit4ID s.r.l., Naples, Italy

Abstract. Allowing cross-border health-care data exchange by establishing a uniform QoS level of health-care systems across European states, represents one of the current main goals of the European Commission. For this purpose epSOS project was funded with the objective to overcome interoperability issues in patients health information exchange among European healthcare systems. A main achievement of the project was the OpenNCP platform. Settled over the results of the epSOS project, KONFIDO aims at increasing trust and security of eHealth data exchange by adopting a holistic approach, as well as at increasing awareness of security issues among the healthcare community. In this light, the paper describes the KONFIDO project's approach and discusses its design and its representation as a system of interacting agents. It finally discusses the deployment of the provided platform.

1 Introduction

The health-care sector has been impacted by the extraordinary evolution of electronic Health (eHealth) applications able to implement health-care practises supported by electronic processes and communication. There are many examples of technology adoption in this area: (i) Electronic Health Records (EHR); (ii) Tele-monitoring Solutions; (iii) Mobile Health (mHealth) applications and (iv) Coordinated care. The implementation of these innovative technologies has been extending the boundaries of national health care systems, but realizing an effective cross-border healthcare data exchange remains hard to achieve. In order to carry out health care services able to operate across countries, issues related to security and privacy, as well as legal constraints, must be faced. The increased number of people traveling for business, education and leisure purposes makes these issues more relevant inside the European panorama thanks to the set-up of

E. Gelenbe et al. (Eds.): Euro-CYBERSEC 2018, CCIS 821, pp. 11–27, 2018.
https://doi.org/10.1007/978-3-319-95189-8_2

the so called Shengen Area[1]. In addition, to reach a high level of human health protection within the European Union, the Directive 2011/24/EU[2] establishes the right for EU citizen to access to the same level of health-care provisioning when they travel across all the EU Member States. EpSOS project represented the first attempt in order to achieve interoperability among Member States while complying with both National and European laws. In particular, by developing the OpenNCP platform it tried to overcome interoperability issues in patients health information exchange among European healthcare systems. However, the growing use of eHealth solutions has led to many advantages in terms of patients life expectancy, but simultaneously has resulted in a proliferation of cyber-crime and in the creation of malicious applications aiming at accessing sensitive health-care data, the privacy and confidentiality of which must be guaranteed. In recent years, several malicious attacks have been indeed observed such as: (i) 100 million Electronic Health Record accessed by hackers in 2015; (ii) 90% of industries outside healthcare are affected by data breaches disclosing health related data they are unaware to store; (iii) 48 National Health Service Trusts affected by the ramsonware WannaCry in May 2017. It is relevant to underline that security problems in health care sector are especially due to the lack of awareness among people. Focusing on the patients, health workers pay less attention to the risks connected to the digital security. In this light, the epSOS European Project aimed by implementing the OpenNCP Platform to guarantee secure access to patient health information between European healthcare systems. It was a relevant step forward the security goal, but a holistic approach to this issue is still a faraway target. Started from the results of OpenNCP, the KONFIDO project aims to increase trust and security of eHealth data exchange as well as to increase awareness of security issues among the healthcare community, adopting a holistic approach. In this light, the KONFIDO solution provides first of all a reference scenario with basic context information on the eHealth data exchange platform provided by the epSOS project; then, we provide a description of the KONFIDO deployment architecture in the context of the OpenNCP platform, by highlighting how the security of OpenNCP data exchange is improved by using KONFIDO; we describe in detail the interaction among the KONFIDO components and we finally give our conclusions. Other aspects of the KONFIDO project are discussed in detail in other recent papers. In particular, the ethical framework that covers such transborder or inter-regional health data exchanges is discussed in [6]. The important issue of user requirements is developed in [11]. Specific physical-based techniques that can be used to generate seeds for cryptography are proposed in [1]. The potential use of the novel technology of blockchains in this context is investigated in [2].

[1] https://ec.europa.eu/home-affairs/what-we-do/policies/borders-and-visas/schengen_en.

[2] http://eur-lex.europa.eu/LexUriServ/LexUriServ.do?uri=OJ:L:2011:088:0045:0065:en:PDF.

2 Cross-Border eHealth Data Exchange in Europe: epSOS/OpenNCP Project

The **epSOS**[3] project (Smart Open Services for European Patient I & II 2008–2014) has provided a practical eHealth framework and ICT infrastructure, based on existing national infrastructures, that enables secure access to patient health information, particularly with respect to a basic Patient Summary (patient general info, clinical data, prescribed medicines, etc.) and ePrescription/eDispensing (electronic prescribing of medicine/retrieving prescriptions), between European healthcare systems. The key aspects used in the epSOS project to guarantee eHealth Interoperability in EU have been the following: (i) Existing national healthcare infrastructures/legislation remain unchanged; (ii) Trust among Member State (MS) is based on contracts and agreed policies; (iii) Information is exchanged but not shared.

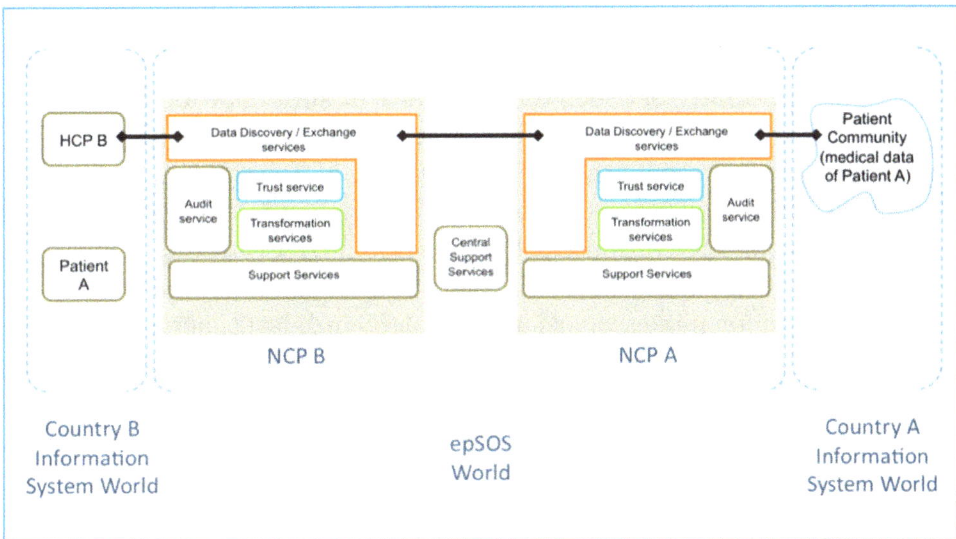

Fig. 1. epSOS logical view (epSOS documentation).

The epSOS architecture is implemented as a set of interacting National Contact Points (NCPs) built on top of Web technologies (SOAP). The platform model adopted by epSOS can be viewed as a federations of services connected with service interfaces defined by specified contracts (a SOA system) (see Fig. 1). In epSOS, the NCP is the main module of cross-border interoperability, exploiting the role of connection the National Infrastructure (NI) to the European Level environment. The components of an NCP can be viewed as a logical wrapper of the different NI. As seen in Fig. 1, the main NCP components are:

[3] http://www.epsos.eu.

- Data discovery exchange services: establish the communication in order to exchange patient data and retrieve information;
- Trust services: ensure the circle-of-trust, i.e. the validation, verification, signing, mapping of messages;
- Transformation services: needed to transform clinical document, i.e. their translation and mapping of taxonomy;
- Audit services: assuring the operations audit and the logs traceability;
- Support services: ensure response time, guaranteed message delivery and session, response time.

The basic blocks of the architecture (epSOS profiles) are built upon three main operations: Query, Retrieve and Notify. Those operations are the unitary blocks needed to perform data exchange between countries in the openNCP context. The approach implemented by epSOS is based on the mediation performed by the NCP. A Health Care Professional (HCP) requests specific information (like a patient summary) from the NCP (or to the NI) of its country. The NCP is in charge of interacting with the other NCPs to retrieve the required information, pivoting the documents (changing the position of information to allow for example the compatibility between different patient summary formats), encoding the pivoted document in the national structure, and interact with the NI.

This approach implements the so called "Circle of Trust". Within epSOS, the consumer (performing query operations) and the provider (retrieve operations) do not know each other. On national side, a Member State may have multiple gateways outside the NCP - representing Member State's health information systems, such as regional ones in order to identify and, later, access patient data. The Circle of Trust is among NCPs. They are solely able to establish mutual trust relationships. An NCP acts as a legal entity which creates a secure link between the epSOS trust domain from the national trust domain. It is the only component that has an identity in both domains. The framework implemented by epSOS to achieve the aforementioned scope has been named OpenNCP.

epSOS Security Aspects. In epSOS, the security of communications is ensured by employing cryptography and secure protocols. The security of communicating parties is not enforced by technical means; it is instead provided by legally binding agreement. Furthermore, epSOS does not offer any protection against the propagation of cyber attacks, because they are out of the project scope. Therefore, attacks which succeed in compromising a NI can exploit the NCP to propagate to other countries. This means that, due to this chain of trust between the NCPs, if one NCP states that someone is authenticated, this will be accepted by the NCPs of other countries. Thus, compromising one NCP (having control of it) can potentially affect the whole infrastructure. In particular, looking at the Patient Summary response process (see Fig. 2), we can observe that the medical data is in plain text in almost all phases performed by the NCP. This means that the security level of these phases is the same as the NCP itself and, hence, an NCP vulnerability can be exploited to generate a data breach on the OpenNCP processes. The KONFIDO toolbox can be used to overcome the

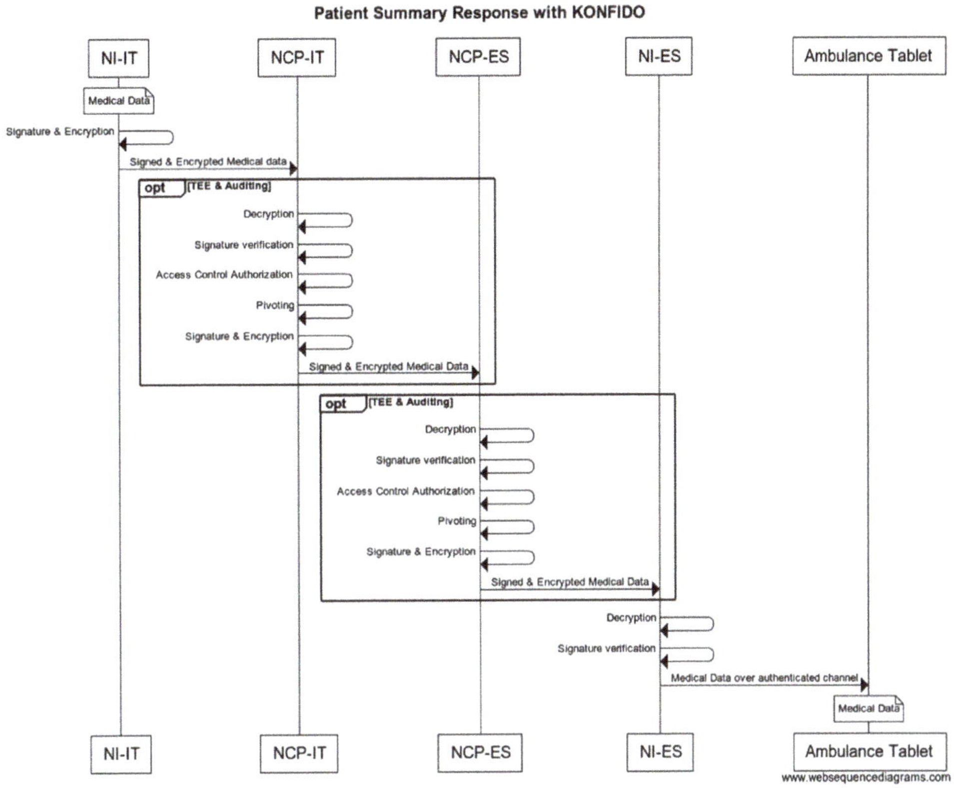

Fig. 2. Patient Summary response with KONFIDO on-top of OpenNCP processes. The *opt* rectangles highlight the actions that will be performed in a Trusted Execution Environment (TEE) and supported by the other KONFIDO technologies. In particular, these actions will be executed in a TEE to guarantee a trust and secure processing of the data, transmitted via a secure communication channel, and supported by an efficient auditing mechanism.

identified vulnerabilities by deploying a set of functionalities to guarantee, for example, that the health data will be never exposed as plain text in an insecure area.

3 Secure and Trusted Paradigm for Interoperable eHealth Services: KONFIDO

KONFIDO[4] is a H2020 project [5], that aims to advance the state-of-the-art of eHealth technologies by providing a scalable and holistic approach for secure inner- and cross-border exchange, storage and overall handling of healthcare data in a legal and ethical way both at national and European levels. In order to address these challenges, KONFIDO takes on a holistic approach by targeting all architectural layers of an IT infrastructure, such as storage, dissemination, processing and presentation.

4 http://www.konfido-project.eu.

More specifically, KONFIDO will provide a modular set of tools that can be composed to improve the resilience of eHealth data-exchange applications by allowing to address a wide range of possible eHealth scenarios (not only the ones related to OpenNCP) and to solve vulnerabilities in the exchange and processing of health data. As a first step, KONFIDO performed a gap analysis for information security in interoperable solutions at a systemic level [13].

The toolbox offered by KONFIDO includes the following tools/services:

- Trusted Execution Environment (TEE): the new security extensions provided by some of the main CPU vendors;
- Physical Unclonable Function (PUF)-based security solutions that are based on photonic technologies;
- Homomorphic Encryption (HE) mechanisms;
- Customized extensions of the selected Security Information and Event Management (SIEM) solutions;
- A set of disruptive logging and auditing mechanisms developed in other technology sectors such as blockchain and transferred to the healthcare domain;
- A customized eIDAS implementation;
- Publish/Subscribe communication channel;
- TEE communication channel.

The high modularity of the KONFIDO toolbox, allows to address a wide range of possible eHealth scenarios (not only the ones related to OpenNCP) and to solve many vulnerabilities in the exchange and processing of health data.

Trusted Execution Environment. The Trusted Execution Environment (TEE) is created starting from security Software Guard eXtension (SGX[5]) of Intels CPU that allows the creation of protected areas of memory inside the address space of an application. These TEEs, known as *Secure Enclaves* in SGX jargon, provide strong protection of code and data residing inside through encryption and integrity checks of their memory range, performed directly by the CPU. SGX can be considered as a *reverse sandbox*, i.e., it protects applications from the untrusted system outside, comprising the OS, implying that system calls cannot be performed into the enclaves. In KONFIDO, we want to perform specific functions of OpenNCP in SGX enclaves. More precisely, we focus on the enhancement of the NCP host, which is the national gateway in charge of transforming Patient Summaries (PS) from one language to another and where most critical operations take place. As mentioned above, during the PS exchange, in fact, the patient health record is exposed to attacks (see Fig. 2), when it is unencrypted and re-encrypted into the NCP. That is, when the NCP-A receives from the NI-A (National Infrastructure of Country A) a encrypted PS and needs to decrypt, transcode, and re-encrypt before sending it towards another NCP or HCP, an attacker landed on the NCP host may steal or tamper the sensitive patient data by duping the memory content. Hence, the idea is to perform decryptions, transformations, and encryptions of PS into the TEE provided by SGX by integrating

[5] https://software.intel.com/en-us/sgx.

part of the transformation and security modules into an enclave. We also take advantage of an additional important feature of SGX provided by the Remote Attestation (RA) mechanism, which enables service providers to provision applications, and to know with confidence their secrets are properly protected. In this way, an enclave must convince the other enclave with which it is communicating that it has a valid measurement hash, running in a secure environment and that it has not been tampered by establishing trusted channels between end-nodes via the remote attestation of enclaves in order to ensure secure communication among NCP nodes belonging to the community.

PUF-Based Random Number Generator. A photonic device will be designed and developed to enable trusted data sharing and exchanging at cross-border level. The operational properties of this device are based on the intrinsic physical mechanisms that are enabled by a photonic Physical Unclonable Function (p-PUF) [10]. The complexity of the utilized function makes it practically impossible for someone to predict or manipulate the random numbers generated by this device. In more detail, p-PUF devices will be employed in the NCP that will operate as true random number generators and key generators. More specifically, the p-PUF module will be used for generation of:

- True random numbers following either a uniform or a normal distribution for the needs of the HE cryptosystem scheme based on TFHE library.
- Special key triples for the needs of the HE cryptosystem based on the FV scheme. These keys will be delivered to HE module through the TEE module over an SSL enabled channel.
- Keys for enabling SSL communication of the TEE with other TEEs running on different NCP systems.
- True random bits that will be used to increase the entropy of the NCP system, enabling all applications running on the system to have access to a large source of entropy of decent quality, in terms of randomness.

The true random numbers generated by the PUF module will have excellent unpredictability properties, verified by NIST/DIEHARD test suites. They will be used directly or indirectly, through special key generation or system entropy increase, by all other system modules in an effort to increase the security of the entire system.

Homomorphic Encryption Component. Homomorphic encryption (HE) is a recent cryptographic method allowing to perform computations directly on encrypted data, without the need of decrypting it. As such, the encryption schemes possessing homomorphic properties can be very useful to construct privacy-preserving protocols, in which the confidential data remains secured not only during the exchange and the storage, but also for the processing. The Fully Homomorphic Encryption (FHE) schemes are capable to perform additions and multiplications over homomorphically encrypted data (ciphertexts), which correspond to addition and, respectively, multiplication operations over the clear text messages (plaintexts). Therefore, since any function can be expressed as a combination of additions and multiplications, FHE cryptosystems could compute, in theory, any arbitrary function. The first barrier to the adoption of FHE cryptosystems in real-world applications remains the computational overhead induced by the actual execution on homomorphically encrypted data. However, making use of recent dedicated compilation and parallelism techniques, it is possible to mitigate the performances overhead for a series of real, yet lightweight, applications. CEA crypto-compiler and run-time environment Cingulata[6] (previously known in the research field as Armadillo) allows to easily make the connection between the algorithms written in a high-level programming language and the low-level execution environment required for homomorphically encrypted data and, thanks to dedicated optimization and parallelism techniques, it achieves acceptable performance and security levels. For the KONFIDO project, the HE component used for protecting the exchange and the processing over sensitive patient data provides services at NI level, while for the NCP it is based on a new and ameliorated version of Cingulata. A first step towards its improvement consists in the release of Cingulata in an open source mode. In the context of KONFIDO, another amelioration is the design of a generic interface for different FHE cryptosystems and its support in Cingulata.

SIEM System. The KONFIDO SIEM will extend some existing SIEM solutions [3,4], and customize them based on the specific requirements of a federated environment compliant to the OpenNCP model. The KONFIDO SIEM will be able to analyse information and events collected using a holistic approach at the different levels of the monitored system to discover possible ongoing attacks, or anomalous situations. Considering the high number and heterogeneity of events to be collected and the specific solutions adopted for security provisioning, the development of a SIEM solution customized for such a deployment is required. In particular, the SIEM solution will be able:

- To treat homomorphically encrypted data: The use of homomorphic encrypted data allows for processing of sensitive information without disclosing their content with respect to the privacy requirement of the information;
- To communicate with secure enclaves: The communication capabilities with secure enclaves allows the KONFIDO SIEM to acquire data from a trusted entity in different formats, i.e. homomorphical encrypted data in case of sensitive information, plain data in the other cases;
- To deal with the federated deployment characteristic of OpenNCP-compliant scenarios and, thus, to support a distributed analysis of high volumes of data;
- To provide encrypted output using a PUF base encryption technique: The capability to provide an encrypted output based on PUF technologies allows the SIEM to disseminate sensitive monitoring results readable only to authorized entities.

[6] https://github.com/CEA-LIST/Cingulata.

Applying SIEM solutions to a federated eHealth system, such as the one addressed by the KONFIDO project, poses a number of challenges and requires the development of ad-hoc solutions. First of all, the lack of an individual owner of the overall infrastructure requires that the KONFIDO solution must be opportunely thought. The solution that will be implemented to overcome this problem is that each NI had a dedicated SIEM and each SIEM is interconnected with other ones to exchange security metrics via a secure publish subscribe communication channel. The KONFIDO SIEM will be designed to use both misuse-based approaches and anomaly-based ones. The designed algorithms will include both automatic anomaly detection methods, able to distinguish between normal and abnormal operations, and visual analytics methods, able to visually depict characteristics that assist the human operator to discover attacks and their causes (e.g. which users initiated an attack). In particular, the KONFIDO SIEM will be integrated with a Visual Analytics Module for analysing large amounts of data, containing multiple types of information, and detecting anomalies, utilizing both automatic anomaly detection algorithms, such as Local Outlier Factor and Bayesian Robust Principal Component Analysis [7], and visual analytics methods, such as k-partite graphs and multi-objective visualizations.

Blockchain Based Auditing System. The blockchain-based auditing mechanism developed in the framework of KONFIDO is a legally binding system that allows to prove that eHealth data have been requested by a legitimate entity and whether they have been provided or not. The main scenario includes the NCP of one country that requests eHealth data for a patient from the NCP of another country; in this case, both countries need to keep an unforgeable copy of the transaction, in order to be able to prove that the other NCP has requested and/or received the data. To solve this issue, we employ a blockchain (i.e., a distributed data structure) that links each block to its predecessor via cryptography. The OpenNCP node generally interacts with 2 different types of counterparts: the national infrastructure (to retrieve patient data from the national healthcare system) or another OpenNCP node (to retrieve patient eHealth data from another country). Each event of this type is stored as a log file and OpenNCP provides a web-based interface to view registered events and critical logs. In order to capture, filter, timestamp and encrypt the most critical logs that refer to cross-border data exchange between two NCP nodes in different countries, we will adapt the SmartLog log management system. The encrypted log files will then be stored on the KONFIDO distributed ledger. Given the fact that only authorised nodes will participate in the KONFIDO blockchain, we will employ a permissioned blockchain, where an access control mechanism will define who can join the system. The KONFIDO blockchain-based auditing mechanism will interact with the SIEM system to report any abnormal activity on the blockchain and the TEE to perform encryption of log files that contain sensitive information.

eIDAS Based Authentication System. OpenNCP will be extended to provide eIDAS-compliant authentication for its users. eIDAS-compliant authentication will take two different forms, considering the two different kinds of users in the system:

a Healthcare providers, like physicians and pharmacists, that must access the system with a strong digital identity, issued by their country of residence;
b Patients, that could access the system using an eIDAS cross-border authentication.

For each one of the three piloting countries, at least one authentication scheme will be supported. The deployment of the eIDAS Nodes for each of the eIDAS-participating countries is still at the beginning, so a sketchy eIDAS Node to manage the authentication requests for patients from the three piloting countries will be developed. This node will be based on the CEF eID sample implementation of the eIDAS Node, that is freely available to be customized. OpenNCP authentication takes place in the Portal component, which is a Liferay Community Edition application server. The Liferay authentication process is based on a modular and extensible approach, that shows how it is possible to have different authenticators. As such, two different authenticators will be implemented: one that authenticates locally, for healthcare providers, and one that authenticates with a remote eIDAS Node.

3.1 KONFIDO Deployment Architecture

Considering the OpenNCP scenario and the relative vulnerability assessment, the deployment architecture and distribution of the KONFIDO toolbox is presented in Fig. 3. The KONFIDO toolbox is deployed in all actors of the scenario with varying functionalities depending on the actions to be taken and on the hardware available. In particular:

- In each NCP, the entire KONFIDO solutions will be deployed. A TEE will be used to secure all actions needed to achieve a secure patient summary exchange; a PUF component will be deployed and integrated to achieve an unclonable key generator that can be used to generate keys, certificates and to secure the communication channels; an eIDAS service will be used to improve the actors authentication; the Auditing Services will be used to be compliant with log management/storing regulations; a HE technique will be used to allow the data processing for example of the PS without having to use the relative plain text.
- In each NI, a light version of the KONFIDO toolbox will be installed. The minimum set of KONFIDO solutions that must be installed is composed by the TEE. The TEE is needed to secure the transmission of the patient summary. Other tools are optional, in particular for the PUF component

(considering that an additional hardware is needed), its installation is required only on the corresponding NCP. The NCP will provide the PUF services to the NI via specific APIs offered by the TEE.
- In each terminal device, a KONFIDO client can be installed to allow a secure communication with the NI (optional).

Considering the high number of heterogeneous devices that can be involved in the OpenNCP scenario, the specific solutions adopted for security provisioning and their hardware requirements, KONFIDO will provide different communication channels to cover all possible situations:

- TEE communication channel: It is a trusted channel established using remote attestation between TEE based on Intel SGX technology. This communication channel allows the data exchange between SGX enclaves using PUF technologies for the keys used during the remote attestation.
- SSL communication channel between SGX-based TEE and other TEEs: It is a secure communication channel (SSL) to allow the communications between TEEs based on different technologies like Intel SGX and ARM Trust Zone (ARM TZ).
- HE+SSL communication channel: It is a homomorphic encrypted SSL communication channel to be used when TEE technologies are not available (for example in mobile devices or in NCP without TEE support).
- SSL communication channel: It is a standard communication channel used only for local data exchange like the communication between the PUF hardware and the TEE.
- OpenNCP communication channel: It is the standard OpenNCP communication channel.

Furthermore, in order to protect the OpenNCP infrastructure from distributed attacks (e.g. DDoS), a SIEM solution is needed. Considering the management/hosting issues and national regulations coming from a centralized SIEM, only a distributed solution is applicable: each NCP will have its SIEM that looks at corresponding NI and that is interconnected with other SIEMs to exchange security metrics via a publish-subscribe communication channel (Fig. 3). Two specialized TEE data hooks will be available for the SIEM, one providing plain data, and the other providing homomorphic encrypted data. The second one is needed to allow the data processing of sensitive data (respecting the privacy requirement) in terms of data threshold comparison, structure coherence and so on without access to the relative plain text.

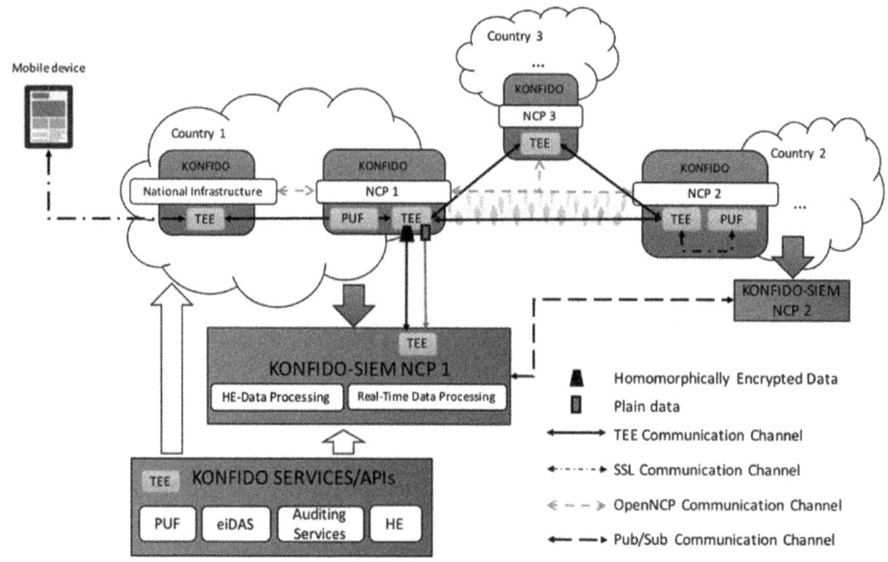

Fig. 3. KONFIDO architecture

4 An Agent-Based View of KONFIDO

The KONFIDO architecture can also be viewed as a system of interacting agents as shown schematically in Fig. 4, and in this section we describe a generic KONFIDO interface template, structured as a multi-agent Agent System (AS). This AS would be resident at each individual national or regional access point. Each AS can communicate with other similar ASs in the same or in different countries or regions, i.e. at the same local site or at remote sites, via a system such as OpenNCP. The ASs can also communicate directly with each other through the Internet. Each AS will be composed of several specialized agents (SA):

- Within the AS, the SAs can communicate with each other;
- One of these SAs is designed to communicate with the local NI;
- Other SAs are specialized in communicating with other SAs at other national access points, and one can imagine that within an AS there would be a distinct SA that is designed specifically to communicate with the SA at each specific country, and the agents can learn and adapt individually to their specific environment [9].

For each of the SA's, an automaton-like input-state-output graph specifies and describes its interaction with messages that enter the SA and which are aimed in particular at this SA, and with other agents outside and inside this particular SA. This graph represents states as nodes, and each distinct input is represented by an arc leading into another node. An input-state pair will then produce a new state (the next state) and an output.

Within each AS, there would be at least one SA which is specialized for security surveillance and reaction (i.e. the Security Surveillance Agent SSA):

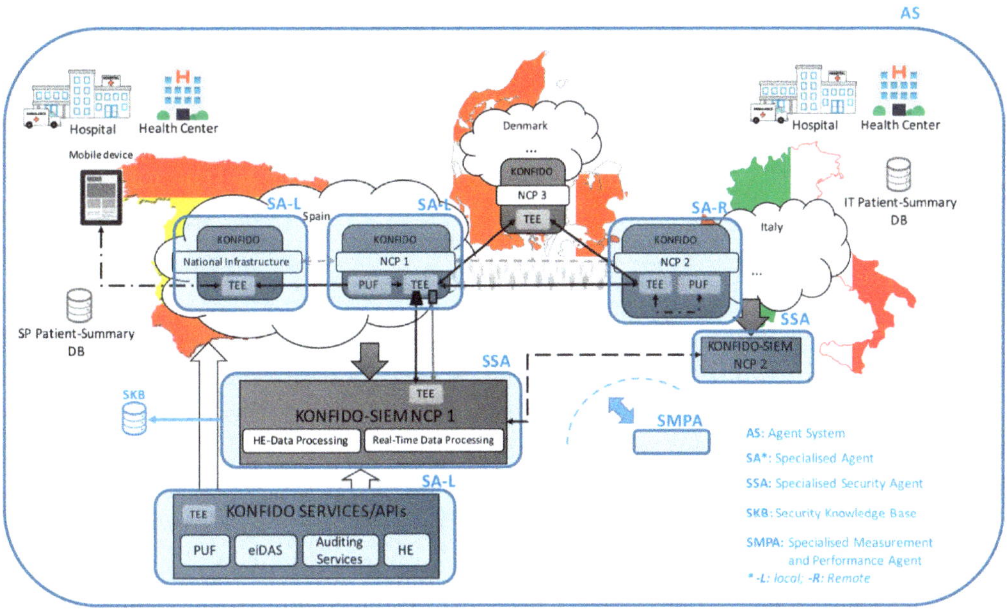

Fig. 4. The KONFIDO architecture as a system of interacting agents

- We can imagine that different SSAs can be specialised in keeping track of specific communications with the national health infrastructure, or the various communications that are being conducted.
- In addition, a Security Knowledge Base (SKB) which is local to each AS will store security related data that is relevant to that AS.

4.1 Advantages of the Multi-agent System Architecture

The AS architecture has several advantages over other approaches:

- It allows the designer to introduce new functionalities by introducing new SAs;
- This architecture allows for negotiations and economic exchanges between agents, that can offer means for distributed decision making;
- It simplifies the documentation since each AS with its collection of SAs follows the same standard template. Each AS, and each SA, is designed starting from the same core template and code, which should be portable between different countries, regions and access points;
- Code and agents can be shared as needed across multiple countries and access points;
- It allows for the separate concurrent execution of the SA within the same AS, so that we can benefit from parallelism to reduce execution times and also to limit the sequential dependence between different SAs;
- Each SA can be separately stopped and restarted as needed, or deleted, independently of the other SAs. Each individual agent can use its own access controls and attack detection [12] and we can monitor energy and resource usage for each agent separately [8];

- The automaton-theoretic representation proposed for each SA allows the input sequence, i.e. the sequences of messages that are directed to any specific SA, to be processed using standard parsing and interpretation algorithms both off-line, for instance during system development, or when one simulates a given AS to test and evaluate its operation. The same is true for the output message sequences.

Some of these advantages also relate directly to security:

- This also allows us to design the security surveillance for each SA based on standard parsing and formal language interpretation techniques which are 'real-time algorithms' for finite-state automata, and are also real-time for extensions such as push-down automata.
- Specifically, the output sequences from some remote SA, which arrive to a given SA at another location, can also be monitored for compliance with regard to the remote SA's finite-state-machine specification, and likewise the local SA's state and output behaviour can be monitored for compliance to its own specifications.

The AS, can thus comprise a Knowledge Base which includes the automaton specification of each of the SA that it contains, as well as those with which may be remotely located and with which it exchanges message sequences.

4.2 The Specialised Security Agents (SSA)

SSA are simply SAs in a given AS that are in charge of monitoring security and taking decisions that result from this monitoring activity. One of the roles of the SSA's in a given location's AS can be to test the arriving input sequences for compliance with the security requirements and as a way to detect unusual, unexpected or unspecified behaviours. Similarly, once a SSA has accepted an input sequence begin sent by some remote SA-R to a local SA-L as being valid, it can verify the behaviour of the receiving local SA-L with respect that SA-L's specification, in order to detect unusual behaviours. A SSA can similarly have the role of monitoring the output sequences of some local SA-L with respect to the input sequences it receives.

The output of this analysis, such as the type and number of correct or incorrect message sequences, e.g. where correctness can be viewed as recognition by the parsing algorithm, can be fed into a learning type algorithm which is used to detect threats, and threat levels, and also provide data to the local Security Knowledge Base (SKB) which is resident in each AS.

The SSA will have the ability to provide threat assessments and will be able to modify its perceived risk levels for different SAs or for different current (open) or past sessions.

Certain SSA will be considered to have higher priority, and they will be called SSA-H agents. They will be able only to trigger specific reactions such as blocking certain agents, re-starting agents that appear to be compromised, and blocking certain communication ports. We note that an SSA-H will have the ability to call upon certain operating level procedures, contrary to the other SAs which operate at the level of the AS rather than at the level of the underlying software infrastructure.

4.3 Specialised Measurement and Performance Agents (SMPA)

Of course, once the system operates effectively and in a secure manner, it is also necessary that it operates promptly so that delays and congestion are managed as effectively as possible without undue delays and bottlenecks are avoided. Thus we would expect that each AS will typically contain at least one agent, the SMPA, that will measure relevant quantities such as the delay for the execution of requests, the throughput in number of requests processed per unit time, volumes of data transferred, the levels of transmission errors and repetitions, and possibly also data regarding the congestion or load of the physical infrastructure.

Such data can be used to report on end user satisfaction, but we can imagine that it can also be used to adaptively manage the infrastructure and the different SAs, including to prioritise or defer certain requests, so that overall system performance is optimised.

5 Conclusions

In this paper, we presented the KONFIDO approach for secure cross-border health-care data exchange across Europe. KONFIDO aims to deliver a secure and trust toolbox for enabling seamless interoperable cooperation of underlying medical services provided by numerous eHealth applications. Such cooperation requires a high level of security and also an high level of modularity to overcome the heterogeneity of the involved devices. This paper discussed the proposal architecture that will be implemented in the 36-month EU-funded KONFIDO project. In particular, we presented the overall KONFIDO architecture following a bottom-up approach. We started from a description of the reference scenario in the context of the eHealth data exchange provided by OpenNCP platform as outcome of the epSOS project. We presented the KONFIDO components and how these are combined in a holistic approach aiming at improving the security of OpenNCP eHealth data exchange. The main advantage of the KONFIDO solution is that it is designed and implemented as a toolbox composed by different services and tools the combination of which can be used to address a wide range of possible eHealth scenarios (not only the ones related to OpenNCP) and to solve many vulnerabilities in the exchange and processing of health data.

Acknowledgments. The research leading to these results has received funding from the European Union's (EU) Horizon 2020 research and innovation programme under grant agreement N727528 (Action title: KONFIDO - Secure and Trusted Paradigm for Interoperable eHealth Services, Acronym: KONFIDO). This paper reflects only the authors' views and the Commission is not liable for any use that may be made of the information contained therein.

References

1. Akriotou, M., Mesaritakis, C., Grivas, E., Chaintoutis, C., Fragkos, A., Syvridis, D.: Random number generation from a secure photonic physical unclonable hardware module. In: Gelenbe, E., et al. (eds.) Euro-CYBERSEC 2018. CCIS, vol. 821, pp. 28–37 (2018)
2. Castaldo, L., Cinque, V.: Blockchain based logging for cross-border exchange of ehealth data. In: Gelenbe, E., et al. (eds.) Euro-CYBERSEC 2018. CCIS, vol. 821, pp. 46–56 (2018)
3. Coppolino, L., D'Antonio, S., Formicola, V., Romano, L.: Integration of a system for critical infrastructure protection with the OSSIM SIEM platform: a dam case study. In: Flammini, F., Bologna, S., Vittorini, V. (eds.) SAFECOMP 2011. LNCS, vol. 6894, pp. 199–212. Springer, Heidelberg (2011). https://doi.org/10.1007/978-3-642-24270-0_15
4. Coppolino, L., D'Antonio, S., Formicola, V., Romano, L.: Enhancing SIEM technology to protect critical infrastructures. In: Hämmerli, B.M., Kalstad Svendsen, N., Lopez, J. (eds.) CRITIS 2012. LNCS, vol. 7722, pp. 10–21. Springer, Heidelberg (2013). https://doi.org/10.1007/978-3-642-41485-5_2
5. Coppolino, L., D'Antonio, S., Romano, L., Staffa, M.: KONFIDO project: a secure infrastructure increasing interoperability on a systemic level among eHealth services across Europe. In: Preceedings of ITASEC 2017, 20 January 2017, Venice, Italy (2017)
6. Faiella, G., Komnios, I., Voss-Knude, M., Cano, I., Duquenoy, P., Nalin, M., Baroni, I., Matrisciani, F., Clemente, F.: Building an ethical framework for cross-border applications: the KONFIDO project. In: Gelenbe, E., et al. (eds.) Euro-CYBERSEC 2018. CCIS, vol. 821, pp. 38–45 (2018)
7. Fan, J., Vercauteren, F.: Somewhat practical fully homomorphic encryption. IACR Cryptology ePrint Archive 2012, 144 (2012). http://dblp.uni-trier.de/db/journals/iacr/iacr2012.html#FanV12, informal publication
8. Gelenbe, E., Caseau, Y.: The impact of information technology on energy consumption and carbon emissions. Ubiquity **2015**(June), 1 (2015)
9. Gelenbe, E., Seref, E., Xu, Z.: Simulation with learning agents. Proc. IEEE **89**(2), 148–157 (2001)
10. Herder, C., Yu, M.D.M., Koushanfar, F., Devadas, S.: Physical unclonable functions and applications: a tutorial. Proc. IEEE **102**(8), 1126–1141 (2014)
11. Natsiavas, P., Kakalou, C., Votis, K., Tzovaras, D., Maglaveras, D., Koutkias, V.: User requirements elicitation towards a secure and interoperable solution for health data exchange. In: Gelenbe, E., Campegiani, P., Czachorski, T., Katsikas, S., Komnios, I., Romano, L., Tzovaras, D., (eds.) Proceedings of the 2018 ISCIS Security Workshop, Imperial College London. Springer, Heidelberg (2018)
12. Oke, G., Loukas, G., Gelenbe, E.: Detecting denial of service attacks with Bayesian classifiers and the random neural network. In: IEEE International Fuzzy Systems Conference, FUZZ-IEEE 2007, pp. 1–6. IEEE (2007)
13. Rasmussen, M., et al.: Gap analysis for information security in interoperable solutions at a systemic level: the KONFIDO approach. In: IFMBE Proceedings of the International Conference on Biomedical and Health Informaticsn, Greece, 18–21 November. Springer, Heidelberg (2017, in press)
14. Staffa, M., Sgaglione, L., Mazzeo, G., Coppolino, L., D'Antonio, S., Romano, L., Gelenbe, E., Stan, O., Carpov, S., Grivas, E., Campegiani, P., Castaldo, L., Votis, K., Koutkias, V., Komnios, I.: An openNCP-based solution for secure

eHealth data exchange. J. Netw. Comput. Appl. **116**, 65–85 (2018). https://doi.org/10.1016/j.jnca.2018.05.012. https://www.scopus.com/inward/record.uri?eid=2-s2.0-85048715942&doi=10.1016%2fj.jnca.2018.05.012&partnerID=40&md5=81c9e20e7d35684f36599f4d8163bf98

Random Number Generation from a Secure Photonic Physical Unclonable Hardware Module

Marialena Akriotou[2(✉)], Charis Mesaritakis[1,2], Evaggelos Grivas[1], Charidimos Chaintoutis[1,2], Alexandros Fragkos[1], and Dimitris Syvridis[2]

[1] Eulambia Advanced Technologies, Ag. Ioannou 24, 15342 Athens, Greece
[2] Department Informatics and Telecommunications, National and Kapodistrian University of Athens, Panepistimiopolis Ilisia, 15784 Athens, Greece
makriotou@di.uoa.gr

Abstract. In this work, a photonic physical unclonable function module, based on an optical waveguide, is demonstrated. The physical scrambling mechanism is based on the random and complex coherent interference of high order optical transverse modes. The proposed scheme allows the generation of random bit-strings, through a simple wavelength tuning of the laser source, that are suitable for a variety of cryptographic applications. The experimental data are evaluated in terms of unpredictability, employing typical information theory benchmark tests and the NIST statistical suit.

Keywords: Physical unclonable function · Random number generator
Optical waveguide

1 Introduction

The rapid development of technology and the advent of Internet of Things (IoT) have already rendered the interconnection between heterogeneous devices possible, making the remote access and control of our private information an aspect of our everyday life. However, with the existing forms of hardware security, and taking into consideration the size/cost restriction of such devices, the IoT ecosystem can be compromised by numerous threats, thereby imposing a perpetual hunt of new protection schemes that could be utilized. Within the last decade, Physical Unclonable Functions (PUFs) - a physical feature of an object that it is practically impossible to duplicate, even by the manufacturer - have been proven an innovative approach for the successful solution of the aforementioned issues.

Essentially, a PUF is the hardware analogue of a one-way mathematical function, which is not based on a common hashing transformation but rather on a complex and non-reproducible physical mechanism [1]. Its directionality is preserved through the complexity of the physical system employed, which renders brute force attacks computationally infeasible, while the random physical process involved in its realization

E. Gelenbe et al. (Eds.): Euro-CYBERSEC 2018, CCIS 821, pp. 28–37, 2018.
https://doi.org/10.1007/978-3-319-95189-8_3

nullifies the possibility of cloning. These two key advantages, combined with the deterministic (time-invariant) operation of their physical system, place PUFs as excellent candidates for cryptographic key generation modules, through which keys can be produced on demand, eliminating the need for secure non-volatile storage.

Currently, state of the art devices rely on electronic implementations, mainly depending on the low manufacturing yield of various components like SRAMS, latches etc. However, despite the fact that such schemes are resilient to noise, they have been proven vulnerable to a plethora of machine learning and side channel attacks, which has been attributed to their low physical complexity [2]. Furthermore, implementations that are based on the inherent randomness of nanofabrication procedures, like memristors and surface plasmons [3], have shown great promise and potential, but the technology is still immature.

Photonic implementations of PUFs utilize the coherent interaction of a laser beam with a medium characterized by inherent random inhomogeneity. In these implementations, a laser source illuminates (challenge) a transparent material that has a set of randomly positioned scatterers, the goal being the creation of unique interference patterns (speckle) which are subsequently captured as images (responses). As stated explicitly [6] in the literature a significant number of parameters can vastly affect the responses, for example: the angle and number of incident beam(s), their wavelength, and the beam diameter(s).

The recorded images (responses) go through post-processing via a hashing algorithm to produce distinct binary sequences. Their recovery is achieved through a Fuzzy Extractor scheme [4, 5]. The Fuzzy extractor scheme essentially maps every hashed response to a unique bit-string output and it is comprised of two phases; the enrollment and the verification phase. The former corresponds to the first time that a challenge is applied whereby the output string is generated along with a set of public helper data, while the latter represents the error-prone rerun of the measurement during which the same result is recreated by using the helper data produced in the enrollment phase.

The physical complexity of a photonic PUF can be mainly attributed to multiple scattering of light in the Mie regime. The Mie regime concerns particles of similar size compared to the wavelength of the incident radiation, rendering the exact solutions of the Maxwell equations necessary for an adequate description of the resulting electromagnetic (E/M) field distribution. The computational arduousness of this endeavor, combined with the fact that any modification in the inherent structure of the medium or the illumination conditions require a new set of equations, has the effect of the system being highly unpredictable and therefore immune to statistical attacks [6].

In this paper, we propose an alternative PUF configuration, using a transparent optical medium which allows multi-path propagation of the incident laser beam. That medium allows the random excitation and the simultaneous guiding of a high number of transverse optical modes, which can be perceived as the E/M field distribution governed by the Maxwell equations and boundary conditions of the medium [7]. Some representative intensity distribution patterns of transverse modes are presented in Fig. 1. Each mode is characterized by a different propagation constant, which signifies the phase change per length unit. This enables the coherent interaction between the modes (amplitude and phase), generating the unique speckle patterns.

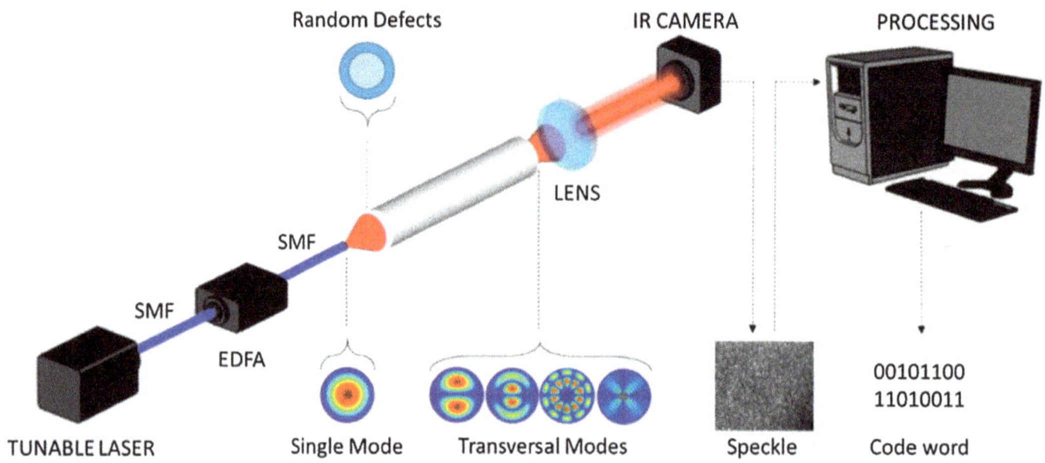

Fig. 1. The experimental setup used for the generation of the binary strings. EDFA stands for Erbium Doped Fiber Amplifier, whereas SMF for Single Mode Fiber

The experimental setup, as illustrated in Fig. 1, employs a tunable single mode laser with a central wavelength of λ = 1540 nm, the waveguide specimen (PUF) and a vidicon camera. The captured images are stored and processed offline, as proposed in [4]. The product of that post-processing are the distinct binary sequences. The suitability of the generated bit-strings to be used as cryptographic keys is evaluated through standard NIST tests and established mathematical metrics like the Hamming/Euclidean distances, conditional information entropy, and minimal conditional entropy.

The use of bulk optics and a full size Vidicon camera, renders the current lab prototype non-miniaturized (30–50 cm across); however, in the near future, miniaturized components (CCD camera) and spatial optimization will lead to a second prototype of drastically reduced dimensions (3–10 cm across). Using the current prototype, each image acquisition, digitization and post-processing, on average, requires less than a second. Generating an entire data set is highly dependent on the number of measurements and the selected delay between measurements, which can vary from a few seconds to a few minutes. Nonetheless, prototype optimization and the inclusion of a dedicated micro-controller responsible for challenge-response generation/acquisition, alongside a typical frame rate of 60fps can allow the generation of 60 high definition speckle patterns per second, thus enabling the generation of approximately 480000 binary sequences per second.

Our proposed PUF is being developed under the framework of the KONFIDO project. An overview of the KONFIDO project is presented in [8]. Other recent work regarding the KONFIDO project can be found in some recent papers. While in [9] the authors consider the ethical issues related to transborder data exchanges, user requirements are still being investigated while logging the transactions via blockchain is proposed in [10].

2 Experimental Results and Analysis

The first leg of the experimental procedure was performed by varying the wavelength of the laser by 100 pm, beginning at 1540 nm and reaching up to 1570 nm, and recording the corresponding speckle patterns produced by a single waveguide (constant random defects). The result of this process was the acquisition of 300 images, with a resolution of 340 × 340 pixels. The unpredictability of the system was assessed by calculating the magnitude of variation of these images. Moving forward, the resiliency of the system to noise was studied by keeping the waveguide and the illumination conditions constant, and acquiring multiple images (60) over a period of several minutes.

The Euclidean distances calculated between the standardized images of the two aforementioned datasets are presented in Fig. 2a. The left histogram of this graph represents the noise-induced dissimilarities between speckles obtained under identical experimental conditions, while the right one shows the discrepancies between images recorded by varying the wavelength of the incident beam. As can be seen, there is significant difference in the mean value of the two distributions ($\mu_{noise} = 46.47 \pm 9.8$ and $\mu_{wave} = 380.47 \pm 9.8$) and clearly they do not overlap. This separation of distributions is a prerequisite for the proper and efficient operation of such systems during verification [1] in order to eliminate the possibility of two different illumination conditions (two different challenges) of the PUF to be falsely considered the same challenge, only affected by noise (false positive), or two different measurements under the same conditions to be falsely registered as different challenges (false negative).

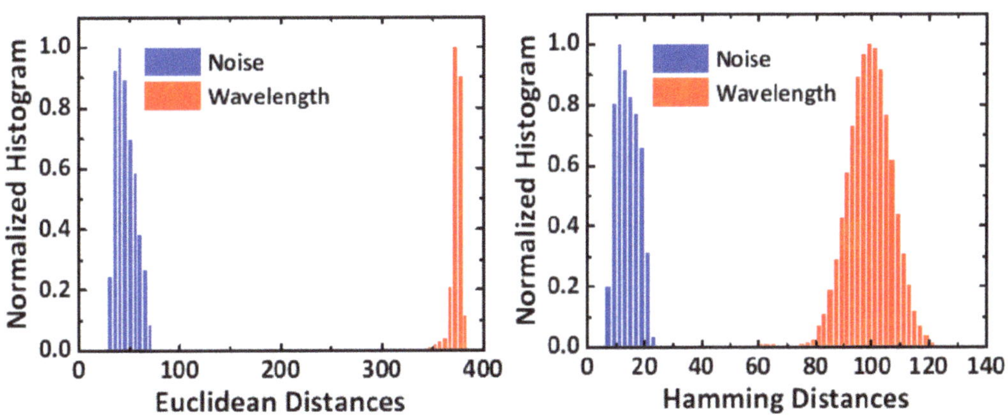

Fig. 2. (a) Normalized histogram of the Euclidean distances for system noise and for different illumination conditions (b) Hamming distance for the same cases.

Figure 2b shows the Hamming Distances of their corresponding hashed bit-strings (255 bit long) extracted via the Random Binary Hashing Method of [4]. The Random Binary Hashing Method can be summarized through the relation $\bar{y} = sign[(SFU)y]$, where y is the PUF response converted to a one-dimensional array of size N, $\bar{y}$ is the resultant hashed bit-string of length M $\leq$ N, U is a diagonal random table (N × N), containing the values ±1 with Pr [Uii = 1] = Pr [Uii = −1] = 0.5, and F is the discrete

Fourier table of (N × N) dimensions. S represents a matrix containing M entries randomly chosen from a uniform distribution (0, N), which are the indices of the elements being extracted to constitute the hashed bit-string. Finally *sign* is the quantization function, which is defined as:

$$sign(\lambda) = \begin{cases} 1 & for \quad \lambda > 0 \\ 0 & for \quad \lambda < 0 \end{cases}$$

As a preliminary analysis of the experimental setup, in order to find the necessary wavelength step, the laser wavelength was initially varied by 10 pm, starting at 1540 nm and reaching up to 1552 nm, still employing a single waveguide, albeit different to the one used prior. This process was repeated for different wavelength steps (i.e. 20, 30, 50, 60, 80 and 100 pm) and as a result, seven distinct sets of images with a resolution of 340 × 340 pixels were acquired.

Two representative histograms of Euclidean Distances, as calculated for the standardized images of the datasets acquired with 10 pm and 100 pm respectively, are presented in Fig. 3a. As can be seen, the distribution corresponding to the 10 pm measurements, compared to the 100 pm results, exhibits a pronounced tail, indicating an increased similarity between pictures and, subsequently, between the yet-to-be-calculated keys. This increased similarity is also verified via the cross-correlation coefficients (Fig. 3b) and can be attributed to a large number of excited modes being common throughout the challenges applied, due to the small wavelength variation used. In particular the cross-correlation coefficient for two consecutive images obtained with 10 pm and 100 pm wavelength difference was found to be 0.98 and 0.69 respectively. Therefore, the 100 pm wavelength step was selected, due to the fact that the cross-correlation coefficient for that step is low enough to provide sufficient differentiation between challenges.

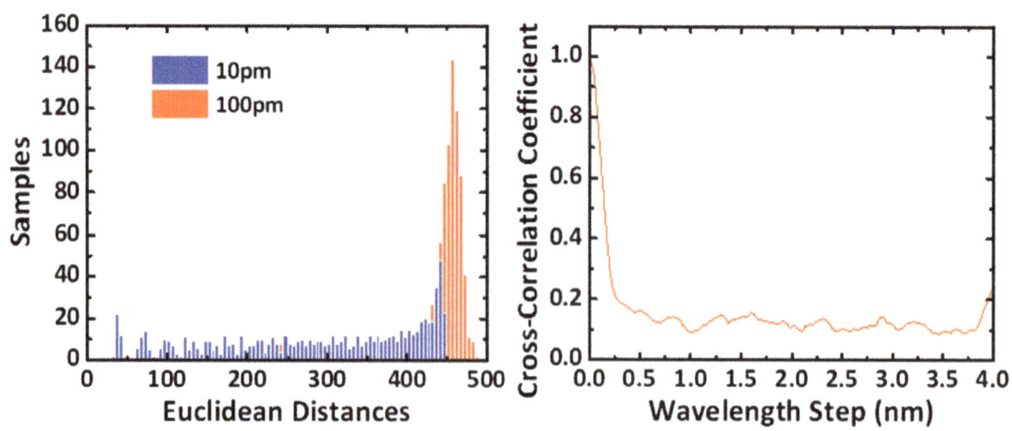

Fig. 3. (a) Euclidean distances of 40 images obtained for a single wavelength, with 10 pm and 100 pm wavelength step size respectively. (b) Cross-correlation coefficient of a single image, obtained under 1540 nm, and its subsequent responses, produced by increasing the laser wavelength in 10 pm step.

It should be noted that, between the unpredictability measurements ($\Delta\lambda$ = 100 pm) presented in the histograms of Figs. 2a and 3a, the specimen used was changed; therefore, the two distributions exhibit close but different mean values, due to the unique non-replicable defects used.

The unpredictability of the generated binary sequences is a critical performance metric, which evaluates the system's resiliency to brute force attacks that aim in exploiting a statistical anomaly or bias of the generated code words. Under that light, a fundamental tool used by the cryptographic community is the NIST random number evaluation test suite. Using this suite of tests, the random sequence under consideration is being benchmarked against the statistical behavior of a known true random number source. The requirements of the NIST suite, regarding the length and number of the sequences, depend on the desired level of certainty (in our case $\alpha = 0.01$) and are different for every test. For the level of certainty that was chosen in our case, the data set being tested should contain at least 1000 sequences, each 1Mbit in length.

So as to construct such a dataset, 30000 experimental images were utilized, each of which was processed through the Random Binary hashing method 30 distinct times. Each time, a unique matrix S was used for the selection of 1024 different pixels. The number of common pixels at the selection stage for all the matrices was chosen so as not to surpass 1 pixel per matrix. The extracted binary strings, of 1024 bit-length, from all images were then concatenated, in order to form a single matrix containing 1 Gbit of data. The outputs of the NIST tests are presented in Table 1.

Table 1. The results of the NIST suit P-value corresponds to the uniformity of the results whereas proportion corresponds to the percentage of 1000 bit strings that passed the test. *Multiple tests present, the worst results are presented.

NIST Tests	P-value	Proportion
DFT	0.0354	99.1%
Rank	0.7617	98.8%
Longest run	0.0019	99.2%
Non-overlapping templates	0.081	98.2%*
Block frequency	0*	100%
Cumulative sums	0*	100%
Frequency	0*	100%
Serial	98.9%	98.9%
Entropy	0.6931	99.3%
Linear complexity	0.4788	98.6%
Maurer's universal	**0**	**96.4%**
Non-periodic template	0.004	98.3%
Random excursions	0.043	98.4%*
Random - excursion variant	0.003	97.8%*
Runs	0.00012	98.3%

The data sequences generated by our system, as illustrated in Table 1, have succeeded in the majority of the tests of the NIST suite (14/15 passed), only marginally failing to pass Maurer's Universal test (proportion of success equal to 96.4%). However, that specific test is known to have generated false negatives on other, widely used, random sequences. Therefore, the proposed PUF can be considered as an adequate random number generator. Furthermore, the sequences which passed three of the tests which involve the percentages of 1 s and 0 s in the bit sequences, (100% of bit-strings passed the tests), failed at the uniformity test (P-value) nonetheless. The distribution of p-values for the frequency test is presented in Fig. 4b. These tests do not produce marginal results (low p-values), as can be seen in the results but, on the contrary, success rate is too high, which implies a highly balanced percentage of 1 s and 0 s in the bit sequences. The two histograms of Figs. 4b and c can be directly compared to each other, Fig. 4c being Maurer's Universal test where the singular fail occurred. Nonetheless, this is a statistical anomaly which does not impose a security breach, due to the fact that an adversary has no indication regarding the probability of bit-flips. Furthermore, the fact that we re-hash images using unique pixel selection matrices with

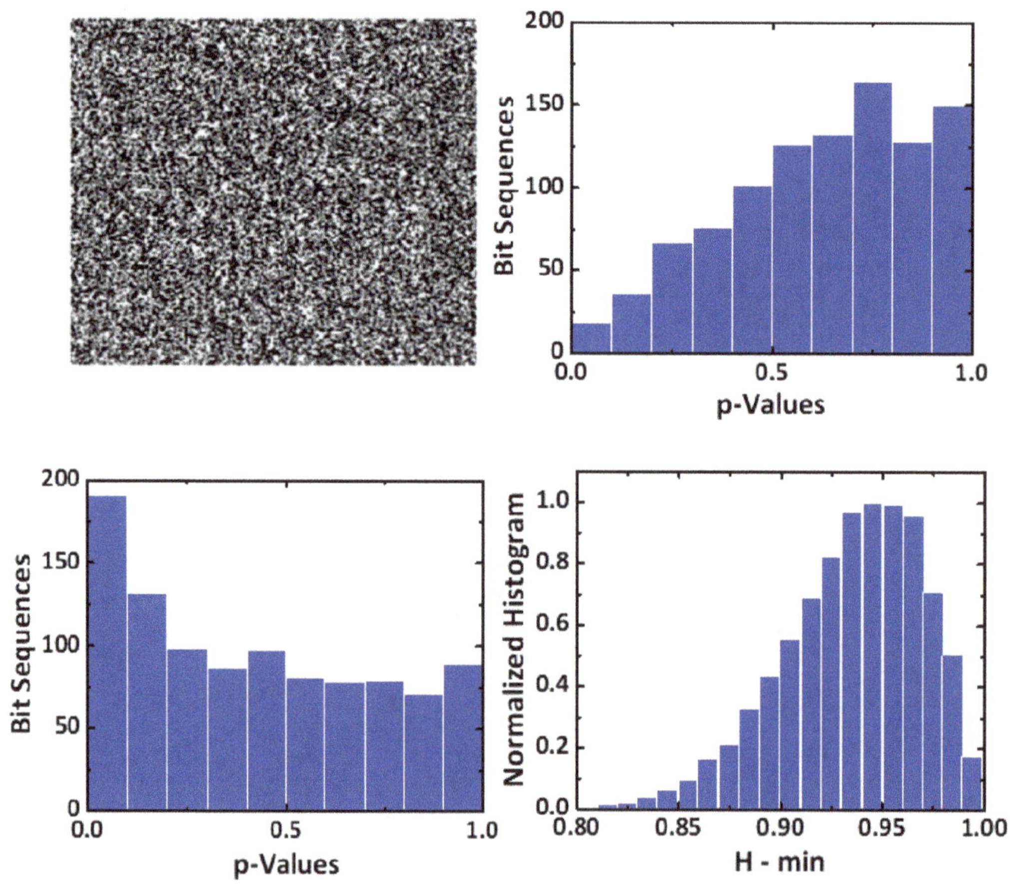

Fig. 4. (a) Representation of the experimental bit-strings, black corresponds to "0" whereas white to logical "1". No pattern can be visually identified. (b) P-Values distribution for the frequency test (NIST-success), (c) P-value distribution of the Maurer's test (NIST-marginal fail). (d) Minimum conditional entropy distribution

zero-pixel repetitions removes any potential experimental bias and forces the system to exhibit a "perfect" gaussian distribution. This feature, in turn, dictates a perfectly balanced number of logical '1' and '0' and potentially is the reason behind the anomaly in uniformity.

In the quest to further fortify our claim to unpredictability, we recruit the help of the computation of the minimum conditional entropy (H-min), for all the pairs of bit-strings. The H-min is a typical conservative measure for unpredictability between pairs of code-words. In this case, we made use of the preexisting and aforementioned sample, which consisted of all challenges from a single PUF (Fig. 4a). It is evident that the mean value is exceptionally high (mean = 0.929), thereby confirming the suitability of a photonic PUF to be used as a cryptographic key generator. In Table 2, we include the minimum conditional entropy and the conditional entropy of various silicon-cast PUFs as well as those of a popular pseudo-random algorithm (Ziggurat), for comparative reasons. As is clearly illustrated, the proposed scheme offers comparable performance to both the Ziggurat algorithm as well as the best of what the silicon-cast PUFs have to offer, all the while vastly outperforming every other implementation.

The aforementioned results provide insight that the proposed PUF can operate as a random number generator without the vulnerabilities of typical approaches. On the other hand, these results are generated by exploiting different PUF instantiations, different challenges and by varying the pixel selection procedure (so as to generate 1 Gbps of data). This approach is not practical and demands the integration of a significant number of PUFs in the same device or the use of more sophisticated processing schemes. Nonetheless, the demonstrated sensitivity of the responses to the laser's wavelength alongside the ability to simultaneously spatially modulate the incoming illumination can offer similar results in terms of performance without the cumbersome use of multiple PUFs.

Ultimately, it is important to note that the proposed system can generate bit-strings of any size which can be used as symmetric keys or as random seeds for an algorithmic pseudo-random generator with no additional processing. In the case of random number generation for asymmetric key encryption (private/public), where key requirements exist, like the PUF generated private key to be a large primary number, further operations can be performed during post-processing.

Table 2. Conditional entropy (H-Cond) and minimum conditional entropy (H-min) for silicon cast PUFs, the proposed scheme and a popular pseudo-random algorithm. *The proposed implementation

PUF type	H-min	H-Cond
SRAM	0.937	1
DFF	0.4	0.875
Latch	0.211	0.68
Arbiter	0.01	0.053
RO	0.104	0.765
Optical-PUF*	0.929	0.99
Ziggurat	0.928	0.99

3 Conclusion

The proposed photonic PUF is based on an alternative scrambling mechanism compared to conventional approaches that is based on the random excitation and power distribution of a high number of transverse optical modes in a guiding medium. The proposed scheme allows the generation of binary sequences compatible with the NIST test, while at the same time offers higher performance compared to state of the art approaches in terms of Hamming- Euclidean distance and minimum conditional entropy. These results provide insight that further development of the proposed scheme could provide a secure standalone module for random number generation that does not share the vulnerabilities of pseudo-random algorithms or conventional PUFs and does not need secure nonvolatile storage. In near future implementations, the cumbersome tunable laser can be replaced with a spatial light modulator, thus allowing an exponentially larger challenge space (number of inputs), with similar or higher performance.

Acknowledgements. The research leading to these results has received funding from the European Union's Horizon 2020 research and innovation programme under grant agreement No. 727528 (KONFIDO—Secure and Trusted Paradigm for Interoperable eHealth Services). This paper reflects only the authors' views and the Commission is not liable for any use that may be made of the information contained therein. Part of this work was implemented by scholarship from the IKY (State Scholarships Foundation) act "Reinforcement of research potential through doctoral research" funded by the Operational Programme "Human Resources Development, Education and Lifelong Learning", 2014–2020, co-financed by the European Commission (European Social Fund) and Greek state funds.

References

1. Pappu, R., Recht, B., Taylor, J., Gershenfeld, N.: Physical one-way functions. Science **297**, 2026–2030 (2002)
2. Katzenbeisser, S., et al.: PUFs: Myth, fact or busted? A security evaluation of physically unclonable functions (pufs) cast in silicon. In: Prouff, E., Schaumont, P. (eds.) CHES 2012. LNCS, vol. 7428, pp. 283–301. Springer, Heidelberg (2012). https://doi.org/10.1007/978-3-642-33027-8_17
3. Gao, Y., Ranasinghe, D.C., Al-Sarawi, S.F., Kavehei, O., Abbott, D.: Memristive crypto primitive for building highly secure physical unclonable functions. Sci. Rep. **5**, 12785 (2015)
4. Armknecht, F., Maes, R., Sadeghi, A.R., Standaert, F.X., Wachsmann, C.: A formal foundation for the security features of physical functions. In: IEEE Symposium on Security and Privacy (SSP), pp. 397–412. IEEE Computer Society (2011)
5. Shariati, S., Standaert, F., Jacques, L., Macq, B.: Analysis and experimental evaluation of image-based PUFs. J. Crypt. Eng. **2**, 189–206 (2012)
6. Rührmair, U., Urban, S., Weiershäuser, A., Forster, B.: Revisiting optical physical unclonable functions. ePrint Archive, pp. 1–11 (2013)
7. Pain, H.J.: The Physics of Vibrations, vol. 570, 6th edn. Wiley, Hoboken (2005). https://doi.org/10.1002/0470016957

8. Staffa, M., et al.: KONFIDO: An OpenNCP-based secure eHealth data exchange system. In: Gelenbe, E., et al. (eds.) Euro-CYBERSEC 2018. CCIS, vol. 821, pp. 11–27. Springer, Cham (2018)
9. Faiella, G., et al.: Building an Ethical Framework for Cross-border applications: the KONFIDO project. In: Gelenbe, E., et al. (eds.) Euro-CYBERSEC 2018. CCIS, vol. 821, pp. 38–45. Springer, Cham (2018)
10. Castaldo, L., Cinque, V.: Blockchain-based logging for cross-border exchange of eHealth data in Europe. In: Gelenbe, E., et al. (eds.) Euro-CYBERSEC 2018. CCIS, vol. 821, pp. 46–56. Springer, Cham (2018)

Check for updates

Building an Ethical Framework for Cross-Border Applications: The KONFIDO Project

G. Faiella[1(✉)], I. Komnios[2], M. Voss-Knude[3], I. Cano[4], P. Duquenoy[5], M. Nalin[6], I. Baroni[6], F. Matrisciano[1], and F. Clemente[1,7]

[1] Fondazione Santobono Pausilipon Onlus, Naples, Italy
giuliana.faiella@gmail.com
[2] Exus Software Ltd., London, UK
[3] Sundhed.dk, Copenhagen, Denmark
[4] IDIBAPS, Hospital Clinic de Barcelona, Universitat de Barcelona, Barcelona, Spain
[5] Department of Computer Science, Middlesex University, London, UK
[6] Telbios S.r.l., Milan, Italy
[7] CNR-Istituto di Cristallografia, Rome, Italy

Abstract. Innovative eHealth technologies and solutions are changing the way healthcare is delivered, raising many challenges regarding the ethical concerns that need to be addressed. There is a growing demand for tools that enable the assessments of the ethical impact in order to assure compatibility or highlight areas of incompatibility. This paper aims to address the ethical challenges that will arise during KONFIDO EU-funded project. KONFIDO project aims to develop tools and procedures to create a paradigm for secure inner and cross-border exchange of healthcare data in a legal and ethical way at both national and European level. The paper proposes an ethical framework that consists of a set of ethical principles derived from recent literature and European regulation and a supporting checklist. The ethical framework represents a concrete and practical guidance for healthcare professionals and developers in order to build ethically acceptable KONFIDO solutions.

Keywords: eHealth · Cross-border healthcare data exchange
Ethical framework

1 Introduction

Recent European level plans in healthcare include the means to implement cross-border healthcare solutions in the European Union. This raises awareness towards the need for secure interoperable eHealth technologies and solutions, including electronic health records (EHRs), electronic prescribing (ePrescription), mobile health (mHealth) devices and applications [1, 2]. The related documents can include sensitive information that patients might not wish to reveal. The need for a pragmatic approach and tools for handling ethical access issues has been well recognized in the health research

E. Gelenbe et al. (Eds.): Euro-CYBERSEC 2018, CCIS 821, pp. 38–45, 2018.
https://doi.org/10.1007/978-3-319-95189-8_4

community. eHealth research projects are conducted by large consortia formed of public-private partnerships that operate in multinational settings that are increasingly attempting to bring together large data sets utilising patient's computerised medical record data for cross-border applications. The EU-funded KONFIDO project (http://konfidoproject.eu/) [8–10] presented in the present volume [7], aims to develop tools and procedures to create a scalable and holistic paradigm for secure inner and cross-border exchange of healthcare data in a legal and ethical way at both national and European level. KONFIDO requires assessing the ethical dimensions that concerns the collection, storage, transmission and dissemination of personal data. As a result, the KONFIDO landscape of potential ethics issues is very complex. In order to address these issues, an ethical framework and other supporting tools were defined as a guide to provide a direction on the cross-border eHealth applications involved into KONFIDO.

2 Building the Ethical Framework: The Methodology

In order to understand what ethical principles have already been identified and discussed in the context of eHealth, a comprehensive analysis of recent literature and European Regulations (see Table 1) has been conducted in order to identify relevant references related to the ethical aspects of eHealth using specific search terms (e.g., eHealth ethics & framework, ethics & cross-border healthcare, etc.).

Table 1. Ethical principles in literature findings

Document title	Ethical principles
de Lusignan et al. [3]	1. Autonomy 2. Respect rights and dignity of patients 3. Respect clinical judgment of clinician 4. Duty to provide care 5. Protection of the public from harm 6. Beneficence 7. Justice 8. Non-maleficence 9. Reciprocity 10. Solidarity 11. Stewardship 12. Trust 13. Lawfulness 14. Transparent project approval process

(continued)

Table 1. (*continued*)

Document title	Ethical principles
ETHICAL Project (EHTEL - ETHICAL Principles for eHealth - Briefing Paper) [4]	1. Trust in data sharing 2. Privacy and security 3. Ownership and data control 4. Dignity 5. Equity 6. Proportionality
eHealth Code of Ethics [5]	1. Candor & Honesty 2. Quality 3. Informed Consent 4. Privacy 5. Professionalism 6. Accountability
General Data Protection Regulation (Regulation (EU) 2016/679) [2]	1. Lawfulness, Fairness & transparency 2. Purpose limitation & Data minimization 3. Data accuracy 4. Storage limitation 5. Data integrity 6. Data confidentiality 7. Accountability 8. Data protection by design and by default

The main findings in Table 1 can be aggregated for similarity of concepts as shown in Fig. 1. The ethical principles that are highlighted in grey are those included into KONFIDO ethical framework. They are described in the following with suggested actions.

Trust

The ethical principle of trust is based on consent and confidentiality principles.

Data subjects should be informed when their identifiable data are sent or compromised abroad and an informed consent should be obtained for sharing identifiable data or for sharing data across a network that may be unsecure. Another aspect of trust is related to data quality. In fact, this principle ensures that individuals cannot be incorrectly identified and false conclusions cannot be drawn.

Suggested Actions

In order to respect the principle of trust, the software processing systems should include appropriate data quality mechanisms and integrity checks. Data needs to be collected in a standardised way so that it can be comparable and usable. The healthcare

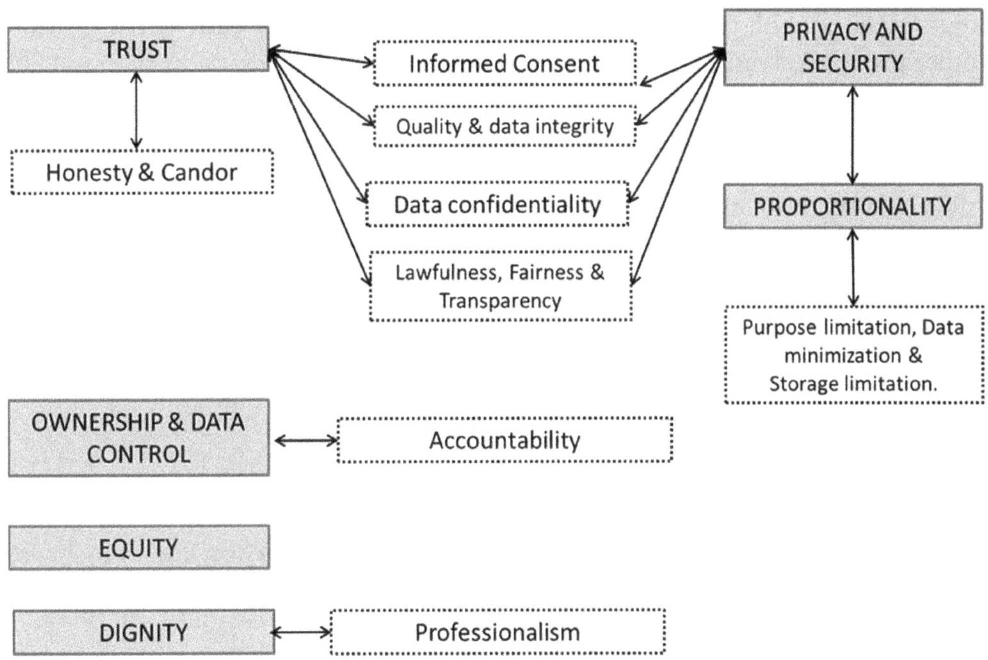

Fig. 1. Aggregation of literature findings: KONFIDO ethical principles.

organisation should provide, in clear and understandable language, general descriptions of policies and practices regarding the collection, storage, and use of identifiable health care information. Moreover, it has to inform the patients regarding potential breaches of data security.

Privacy and Security

Privacy and Security principles are related to two main areas of consent and confidentiality. The eHealth solution developer should perform a risk analysis in order to identify the security measures to protect data. The patient has to receive a document (e.g., information sheet) with details regarding the security mechanisms in place.

Suggested Actions

Perform a risk analysis to identify the principle dangers and related remedies. Prepare an information sheet with details about the security measures.

Proportionality

The principle of proportionality is fundamental when considering eHealth applications with specific reference to data collection, use and storage. According to the proportionality principle healthcare data should not be stored longer than necessary in the recipient country in order to avoid risk of disclosure and the data should be shared via an unsecured network only in life-threatening emergencies. Those responsible for the deployment of eHealth applications will need to balance the excessive use of security and other procedural protection that can greatly increase the cost of providing eHealth solutions and introduce delay.

Suggested Actions
The data sharing mechanisms should guarantee that the data are not stored longer than necessary in the recipient country and the information is unobstructed when there is an urgent need to obtain data, particularly to prevent loss of life.

Ownership and Data control
The patients are the owners and controllers of their healthcare data, with the right to make decisions over access and to be informed about how it will be used.

Suggested Actions
The patients have to be informed about the processing of the personal data and they must authorise data manipulation (e.g., provide authorisation for the cross-boarding data sharing).

Equity
eHealth applications have the potential to promote equality and reduce inequalities in healthcare. The provision of tools for self-management enables people with chronic diseases to have more control over their conditions. Remote monitoring can also improve the quality of life for certain groups in society enabling them to keep living in their own homes rather than being treated or cared for in nursing homes or other care centres. All of these features can work towards reducing health inequities.

Suggested Actions
KONFIDO services should contribute to equality in healthcare and it should be suitable to be used in every EU member country.

Dignity There is no doubt that eHealth has the potential to bring significant benefits. However, there is a risk that the human aspects are ignored and the patients do not have the power to influence the development of eHealth applications and become a simple component in an eHealth machine. In order to prevent this, eHealth applications need to be reviewed with input from end-users that should have the accountability to give their feedback about the data management system.

Suggested Actions
Design KONFIDO without ignoring the human aspects, with the patient at the centre of the healthcare processes. Introduce mechanisms that enable a continuous revision of KONFIDO applications according to end users feedbacks.

3 Ethical Framework Flowchart

The ethical framework is proposed in the form of a flowchart based on the H2020 Guidance—How to complete your ethics self-assessment v5.2 [6]. In the flowchart (Fig. 2), the grey boxes represent the activity performed by KONFIDO applications and the dotted boxes contain the suggested actions and the support documents. The implementation of ethical principles should include a participatory and person-centred approach. In this sense, three documents are introduced: an informed consent, an information sheet (i.e., storage procedure, data security measures) and data-sharing authorisation.

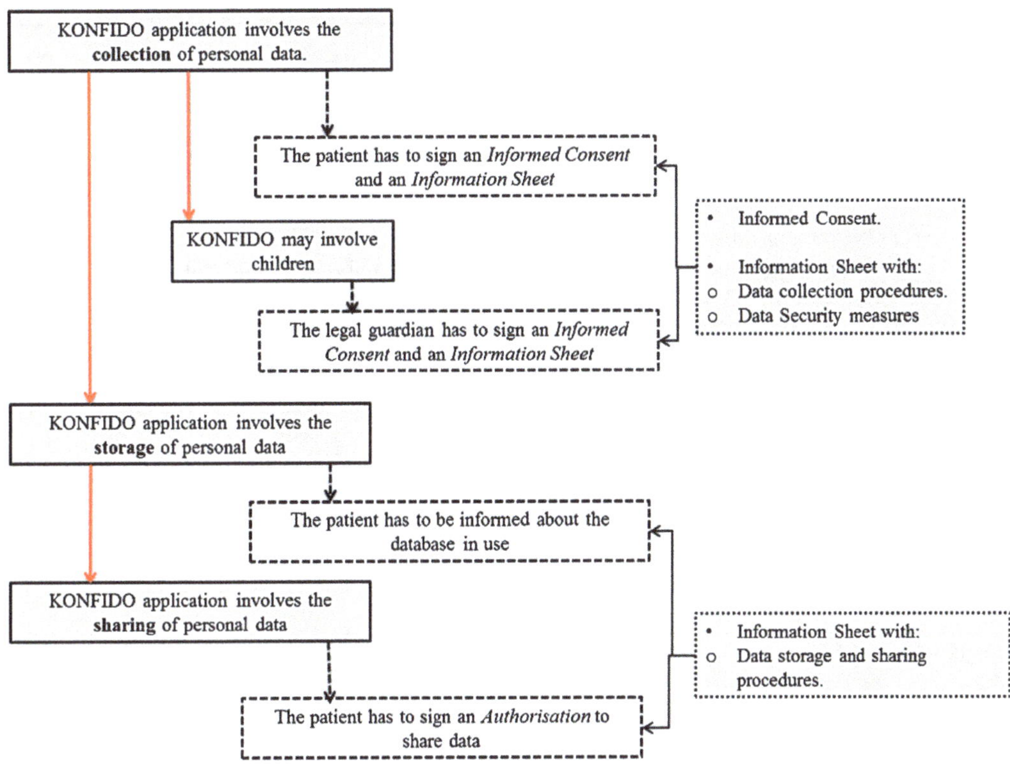

Fig. 2. Ethical framework

4 KONFIDO Architecture Review: A Preliminary Checklist

In order to check if KONFIDO architecture is compliant with the ethical principles, a preliminary survey was developed with the checklist reported in Table 2.

Table 2. Preliminary survey for the review of KONFIDO architecture

Trust in data sharing 1. Has a minimal dataset been defined? 2. Is there any anonymised/pseudo-anonymised information? 3. If yes, which is this information? 4. Is there any encrypted information? 5. Does KONFIDO architecture include data quality mechanisms? 6. Does KONFIDO architecture include appropriate integrity checks?
Privacy and security 1. When sharing identifiable data, is the consent obtained? 2. Is it possible to define collection and storage procedures? 3. Are the risks of sharing process examined (e.g., as a result of a risk analysis)?
Proportionality 1. How long data are stored in the recipient country? 2. Are there any emergency procedures that facilitate data access in case of urgent need?
Ownership and data control 1. Is the patient informed when data is shared abroad (Notification Process)? 2. Is the patient informed when data is compromised abroad (Notification Process)? 3. Does KONFIDO architecture generate records of data processing activities? 4. If yes, which kind of information is stored?
Equity 1. Is the designed architecture always applicable? 2. Are there any conditions in which a KONFIDO application could be difficult or impossible? 3. If yes, could you provide some examples?
Dignity 1. Is it possible to provide feedback and make complaints?

5 Conclusions

Across Europe there is a growing demand for tools that enable ethical impact assessments and comparative analysis of ethical principles related to eHealth solutions for cross-border applications.

This paper proposes an Ethical framework and a set of tools that will enable KONFIDO project to be compliant with a set of ethical principles extracted from recent literature and European Regulation. For each ethical principle, a set of suggested actions have been listed and included into a flowchart that analyses three different operational levels of KONFIDO applications (i.e., collection, storage and sharing).

Acknowledgements. The research leading to these results has received funding from the European Union's Horizon 2020 research and innovation programme under grant agreement No 727528 (KONFIDO—Secure and Trusted Paradigm for Interoperable eHealth Services).

References

1. eHealth Task Force Report: Redesigning health in Europe for 2020. Publications Office of the European Union (2012)
2. Chassang, G.: The impact of the EU general data protection regulation on scientific research. Ecancermedicalscience **11**, 709 (2017)
3. de Lusignan, S., Liyanage, H., Di Iorio, C.T., Chan, T., Liaw, S.T.: Using routinely collected health data for surveillance, quality improvement and research: framework and key questions to assess ethics, privacy and data access. J. Innov. Health Inform. **22**(4), 426–432 (2016)
4. European Health Telematics Association (EHTEL): ETHICAL principles for eHealth: conclusions from the consultation of the ethics experts around the globe (2012). A briefing paper. http://www.ehtel.org/publications/ehtel-briefing-papers/ETHICAL-briefing-principlesfor-ehealth/view
5. Rippen, H., Risk, A.: eHealth code of ethics (May 24). J. Med. Internet Res. **2**(2), e9 (2000)
6. H2020 Guidance: How to complete your ethics self-assessment: V5.2 – 12.07.2016
7. Gelenbe, E.: Some current research on cybersecurity in Europe. In: Gelenbe, E., et al. (eds.) Euro-CYBERSEC 2018. CCIS, vol. 821, pp. 1–10. Springer, Cham (2018)
8. Staffa, M., et al.: KONFIDO: an OpenNCP-based secure ehealth data exchange system. In: Gelenbe, E., et al. (eds.) Euro-CYBERSEC 2018. CCIS, vol. 821, pp. 11–27. Springer, Cham (2018)
9. Akriotou, M., et al.: Random number generation from a secure photonic physical unclonable hardware module. In: Gelenbe, E., et al. (eds.) Euro-CYBERSEC 2018. CCIS, vol. 821, pp. 28–37. Springer, Cham (2018)
10. Castaldo, L., Cinque, V.: Blockchain based logging for the cross-border exchange of E-health data in Europe. In: Gelenbe, E., et al. (eds.) Euro-CYBERSEC 2018. CCIS, vol. 821, pp. 46–56. Springer, Cham (2018)

Blockchain-Based Logging for the Cross-Border Exchange of eHealth Data in Europe

Luigi Castaldo(✉) and Vincenzo Cinque

Bit4id S.r.l., via Diocleziano 107, 80125 Naples, Italy
{lca,vci}@bit4id.com
http://www.bit4id.com

Abstract. On an EU level, the topic of electronic health data is a high priority. Many projects have been developed to realise a standard health data format to share information on a regional, national or EU level. All the projects favour and contribute to the development and improvement of the prerequisites for intra- and cross-border patient mobility. This work presents a new approach for the implementation of disruptive logging: an audit mechanism for cross-border exchange of eHealth data on OpenNCP, providing traceability and liability support within the OpenNCP infrastructure. Relevant parties could be legally obliged to keep a log of all privacy-critical operations performed by OpenNCP users.

Keywords: Cyberecurity · E-Health · Blockchain · Logging

1 Introduction

In the last few years, the number of people travelling across Europe for leisure, business or study purposes has been constantly increasing. In addition, the right of European Union (EU) citizens to seek healthcare in other European countries creates a strong demand for the cross-border exchange of health data. On an EU level, the topic of electronic health data is a high priority. Several projects have been developed to realise a standard health data format to share information on a regional, national or EU level.

With the advent of digital technology and with an increasing number of countries in Europe shifting their priorities towards digital health care, a secure, standard method for exchanging data among member states is needed. Electronic data does not flow freely between most of the EU countries due to a number of barriers, such as a lack of awareness, trust and legal clarity. This has led to the need for increased security implementations, resulting in improved user acceptance of such applications and thus to large-scale adoption of these technologies and to full exploitation of their advantages. Electronic health record (EHR) systems must assure a high level of protection to maintain the confidentiality of patients' data [12].

E. Gelenbe et al. (Eds.): Euro-CYBERSEC 2018, CCIS 821, pp. 46–56, 2018.
https://doi.org/10.1007/978-3-319-95189-8_5

The EU is very active in the development of possible solutions, and several projects have been funded by EU's Horizon 2020 programme. For instance, the KONFIDO [11,17] project is developing a federated architecture, using privacy through design principles. It will enable the secure exchange, processing and storage of health-related data. KONFIDO will make cross-border interoperation of eHealth services provided by individual countries more secure, while allowing each participating entity to enforce specific policies for protection and control of personal health related data.

While some past and current projects have delivered important results, a sound holistic approach to the issue of digital security in eHealth is still a faraway target.

In this work, we present a secure audit mechanism based on blockchain technology. We first provide a general overview of the current situation regarding eHealth data exchange in Europe. Second, we introduce the OpenNCP software, mainly focusing on the log flows inside the platform. We continue with a description of the presented solution, detailing the interaction between the proposed components. Finally, we give our conclusions.

2 eHealth Data Exchange in Europe

Moving toward eHealth is a key goal of the EU. Many health and IT policy documents emphasise the benefits of (and barriers to) pursuing the digital agenda. In 2004, the European Commission initiated its first eHealth Action Plan, requesting a commitment from Member States to work together on eHealth. Over the last decade, progress toward eHealth within the 27 EU Member States has been inconsistent [6,9]. The academic literature has primarily focused on issues related to the adoption and diffusion of specific eHealth technologies, such as EHRs, health information exchanges (HIEs), and telemedicine, along with their various benefits and barriers [5].

To increase the efficiency of patient care delivery, healthcare parties must be able to access and exchange patient information independent of their organisational and technological particularities. The European Commission is taking a first step in this direction by defining guidelines for defining and sharing patient summaries across Europe. The European Patient Summary (EPS) [15] is an interoperability infrastructure intended to address this challenge by managing and exchanging patient summaries across European healthcare networks. From a technical perspective, the realisation of the EPS demands powerful middleware technology that guarantees ubiquitous access to distributed and multi-faceted data as well as scalability, persistency and interoperability.

One of the most relevant efforts has been the epSOS [7] Project, aiming at designing, building and evaluating an e-Health framework and ICT infrastructure to allow patient data to be securely exchanged among different European healthcare systems. The epSOS project provided a practical eHealth framework and ICT infrastructure, based on existing national infrastructures, that enables secure access to patient health information, particularly with respect to a basic Patient Summary and ePrescription/eDispensing, between European healthcare systems. The cross-border services are handled by clinical gateways called National Contact Points (NCP) [14].

epSOS introduced a full set of specifications and operational aspects to define an interoperability framework that builds on widely accepted standards, such as Health Level 7 (HL7). epSOS also provided a reference implementation which was changed to an open-source community implementation, OpenNCP [10].

3 OpenNCP

OpenNCP [8] solves the problem of securely exchanging documents for care provisioning abroad, maintaining the clinical/legal value of the original documents. OpenNCP is meant to establish shared eHealth practices with respect to patient data exchange across European member countries. Besides supporting the correct flow of data, the goal of OpenNCP is to ensure the respect of security, legal and interoperability requirements. OpenNCP provides a number of interoperable services, which enable national and regional eHealth platforms to establish cross-border health information networks. Although OpenNCP offers a secure solution to transfer eHealth data across the EU, there is still room for improvements from a security point of view. A key concern is the implementation of a secure and unforgeable audit system.

3.1 Logflow

An OpenNCP node generally interacts with two different types of counterparts: a national infrastructure, to retrieve patients' data from the national healthcare system, and another OpenNCP node, to retrieve patient's health data from another country. This section mainly focuses on identifying the log flows inside OpenNCP, in particular for all the scenarios requiring health data exchange between two different countries. An OpenNCP node interacts externally towards another NCP node for these purposes [16]: (a) Exchange of ePrescription (eP), Patient Summary (PS) and eDispense documents; (b) Patient identification.

Audit Manager. The current implementation of OpenNCP uses an internal component, based on OpenATNA [1], to implement the Audit Trail objectives. This component provides interfaces for the Audit Trail Service, acting as service point to keep track of events to be logged. The Audit Manager has a built-in feature to assure that all the audit messages are sent to OpenATNA and persisted in the database. If something goes wrong while attempting to send an audit message to OpenATNA, the message is stored on the file-system for later handling.

Patient Identification. The workflow between two countries during the identification of a patient in a foreign country (B) and his or her home country (A) can be summarised as follows: the Audit Manager on node B keeps track of the request sent by country B. The same occurs in country A when the message arrives. When country A responds to the request, a new record is created in the Audit Manager and persisted in the database. The same happens in B when the response arrives.

Data Exchange (PS and EP) and Notifications. If a patient has been already identified, a healthcare professional (HP) can query the system to retrieve his or her patient summary and/or prescriptions. Each component performing an operation, in both countries, either going on the National Infrastructure or forwarding to an external NCP node, saves an audit trail in the DB by means of the Audit Manager.

4 Architecture

This work proposes a new architecture to overcome the issues related to the standard logging mechanisms within OpenNCP. It provides traceability and liability through an unforgeable log management system based on blockchain. The aim of this study is to create an architectural model of a centralised blockchain-based solution extending Bit4id's SmartLog [2] platform.

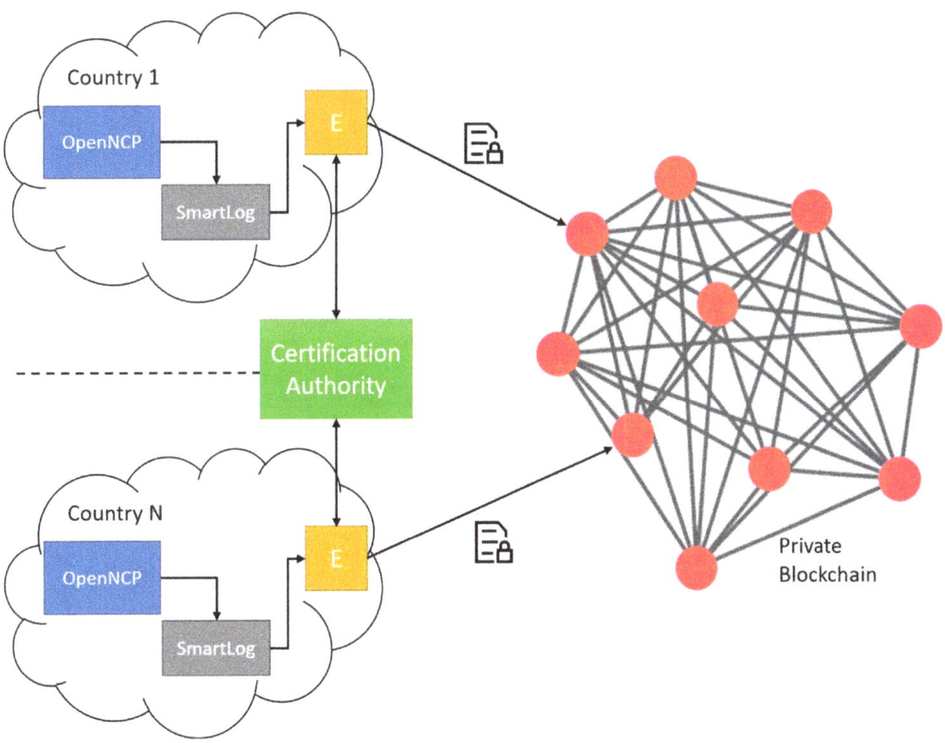

Fig. 1. Log management system architecture.

The proposed architecture is based on three modules (Fig. 1):

- SmartLog: it is able to ensure the origin and integrity of system logs and certain time evidence of log generation (by time-stamping) along with the standard filtering features provided by the most common logging management systems;
- Encryption module (E): all the logs must be properly encrypted before saving them on the blockchain. The encryption is needed for two main reasons: (a) making logs accessible only to the countries involved in the transactions; (b) purging all the logs after a certain amount of time, according to specific regulations;
- Blockchain: it grants distributed access to data, while making information unforgeable and undeletable.

The proposed approach requires deployment of the new modules in each OpenNCP node. For every country, the new logging system requires that a SmartLog and an encryption module directly connected to the OpenNCP node be in use, and a node belonging to a private blockchain must safely store the logs. The Certification Authority, depicted in Fig. 1, is part of the defined encryption mechanism, but it does not need to be deployed in every country. A single element is enough to support the entire architecture (Fig. 2).

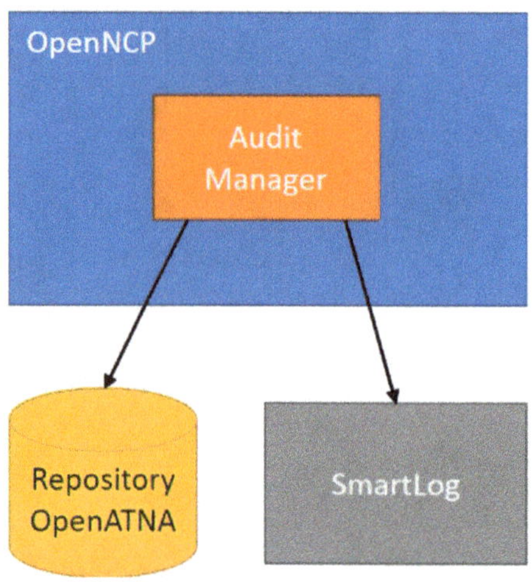

Fig. 2. SmartLog integration.

4.1 SmartLog

SmartLog is a client-server system for log message management, ensuring system log origin, certain time evidence of log generation (by time-stamping), integrity of each message and confidentiality. SmartLog makes it possible to perform efficient and centralised management of the log files. The solution is not invasive and is completely decoupled from pre-existent hardware/software architectures. Moreover, it does not require any intervention on the current OpenNCP architecture or development of an integration module. The product is able to replace the OpenATNA repository used by the platform. In our work, SmartLog receives the logs directly from the Audit Manager, which can be achieved by changing a few parameters in the OpenNCP settings configuration.

SmartLog is based on four main components (Fig. 3):

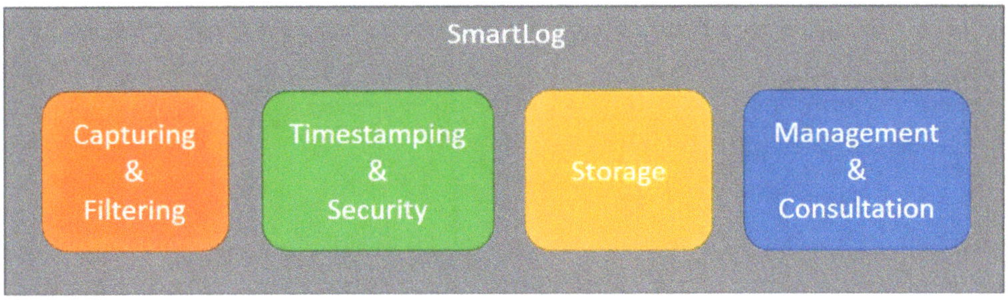

Fig. 3. SmartLog components.

- Capturing and filtering: SmartLog is able to safely acquire and transfer all messages generated by the monitored systems. Any type of event can be enriched and transformed;
- Timestamping and security: the platform generates a timestamp for each log message to ensure a trusted and certain time reference for the log and to level out the time formats (often disparate) between the different systems;
- Storage: SmartLog comes with an internal storage mechanism hosting all the collected logs, without allowing access to the data except for authorised personnel. This work focuses on extending this functionality, storing selected logs directly on a private blockchain through the use of the encryption module described in the next section. This mechanism will be applied only to logs regarding critical operations within OpenNCP;
- Management and consultation: log consultation and management is exclusively available to authorised personnel.

When SmartLog completes its processing on the received logs, it has two possible choices: storing the logs in internal secure storage or, in case the logs referring to ehealth data exchange between two countries, forwarding them to the encryption module for the next steps.

4.2 Encryption Mechanism

Once the critical logs have been filtered and processed by SmartLog, they are ready to be securely stored on the blockchain to make them unforgeable and undeletable. At this point, another problem arises. When something is stored on a blockchain, even a private blockchain, the information becomes accessible to everyone connected to the distributed ledger. In case of eHealth, most often, exchanged data contains patients' sensitive information, and so it cannot be openly exposed to everyone in the system. According to EU regulations, only the entities involved in a transaction should have access to the audit logs of the transaction. Moreover, old logs must be purged after a certain amount of time.

The regulation requirements are partially conflicting with the immutability and undeletable nature of the auditing mechanism and the blockchain technology. For this reason, a specific encryption mechanism has been defined in this work. This mechanism is required to ensure that data are only accessible to the parties involved. An approach with a combination of symmetric and asymmetric encryption enables data sharing between selected entities and yields good performance for the auditing system [13].

Symmetric Encryption. Symmetric encryption mechanisms considerably reduce encryption complexity. Following this method, data are encrypted and decrypted by splitting them into a form of blocks. In its simplest mode, it is possible to split plain text into blocks, which are then fed into the cipher system to produce blocks of cipher text. By handling only small chunks of data, symmetric encryption algorithms yield good performance. The biggest problem with symmetric key encryption is finding a safe way to exchange the ciphering key with the other parties involved in the communication [18].

Asymmetric Encryption. Asymmetric cryptography, also known as public key cryptography, uses public and private keys to encrypt and decrypt data. For asymmetric encryption to deliver confidentiality, integrity, authenticity and non-repudiability, users and systems need to be certain that a public key is authentic, that it belongs to the person or entity claimed and that it has not been tampered with or replaced by a malicious third party. There is no perfect solution to this public key authentication problem. A public key infrastructure (PKI), where trusted certificate authorities certify ownership of key pairs and certificates, is the most common approach.

The encryption module, by design, generates a new key-pair and the corresponding Certificate Signing Request (CSR) every year. The CSR is later submitted to the trusted internal Certification Authority (CA). Upon receiving the CSR, the CA validates the request and responds with a CA Certificate. When the certificate expires, the module takes care of deleting the key-pair associated to it and generates a new one to request a new certificate.

When the encryption module of an OpenNCP node receives a new log from SmartLog, it converts it in the encrypted format depicted in Fig. 4. The encryption process can be summarised as follows:

1. The encryption module extracts meta-data from the log, such as source country, destination country and performed operation. The meta-data are not encrypted and are used to index the messages in the blockchain for future retrieval;
2. Module (E) generates a random symmetric key (K) that is used to encrypt the audit log (M): $[SE(M, K)]$;

3. The key is later encrypted using the asymmetric encryption. The module encrypts the key (K) two times. The first encryption is performed using the public key P_{send} of the source country [$AE(K, P_{send})$], the second using the public key P_{recv} of the destination country [$AE(K, P_{recv})$]. The public keys are always retrieved from the CA, which is the only trusted entity to retrieve public keys;
4. The fully encrypted log is sent to the blockchain to be permanently stored;
5. The module destroys the symmetric key, which from that point on is only available in the message on the blockchain.

=

Metadata	Enc. Key	Message
Sender	$AE(K, P_{send})$	$SE(M, K)$ where: M = message K = symmetric key
Receiver		
Operation	$AE(K, P_{recv})$	
Index Keys		

Fig. 4. Encrypted log structure.

The encryption mechanism described above makes the data stored on the blockchain only accessible to entitled parties. Only the involved parties can access the logs using their private key, if it has not already expired. If one of the countries (A) involved in a transaction needs to get access to a log, it can retrieve the log from the blockchain. The log can only be decrypted in the encryption module, which owns the private key of the country. The private key PR_A is used to decrypt the symmetric key (K) saved in the message, which in turn is used to decrypt the real log. This process safeguards users' privacy and enables the single actors to decrypt the messages on their own in case of disputes. Moreover, changing the encryption key-pairs every year and forcing the deletion of the previous ones for every Member State makes it impossible to decrypt old logs, in accordance with the specific regulations.

4.3 Blockchain

Blockchain is a decentralised transaction and data management technology developed first for Bitcoin cryptocurrency. The interest in Blockchain technology has been increasing since the idea was coined in 2008. The reason for the interest in Blockchain is its central attributes, which provide security, anonymity and data integrity and immutability without any third-party organisation in control of the transactions, and therefore it creates interesting research areas, especially from the perspective of technical challenges and limitations [3].

All the participants are equipotent and equally privileged, and the operational principles of the decentralised database are mutually decided. Blockchain protocols thus ensure that transactions on a blockchain are valid and never recorded to the shared repository more than once, enabling people to coordinate individual transactions in a decentralised manner without the need to rely on a trusted authority to verify and clear all transactions.

After a block has been added to the blockchain, it can no longer be deleted or changed, and the transactions it contains can be accessed and verified by everyone on the network.

Multiple distributed ledger solutions have been evaluated to best fit the flexibility, security and performance prerequisites needed for the proposed approach. Considering the generic purpose of the platform, we decided to use MultiChain [4]. It is an open source technology allowing the implementation of a private blockchain and providing low overhead for the transactions handling.

The MultiChain technology is a platform that helps users to establish a certain private Blockchain. It solves the related problems of mining, privacy and openness via integrated management of user permissions.

Once a blockchain is private, problems relating to scaling are easily resolved, as the chain's participants can control the maximum block size. In addition, as a closed system, the blockchain will only contain transactions which are of interest to those participants.

Privileges. In MultiChain, all privileges are granted and revoked using network transactions containing special metadata. The miner of the first 'genesis' block automatically receives all privileges, including administrator rights to manage the privileges of other users. This administrator grants privileges to other users in transactions whose outputs contain those users' addresses along with metadata denoting the privileges conferred. When changing the administration and mining privileges of other users, an additional constraint is introduced, in which a minimum proportion of the existing administrators must vote to make a change.

Mining. By restricting mining to a set of identifiable entities, MultiChain resolves the dilemma posed by private blockchains, in which one participant can monopolise the mining process. The solution lies in a constraint on the number of blocks which may be created by the same miner within a given window. MultiChain implements this scheme using a parameter called mining diversity.

General Data Storage. MultiChain streams enable a blockchain to be used as a general purpose append-only database. A MultiChain blockchain can contain any number of streams, where the data published in every stream are stored by every node.

5 Conclusions

In this paper, we presented a method for utilising blockchain technology to provide tamper-proof audit logs for cross-border exchange of eHealth data in Europe. Blockchain security properties can guarantee off-the-shelf non-repudiation and integrity for logs without extra efforts. MultiChain technology, without relying on the proof-of-work mechanism, does not suffer from the limitations imposed by the Bitcoin technology regarding the number of transactions, block size and cost per transaction. This approach provides an easy to integrate solution for current OpenNCP issues by providing traceability and liability support within its infrastructure. Our work combines secure storing mechanisms with fine-grained privacy controls in one component, without requiring significant changes to the OpenNCP architecture.

References

1. Openatna. Technical report, MOSS & University of Cardiff (2018). https://ec.europa.eu/cefdigital/code/projects/EHNCP/repos/ehealth/browse/openatna
2. Bit4id: Smartlog (2018). https://www.bit4id.com/en/secure-log-management/
3. Bonneau, J., Miller, A., Clark, J., Narayanan, A., Kroll, J., Felten, E.: Research perspectives and challenges for bitcoin and cryptocurrencies. In: IEEE Security and Privacy, March 2015. https://eprint.iacr.org/2015/261.pdf
4. CoinSciences: Multichain (2018). https://www.multichain.com/
5. Currie, W., Seddon, J.: A cross-national analysis of ehealth in the European union: some policy and research directions. Inf. Manag. **51**(6), 783–797 (2014)
6. Dobrev, A., Jones, T., Stroetmann, V., Stroetmann, K., Vatter, Y., Peng, K.: Interoperable ehealth is worth it-securing benefits from electronic health records and eprescribing. Bonn/Brussels: European Commission on Information Safety and Media (2010)
7. EpSOS-Project: About epsos (2018). http://www.epsos.eu/home/about-epsos.html
8. EpSOS-Project: Openncp (2018). https://openncp.atlassian.net/wiki/spaces/ncp
9. European-Commission: E-health-making healthcare better for european citizens: An action plan for a european e-health area (2004)
10. Fonseca, M., Karkaletsis, K., Cruz, I., Berler, A., Oliveira, I.: OpenNCP: a novel framework to foster cross-border e-health services. In: MIE, pp. 617–621 (2015)
11. KONFIDO-Project: About konfido (2018). http://www.konfido-project.eu/konfido/content/what-konfido-project-about
12. Krummenacher, R., Simperl, E., Cerizza, D., Valle, E.D., Nixon, L., Foxvog, D.: Enabling the European patient summary through triplespaces. Comput. Methods Programs Biomed. **95**(2), S33–S43 (2009)
13. Kumar, Y., Munjal, R., Sharma, H.: Comparison of symmetric and asymmetric cryptography with existing vulnerabilities and countermeasures. Int. J. Comput. Sci. Manag. Stud. **11**(3) (2011)
14. Moharra, M.: Almazán, C., Decool, M., Nilsson, A., Allegretti, N., Seven, M.: Implementation of a cross-border health service: physician and pharmacists' opinions from the epSOS project. Fam. Practice **32**(5), 564–567 (2015)
15. Olsson, S., Lymberis, A., Whitehouse, D.: European commission activities in ehealth. Int. J. Circumpolar Health **63**(4), 310–316 (2004)
16. Ruestchmann, P., de Béjarry, G.: Final epSOS system technical specification. Deliverable D3.3.2, ASIP SANTE, April 2010

17. Staffa, M., Coppolino, L., Sgaglione, L., Gelenbe, E., Komnios, I., Grivas, E., Stan, O., Castaldo, L.: Konfido: An openNCP-based secure ehealth data exchange system. In: Gelenbe, E. et al. (eds.) Euro-CYBERSEC 2018. CCIS, vol. 821, pp. 11–27. Springer, Heidelberg (2018)
18. Thakur, J., Kumar, N.: DES, AES and Blowfish: symmetric key cryptography algorithms simulation based performance analysis. Int. J. Emerg. Technol. Adv. Eng. **1**(2), 6–12 (2011)

Problem Domain Analysis of IoT-Driven Secure Data Markets

Máté Horváth(✉) and Levente Buttyán

Department of Networked Systems and Services,
Laboratory of Cryptography and Systems Security (CrySyS),
Budapest University of Technology and Economics, Budapest, Hungary
{mhorvath,buttyan}@crysys.hu

Abstract. The Internet of Things (IoT) provides us with a vast amount of new data day by day, however, currently, most of these are only stored without utilizing their full potential. The attractive concept of data markets can change this situation in the near future and thus we initiate the study of security aspects of such systems. In this work, as a first step, we analyse the data markets based on the possible security requirements of the different participants. We identify more than 30 possible scenarios and connect these to the relevant areas of cryptography. Our analysis also highlights several open problems motivating further research on certain cryptographic primitives.

Keywords: Cybersecurity · IoT · Data markets · Market mechanisms

1 Introduction

Current technological trends, as the proliferation of smart devices and the Internet of Things (IoT), made the rapidly increasing amount of data a new raw material waiting for utilization. The main barrier of this is that in most cases the collected data is only available for the user and manufacturer of a sensor or smart device. One possible way of exploiting the full potential of this information is to build an ecosystem around it. This is exactly the idea of Data Markets [5], where data brokers (DB) buy data from the owners and resell the collected data (possibly together with computing resources) to a third party that provides some value-added services (VAS) to its users. These services can typically help predictions or support optimization via analysing a wide range of data.

This work was partially performed in the frame of the FIEK_16-1-2016-0007 project, implemented with the support provided from the National Research, Development and Innovation Fund of Hungary, financed under the FIEK_16 funding scheme, and it was also partially supported by the National Research, Development and Innovation Office – NKFIH, under grant contract no. 116675 (K).

E. Gelenbe et al. (Eds.): Euro-CYBERSEC 2018, CCIS 821, pp. 57–67, 2018.
https://doi.org/10.1007/978-3-319-95189-8_6

Our Contribution. The issue of security and privacy arises naturally whenever data get out of the control of its owner. In this work, we investigate the possible security issues related to data markets. Compared to a simple cloud computing scenario, where only two roles (user and cloud service provider) are present, data markets involve parties of three type (data owner, DB, and VAS provider) which can all trust or distrust the others. Based on the level of trust between the parties, we identify 31 different scenarios, some of which can be handled straightforwardly, some are closely related to different areas of cryptography, while others motivate further research on specific problems. We found that the two most interesting open questions are the following. *Is it possible to provide the secrecy of a computation and at the same time verify that it obeys certain restrictions? Can an encryption scheme allow for computation on certain hidden data but not on others such that the admissible data can be determined in a fine-grained manner?* Our work also motivates the adjustment of existing cryptographic primitives to the use-cases provided by data markets.

Related Works. While to the best of our knowledge, the concept of data markets has not been implemented yet, several pioneering projects are approaching towards this goal. Their common property is that only limited information is available about their design (in the form of white papers). These initiatives include the Data Market Austria Project [3]; the pilot study of IOTA Data Marketplace [9]; Ocean Protocol [12] that aims to connect data providers and consumers; the decentralized marketplace of Datum [4]; and the Enigma Protocol [15] based on secure multiparty computation (MPC). Market formation through automatic bidding [6,7] can also be considered in the context of data markets.

2 System Model for Data Markets

The resources of a data market are provided by owners of sensors and "IoT" devices (DO), who provide (sell) data directly to the data broker (DB) and indirectly to VAS providers. In our model, DB is not decentralized but rather a single entity, investing in infrastructure for data storage and executing computations. Naturally, different DBs might compete with each other in the future and most probably also with different distributed systems (improving the service quality), but our focus is the inner working of a single, centralized marketplace (with one DB).

DBs offer their services to different value-added service providers (VASPs) that can utilize data in order to fulfil the various needs of end users (either individuals or companies). It is important to note that we do not want to restrict the scope of offered services, but from statistical analysis to the training of AI (artificial intelligence) models, any service is included. Even if the final goal of such ecosystems is to serve the end users, they are less important in our study as we are interested in the security aspects of data markets. More precisely, all the available information for an end user is a subset of the information handled

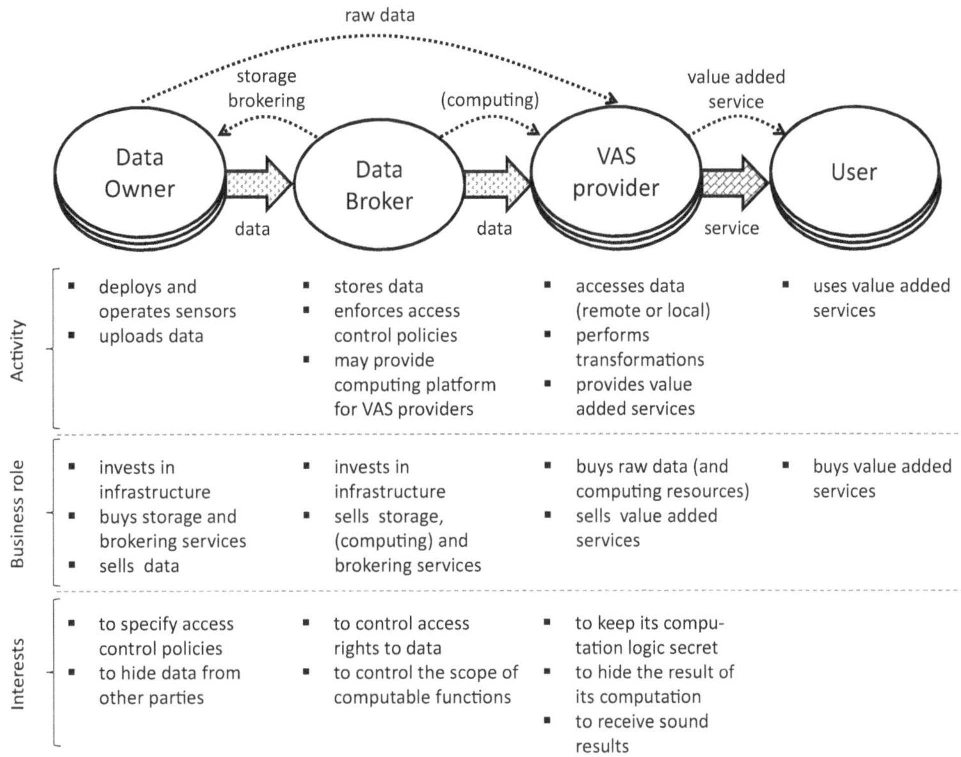

Fig. 1. System model of the envisioned data market.

by the corresponding VASP and vice versa, any information about the end user is exposed in the system through the VASP so for our purposes it is enough to consider VASPs.

The imagined model of the ecosystem is depicted in Fig. 1, containing also the rough business models of the different parties. At the same time, the economic aspects of such system are out of the scope of this work.

3 Related Tools

In this part, we provide a brief and informal description of the concepts appearing later in this work. These are the following.

Trusted Execution Environment (TEE) refers to an isolated processing environment in which computations can be securely executed irrespective of the rest of the system. In a high level, when considering information leakage, outsourced computation that is executed in TEE (by an untrusted party) is equivalent to local computation and thus in the rest of this work we do not differentiate between these two cases. For more details on TEE, see [14].

Differential Privacy is a mathematical framework for the privacy protection of data used for statistical analysis (see [11]). While in some very specific cases it can be useful for privacy protection also in Data Markets, we will not consider this solution because of two reasons. We do not restrict the scope of computable functions to statistics (i.e., individual data values may be of interest instead of only cumulated data) and we are interested in enforcing access control policies belonging to data, while differential privacy does not restrict access to data.

Homomorphic Encryption (HE) enables to execute computations on encrypted data that results in an encrypted output. This capability can be used to make outsourced computation secure, by maintaining the secrecy of inputs and outputs (while the applied function is public). Depending on the supported functions, there exist additively, multiplicatively, somewhat and fully homomorphic encryption schemes. While the latter one supports an arbitrary number of multiplications and additions, in somewhat homomorphic schemes the number of computable multiplications is restricted. See details in [1].

Functional Encryption (FE) is a generalization of traditional (either private- or public-key) encryption schemes that integrates function evaluation into decryption. More precisely, so-called functional secret keys can be issued for a function f, that when used in the decryption of a ciphertext corresponding to a value x, results in the value $f(x)$ without leaking any more information about x, than exposed by $f(x)$. For details, we refer to [8].

Attribute-Based Encryption (ABE) is a subtype of FE, that realizes fine-grained access control. Ciphertexts and secret keys are associated with access control policies and "attributes" (or vice versa) and decryption is possible only if the attributes satisfy the policy.

Oblivious Transfer (OT) and Private Information Retrieval (PIR) are dealing with transmission of data between two parties, such that the receiver does not have to reveal the data, she wants to retrieve from a dataset (PIR). We call this OT when the receiver obtains no other information, besides the desired data, from running the protocol. In the sequel, prime is going to denote that the protocol is non-interactive. For more details about OT and PIR, see [13].

Secure Multi-party Computation (MPC) allow n parties to jointly compute an n variate function on their inputs, often through several rounds of interaction, without revealing their inputs to each other. Among those cryptographic primitives that aim to achieve some form of secure computation, realizations of MPC are the closest to practical usability [10].

Obfuscation (Obf.) is a program transformation that preserves the functionality but alters the description and operation such that the inner workings of the program remains hidden at the expense of some efficiency loss. In other words, the inputs and outputs of an obfuscated program are plaintexts but the computed function is hidden. In spite of several breakthrough results in the past years, obfuscation is still an exotic area within cryptography with several open questions (see [8]).

We emphasize that MPC and FHE are about to protect the input(s) of a given public computation. However, as it is possible "to turn computation into data", with the help of so-called universal circuits[1], these primitives can also be used to conceal the executed computation besides its inputs and outputs (although its overhead is significant). In the sequel, we denote with an asterisk if MPC or FHE is complemented with this tool.

4 Problem Domain Analysis

Our analysis is started with the investigation of the relations between the participants of the system. After identifying their possible goals regarding security (see also Fig. 1), we organize the emerging use-cases and identify the relevant branches of cryptography and also pointing out open problems.

4.1 Trust and Distrust Between the Parties

The main goal of this study is to identify the different scenarios that emerge when some of the actors in a data market does not trust all the other parties. In order to go through all possible cases and identify already solved and still open problems, we investigate the possible forms of trust between data owners, data broker and VAS providers.

DO → DB If the DB is trusted by the DO, then it is straightforward to store the data as a plaintext. In this case, access control policy enforcement can be outsourced to the DB. On the other hand, an untrusted DB should not store its clients' data in the clear but in *encrypted* form together with the corresponding *meta-data in cleartex*. Note that the latter one is necessary for providing the data brokering service. Access control of data becomes more challenging that can be resolved e.g., by solving the key-exchange between DOs and VASPs.

DO → VASP While a trusted VASP may access plaintext data, access control might still be important as most probably only smaller sets of data are sold to the VASP and thus even in this case VASP should have only *conditional access* to data. When the VASP is not even trusted by the DO, it is natural to expect that it has no direct access to any data and it is only allowed to get results of non-trivial computations on some specific data.

DB → DO Trusting DOs from the viewpoint of a DB is equivalent to *trusting the data source* i.e. the DB assumes that the received data is not fake, its source is the claimed sensor and the result of the measurement was not modified. The lack of this confidence can only be remedied partly using algorithmic measures (e.g., by checking the consistency of the data) and thus this type of distrust is out of the scope of this work. At the same time, this problem can be addressed e.g., using pricing based on game theoretic considerations.

[1] A universal circuit can be considered as a programmable function, taking as input a program description (that is going to be executed) and the ordinary input.

DB → VASP As the DB is selling information to the VAS provider, pricing should scale with the amount of provided information that can be measured using two different metrics as well. The first is the available amount of data for the VAS provider that can be controlled using some access control policy for the data. Note that in this regard, the interests of the DO and the DB coincides and thus we assume that either of them enforces a common access policy. The second possible way of measuring the sold information is through the scope of computable functions on the data that is available for a VASP. One natural way of restricting the computing capabilities of the VASP is via providing it with a restricted interface that naturally determines restrictions. However, we are interested in a more general setting, where such limitation is not present, especially because it leaves no room for the interests of the VAS provider (see the next part). Accordingly, we assume that arbitrary function descriptions are forwarded to the DB that are evaluated if they are in an allowed function class (for which the VASP has paid). Alternatively, if the computation of the functions is not outsourced to the DB, it should be solved that the data, sent to the VAS provider, is only useful for the computation of "allowed functions" and cannot be used as input for any other functions.

VASP → DO When purchasing data from DB, the VAS providers naturally rely on the honesty of the DOs, however, the enforcement of honest behaviour is the duty of the DB according to the system model of the data market. Accordingly, this trust relationship is indirect and thus not investigated.

VASP → DB The business model of a VAS provider is built around the functions, that are evaluated on the data, bought from the DB. This highlights the importance of this asset and shows that VAS providers are motivated to hide the computation logic they use even if the computation is executed by the DB as a part of its services. In case of so-called learnable functions, that can be reconstructed merely from input-output pairs, hiding these values is an important pillar of keeping the function private. Moreover, the output alone has also business value as the end user pays for this to the VAS provider. When talking about the input data, it is important to differentiate the data value from the meta-data. If the DB stores plaintext data, VAS providers can only obscure the accessed data if both the accessed values and meta-data remain hidden from the DB. When only encrypted data is available to the DB, typically meta-data can help to feed the proper input to the function of the VASP but hiding both information can be the goal of a deliberate VAS provider.

Depending on which of these four assets are intended to be hidden from the DB, 2^4 different scenarios can occur. For the ease of exposition, we denote a VAS provider's confidentiality goals with 4-tuple (F, I, I', O), where each variable correspond to a binary value, 0 meaning public and 1 denoting confidential. The variables represent the function to be computed (F), its input value(s) (I), meta-data for the input(s) (I') and the output (O) of the computation (e.g., $(1, 0, 0, 0)$ represents that the VASP only wants to hide the computational logic form the DB). Some of the resulting scenarios are contradictory so we ignore them in the rest of the work. These are the following.

- If a function is public then its domain is public as well. Practically, the function description must include the expected input that is described with the help of the meta-data, which then cannot be hidden (ruling out $(0, 0, 1, 0), (0, 0, 1, 1), (0, 1, 1, 0), (0, 1, 1, 1)$).
- Hiding the accessed meta-data from the DB implies that the used data values are hidden as well and accordingly $(1, 0, 1, 0), (1, 0, 1, 1)$ are also meaningless.
- $(0, 0, 0, 1)$ is also contradictory as given a function and its input, the output can be obtained so it cannot be hidden.

In case of outsourced computation, the VASP might also want to verify the soundness of the received output. Variants of publicly verifiable computation can help to enable this (e.g., in case of MPC [15]), however, we assume the DB is only honest-but-curious and not malicious, especially as the DB is motivated to provide reliable service in order to keep its customers.

4.2 On the Used Notations

Having identified the possible requirements of the different parties in the system, we introduce a notation to refer to the possible scenarios that depend on the fulfilled requirements. From the viewpoint of the DOs, four main scenarios, called worlds, can be distinguished based on whether the DB and the VAS provider are trusted or not. Each world can be further subdivided based on the trust between DB and VAS providers. Accordingly, let $\mathcal{S}^{D(V)}_{V(F,I,I',O)}$ denote a scenario, which is specified by the values of the different variables. $D, V \in \{T, U\}$ refer to the DB and the VAS providers and their value shows thether they are considered to be "trusted" (T) or "untrusted" (U) by the DO; $V \in \{0, 1\}$ indicates whether the DB intends to verify the functions, computed by VAS providers (1) or not(0); and finally $F, I, I', O \in \{0, 1\}$ form the 4-tuple, introduced in the previous part, representing the goals of the VASP. When any of the above parameters are not specified in the notation, we always mean a general scenario in which any of the more specific sub-scenarios can occur (e.g., $\mathcal{S}^T$ denotes all the scenarios where the DB is Trusted).

One might miss from the description of the scenarios the specification of the enforcer of an access policy, which can be done either by a DO or by the DB. We find that this question is rather technology related and the effect of the options are the same, so we do not determine this in the use-cases.

In the subsequent parts, we are going to go through the scenarios, discussing their relevance, the related cryptographic solutions, and the open problems.

4.3 Trusted Data Broker

Our first observation is that whenever the DB is trusted $(\mathcal{S}^T)$, it is straightforward to delegate the enforcement of access control policies to the DB. We investigate the arising use-cases, while keeping this in mind. As a second remark, also note that those scenarios are contradictory, where the inputs (of a function from

Table 1. A rough summary of meaningful subscenarios of $\mathcal{S}_U^T$ with the related concepts and open questions.

		VASP cannot have access to plaintext data				
	function	0	1	1	1	1
	input value	0	0	0	1	1
	input metadata	0	0	0	1	1
	output	0	0	1	0	1
DB stores palaintexts (0)	No restriction on the computed function (0)	Outsourced computation or local computation + FE	Obf. / TEE / MPC*	(Obf. / TEE) + output Enc.	(TEE + OT) or (Obf. + OT') or MPC*	(TEE + OT) or (Obf. + OT') + output Enc.
	Limited function queries (1)	Straightforward verification in both cases	Function verification is challenging when the computed function is hidden			

a VASP) are intended to be hidden, while the meta-data of the same input is accessible for the DB ($\mathcal{S}^T_{(0,1,0,0)}, \mathcal{S}^T_{(0,1,0,1)}, \mathcal{S}^T_{(1,1,0,0)}$ and $\mathcal{S}^T_{(1,1,0,1)}$). The reason is that a trusted DB stores data as plaintext and thus the meta-data of the input directly reveal the input value.

Trusted VAS Provider ($\mathcal{S}_T^T$). When DOs trust both the DB and VASPs, the occurring problems are almost trivial to solve. $\mathcal{S}^T_{T(0,0,0,0)}$ corresponds to a scenario where the DB provides value-added services (DB = VASP) and it is trusted by the DO so challenges do not arise. All the other use-cases can be handled if the necessary computations are executed locally by the VASPs and for this plaintext data is accessible. $\mathcal{S}^T_{T(1,0,0,1)}$ represents exactly this case, while in $\mathcal{S}^T_{T(1,1,1,0)}, \mathcal{S}^T_{T(1,1,1,1)}$ the application of PIR can obscure the used inputs from the DB. $\mathcal{S}^T_{T(1,0,0,0)}$ and $\mathcal{S}^T_{T(1,1,1,0)}$ represents such situations where the VASP publishes the computed results (e.g., indirectly by buying specific stocks).

Untrusted VAS Provider ($\mathcal{S}_U^T$). The use-cases that can emerge in the world of trusted DBs and untrusted VASPs are summarized in Table 1. Outsourcing the computation to the DB simply solves $\mathcal{S}^T_{U(0,0,0,0)}$ even if function verification is required, as it is accessible to the DB. Local computation is also possible when DB encrypts the required data using FE and provides the VASP with functional secret keys for the required computation. In order to hide the computation logic, either the approach of TEE can be applied or techniques for obfuscation are necessary. Besides these direct solutions, the usage of MPC together with universal functions is also viable. At the same time, hiding the function endangers its verifiability. Indeed, the compatibility of these properties is a challenging open problem. When further information is intended to be concealed, besides the function, OT or the encryption of the output has to be integrated with a solution that hides the function.

4.4 Untrusted Data Broker

Moving along to the case of untrusted DB, access control to the data is not trivial anymore. The fact that the DB has only access to ciphertexts makes those scenarios meaningless in which the input values of the computed functions are revealed to the DB ($\mathcal{S}^U_{(0,0,0,0)}, \mathcal{S}^U_{(1,0,0,0)}$ and $\mathcal{S}^U_{(1,0,0,1)}$).

Table 2. A rough summary of meaningful subscenarios of $\mathcal{S}_U^U$ with the related concepts and open questions. (The computation, executed in TEE after finishing the OT protocol, is indicated in square brackets.)

		VASP cannot have access to plaintext data only to the results of computations					
	function	0	0	1	1	1	1
	input value	1	1	1	1	1	1
	input metadata	0	0	0	0	1	1
	output	0	1	0	1	0	1
DB owns ciphertexts (1)	No restriction on the computed function (0)	Function revealing FE	HE	Function hiding FE	Locally computed function hiding FE or FHE*	OT + TEE[Decr-Eval]	OT + TEE[Decr-Eval-Enc]or FHE*
	Limited function queries (1)	The verification of public functions is straightforward		Using the above function hiding FE, DO can verify functions		Open question	

Trusted VAS Provider ($\mathcal{S}_T^U$). According to the trust between DO and VASP, the latter one can have access to plaintext data e.g., by using public key encryption (e.g., ABE if fine-grained access control is required). In this case, the DB only stores and sells data but computation is executed locally by the VASPs. Therefore all the scenarios in $\mathcal{S}_T^{U(1)}$ are impossible because VASPs are allowed to access the plaintext data preventing the control of computable functions. Local computation also makes $\mathcal{S}_{T(0,1,0,0)}^{U(0)}$ and $\mathcal{S}_{T(0,1,0,1)}^{U(0)}$ unrealistic while the remaining scenarios (especially $\mathcal{S}_{T(1,1,0,1)}^{U(0)}$) are trivially solved by the separation of DB from the computation (in $\mathcal{S}_{T(1,1,1,0)}^{U(0)}, \mathcal{S}_{T(1,1,1,1)}^{U(0)}$ PIR can hide the accessed metadata from the DB). $\mathcal{S}_{T(1,1,0,0)}^{U(0)}$ and $\mathcal{S}_{T(1,1,1,0)}^{U(0)}$ again represents that the services of VASPs reveal their functions output to the public.

Untrusted VAS Provider ($\mathcal{S}_U^U$). This is the most restricted scenario, where DOs are the only parties having access to (their own) plaintext data values. For a concise summary, see Table 2. $\mathcal{S}_{U(0,1,0,0)}^U$ and $\mathcal{S}_{U(0,1,0,1)}^U$ exactly match the problems that are considered by FE and (F)HE respectively and as the functions of VASPs are not concealed even their verification is straightforward. When the function is intended to kept secret as well ($\mathcal{S}_{U(1,1,0,0)}^U$ and $\mathcal{S}_{U(1,1,0,1)}^U$), a special form of FE, called function hiding FE, can be invoked either with decryption by DB or local decryption (actually computation) by the VASP after having received functional keys (from DO) and ciphertexts (from DB). However, in these cases function verification is possible, unfortunately, the verifier is not the DB but the issuer of functional keys. $\mathcal{S}_{U(1,1,0,1)}^{U(0)}$ can also be handled using FHE* (i.e., homomorphically evaluating a universal function). The strictest requirements can be satisfied by relying on TEE and OT. After running the OT protocol between DB and the TEE the resulting ciphertext is decrypted, the function can be evaluated on it and either the output is returned (in $\mathcal{S}_{U(1,1,1,0)}^{U(0)}$) or its encrypted form (in $\mathcal{S}_{U(1,1,1,1)}^{U(0)}$).

These use-cases highlight that the integration of computation on hidden data and fine-grained access control is an important challenge as in complex scenarios like these the two goals can arise together. While there are attempts to realize Attribute-Based FHE [2], to the best of our knowledge the integration of FE (for secure function evaluation) and ABE is an entirely open problem.

References

1. Armknecht, F., Boyd, C., Carr, C., Gjøsteen, K., Jäschke, A., Reuter, C.A., Strand, M.: A guide to fully homomorphic encryption. Cryptology ePrint Archive, Report 2015/1192 (2015). http://eprint.iacr.org/2015/1192
2. Brakerski, Z., Cash, D., Tsabary, R., Wee, H.: Targeted homomorphic attribute-based encryption. In: Hirt, M., Smith, A. (eds.) TCC 2016. LNCS, vol. 9986, pp. 330–360. Springer, Heidelberg (2016). https://doi.org/10.1007/978-3-662-53644-5_13
3. Data Market Austria Project. https://datamarket.at/en/. Accessed 5 Feb 2018
4. Datum Network - The decentralized data marketplace (White Paper V15). https://datum.org/assets/Datum-WhitePaper.pdf. Accessed 5 Feb 2018
5. Deichmann, J., Heineke, K., Reinbacher, T., Wee, D.: Creating a successful internet of things data marketplace (2016). https://mck.co/2lAIhjk. Accessed 5 Feb 2018
6. Gelenbe, E.: Analysis of single and networked auctions. ACM Trans. Internet Technol. (TOIT) **9**(2), 1–24 (2009)
7. Gelenbe, E., Györfi, L.: Performance of auctions and sealed bids. In: Bradley, J.T. (ed.) EPEW 2009. LNCS, vol. 5652, pp. 30–43. Springer, Heidelberg (2009). https://doi.org/10.1007/978-3-642-02924-0_3
8. Horváth, M., Buttyán, L.: The birth of cryptographic obfuscation - A survey. Cryptology ePrint Archive, Report 2015/412 (2015). https://eprint.iacr.org/2015/412
9. IOTA Data Marketplace. https://data.iota.org/. Accessed 5 Feb 2018
10. Lindell, Y., Pinkas, B.: Secure multiparty computation for privacy-preserving data mining. J. Privacy Confidentiality **1**(1), 59–98 (2009)
11. Nissim, K., Steinke, T., Wood, A., Altman, M., Bembenek, A., Bun, M., Gaboardi, M., O'Brien, D., Vadhan, S.: Differential privacy: a primer for a non-technical audience (preliminary version). https://bit.ly/2HnYmXD. Accessed 5 Feb 2018
12. Ocean Protocol Foundation Ltd.: A decentralized data exchange protocol to unlock data for artificial intelligence (technical primer). https://oceanprotocol.com/. Accessed 5 Feb 2018
13. Ostrovsky, R., Skeith, W.E.: A survey of single-database private information retrieval: techniques and applications. In: Okamoto, T., Wang, X. (eds.) PKC 2007. LNCS, vol. 4450, pp. 393–411. Springer, Heidelberg (2007). https://doi.org/10.1007/978-3-540-71677-8_26
14. Sabt, M., Achemlal, M., Bouabdallah, A.: Trusted execution environment: what it is, and what it is not. In: 2015 IEEE Trustcom/BigDataSE/ISPA, pp. 57–64. IEEE, Helsinki (2015). https://doi.org/10.1109/Trustcom.2015.357
15. Zyskind, G., Nathan, O., Pentland, A.: Enigma: Decentralized computation platform with guaranteed privacy. CoRR abs/1506.03471 (2015)

GHOST - Safe-Guarding Home IoT Environments with Personalised Real-Time Risk Control

A. Collen[1], N. A. Nijdam[1], J. Augusto-Gonzalez[2], S. K. Katsikas[3], K. M. Giannoutakis[4], G. Spathoulas[3], E. Gelenbe[5](✉), K. Votis[4], D. Tzovaras[4], N. Ghavami[6], M. Volkamer[7], P. Haller[8], A. Sánchez[9], and M. Dimas[10]

[1] University of Geneva, Geneva, Switzerland
anastasija.collen@unige.ch
[2] Televes SA, Santiago de Compostela, Spain
[3] Norwegian University of Science and Technology, Gjøvik, Norway
[4] Centre for Research and Technology Hellas, Thessaloniki, Greece
[5] Imperial College London, London, UK
e.gelenbe@imperial.ac.uk
[6] Exus Innovation, London, UK
[7] Technical University of Darmstadt, Darmstadt, Germany
[8] Kalos Information Systems AS, Oslo, Norway
[9] Spanish Red Cross/Tescos, Madrid, Spain
[10] Obrela Security Industries SA, Athens, Greece

Abstract. We present the European research project GHOST, (Safe-guarding home IoT environments with personalised real-time risk control), which challenges the traditional cyber security solutions for the IoT by proposing a novel reference architecture that is embedded in an adequately adapted smart home network gateway, and designed to be vendor-independent. GHOST proposes to lead a paradigm shift in consumer cyber security by coupling usable security with transparency and behavioural engineering.

Keywords: Smart home · Security · IoT · Gateway · Risk assessment

1 Introduction

According to [1], the average IoT device was attacked once every two minutes in 2016. Unfortunately, such botnets as Mirai are taking advantage of the fact that security is still not a priority for device manufacturers, leading to the lack of possibility of automatic firmware upgrades, exposing the devices to simple attacks such as account enumeration and open ports scanning up to unpatched vulnerabilities presence and their exploitation to gain full control.

In addition to forcing the integration of security aspects into IoT devices at the manufacturer level, it is evident that a monitoring solution is essential to protect the end-users. IoT devices are often completely closed, not standardised

E. Gelenbe et al. (Eds.): Euro-CYBERSEC 2018, CCIS 821, pp. 68–78, 2018.
https://doi.org/10.1007/978-3-319-95189-8_7

or openly developed. Hence, the user does not have a clear idea of the potential risks involved. On top of the purely technological and operational cyber security challenges, the end-user behaviour becomes a determinant factor, with the human typically portrayed as the weakest link in security. Indeed, consumers tend to exhibit low tolerance and fatigue in using sophisticated cyber security solutions or practices, while the cyber security industry often addresses usability as at trade-off on security rather than as a security enhancing component. Thus, combining or integrating usability and security requirements is a major research challenge, which recently has been brought forward [2,3], while turning end-user behaviour in favour of cyber security remains a field with a promising exploitation potential [4].

This paper gives an overview of the European Union Horizon 2020 Research and Innovation project GHOST (https://www.ghost-iot.eu/). GHOST aims to increase the level and the effectiveness of automation of existing cyber security services and to enhance system self-defence while prioritising the opening up the cyber security 'blackbox' to consumers and building trust through advanced usable transparency tools derived from end-users' mental models.

The rest of the paper is structured as follows. Section 2 discusses related work. Section 3 presents the GHOST system, whilst Sect. 4 presents the GHOST validation process. Finally, conclusions are summarised in Sect. 5.

2 Related Work

In traditional cyber security, Intrusion Detection Systems (IDS) are taking the main role in detecting any anomalous activity on the network. Best known solutions are Snort [5], Suricata [6] and Bro [7]. While Snort and Suricata are based on pattern matching detection, Bro is relying on semantic matching of the network events. However, these solutions are designed for professional use and are not explicitly aimed at the IoT environment in terms of protocol analysis availability. Global scale architecture with distributed data storage and correlation for IDS was proposed in [8]. While taking advantage of novel technologies and providing wide coverage of monitored data for expert users, this system is not adapted for smart home installation where regular citizens have to understand the usage of this tool. Graphical representation of attack and threats scenes was greatly advanced in [9]. These works are targeting professional analysts with the deep technology knowledge though. Modelling uncertainties in the cyber threat arena was presented in [10], Grey theory application for threat prediction was analysed in [11] and a framework assessing the impact of cyber attacks was described in [12]. Once again, all these advancements are focusing on the expert users, not regular citizens.

2.1 Advancements in IoT Cyber Security Monitoring

Similarly to traditional cyber security IoT ecosystem is vulnerable to the analogous issues as in web, sensor and mobile communications networks, with particular focus on privacy, authentication and access control network configuration, information storage and management, standardisation and data integrity. The most complete classification of the IoT attack vectors is described in [13], referring to the IoT ecosystem as a Web3 or Web of Things phenomenon, where four main categories are provided: Device, Application Service, Network, Web Interface and Data integrity. Developing a cyber security solution targeting to protect all of the identified vectors is a very challenging and crucial task. [14] is raising a necessity to apply the Negative selection and Danger Theory to traditional IDS, to cover ubiquitous nature of the IoT devices and target all attack vectors specified above. Such systems, however, encounter serious limitations in terms computational power and storage requirements. An overview of the Real-time IoT security solutions was provided in [15]. The authors conclude that existing approaches can be divided into two major classes: hardware and software based security. Alternative to IDS approach is described in [16], where SIEM system for IoT environment is proposed.

2.2 Smart Home Cyber Security Frameworks

The authors of [17] analyse existing architectures of smart homes from the security perspective, concluding that gateway architectures are the most suitable to provide key technologies for cyber protection: auto-configuration and automatic update installation. An overview of existing tooling for the implementation of cyber protection in smart homes is also included in their work, however, all these tools are applicable only for newly designed devices to be included in a future smart homes. On contrary, the IDS framework [18], based on Anomaly Behaviour Analysis, approaches this problem for existing and hardly changeable smart home installations. Their focus is given to measuring the activities of installed sensor devices a smart house is equipped with, and detecting any anomalies in the quantity and quality of the collected measurements. The limitation of their work relies in the ability to apply their analysis only on the primitive IoT devices without direct internet access. Similarly to GHOST, traffic monitoring and inspection solution IoTGuard, based on Bro, is presented in [19]. The main drawback of their framework is the requirement to forward all router's traffic to IoT Controller and link each IoT device with the IoT Watchdog. On the contrary, GHOST provides all-in-one solution to be deployed in the existing smart home installations with key focus given to user's experience and understanding of a cyber security solution.

The great interest of developing smart home cyber security solutions is also given by the commercial entities. Already a wide selection of the commercial products is available on the market: F-Secure SENSE [20], Luma smart Wi-Fi router [21], Dojo [22], CUJO [23], Bitdefender [24], Norton Core [25].

3 The GHOST System

The GHOST system is being realised by analysing existing technical infrastructure and existing software components corresponding to the aims of the project. Usability studies have been defined with the aim to establish mental models of the end users. This allows systematical and effective addressing of the human factor with the aim to facilitate end-users' proper decision making in relation to security and privacy issues and adequate usage of the GHOST solution. It also allows the definition of a first set of end-user requirements, which in turn facilitate better specification of the development and integration of core technologies. Since human participants will be involved in the evaluation phase of the project and personal data will be collected, special emphasis is given on elaborating a data management plan for respecting privacy related issues according to national and EU legislation. It should be noted that the access to the collected data will be provided only to the members of the consortium for development and demonstration purposes.

3.1 Development Approach

To keep up with cyber security issues and threats GHOST not only follows guidance documents, best practices and standards (issued by international, European and national stakeholders) at all stages of design and development, but it also scans for emerging threats/issues. To this end, it makes use of security intelligence available within the consortium and outside (e.g. through mining insightful security blogs), as well as related information collected directly from the end-users and the smart home pilots. The development of GHOST follows an iterative approach. Three iterations have been specified for the implementation of the technical components of the infrastructure. These will be evaluated through real life trials and feedback will be reflected back for further refinement and acceptance, according to the validation process discussed in Sect. 4.

3.2 GHOST Software Architecture

GHOST's conceptual design involves advanced data flow analysis on a packet basis to build the context of communication. From this context, data are classified into user and device profiles, which in turn are used in the automated real-time risk assessment. The assessment is based on evaluation, comparison and matching with safe data flow patterns, utilising a self-learning approach. Data analytics and visualisation techniques are deployed to ensure enhanced user awareness and understanding of the security status, potential threats, risks, associated impacts and mitigation guidelines.

The architecture of the GHOST system, shown in Fig. 1, follows a layered approach that allows independent development of the separate components, while preserving a high interdependency within the framework. A brief outline of each layer and its main functionality is presented in this subsection.

3.3 Core Layers

Data Interception and Inspection (DII). Data related to traffic of all network interfaces in a smart home environment is gathered directly from the network. This data is analysed and stored in order to be used by GHOST components. Significant data extracted from traffic packets is stored to a shared

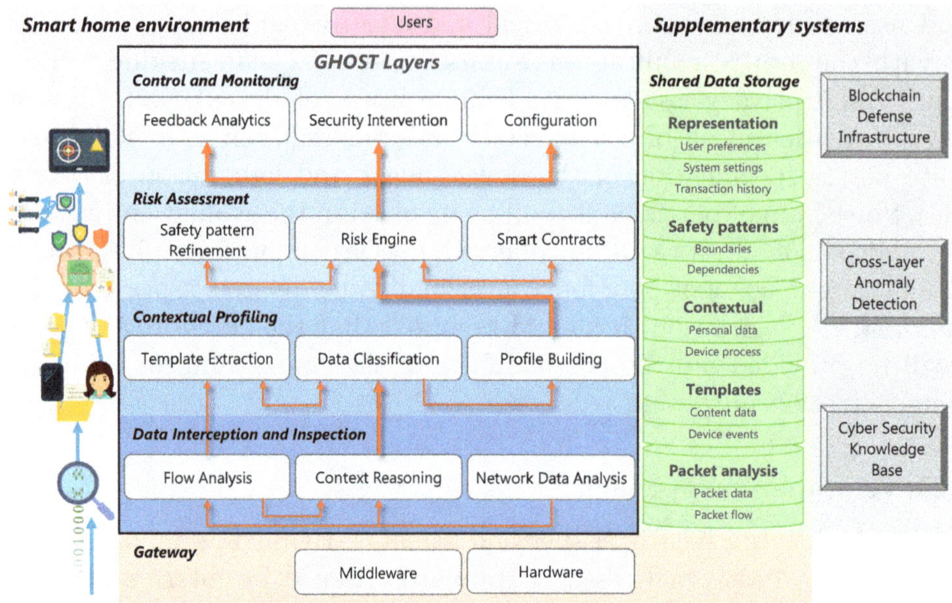

Fig. 1. GHOST architecture

data storage. Additionally traffic packets are aggregated into groups related to specific communications or actions. These groups of packets are also analysed to extract information of a higher abstraction level and store it along with the information produced by single packets analysis. Additionally context information is extracted from traffic data. Recurring patterns of traffic are detected and the causes they are produced by are identified and an initial classification of the data type of traffic is performed. The network traffic may be correlated to actions of people or events in the smart home and the data in the packets are categorised accordingly as personal data or device data.

Contextual Profiling (CP). The classification templates and actual profiles of the typical devices' behaviour are built in this layer, by extracting valuable data from the local network communication already prepared by DII profiles for the normal behaviour of the devices are built in a tree based format for further processing by the risk assessment component. This layer also monitors the communications occurring between any combination of devices including the gateway, along with the status of each device and the status of the gateway. Monitoring is learning based, and models are trained to recognise the normal status of devices and the normal status of communication between them. Random Neural Networks are employed for each pair of devices and reinforcement learning is used to update them through time.

Risk Assessment (RA). This a core layer, which gathers information about the current risks and analyses in real-time current network traffic flows. It correlates device activity on the network with the profiles available from CP layer.

The automatic decision making of the Risk Engine presents transparency of the cyber security solution, informing the end-user only about urgent decisions. Its capabilities is enhanced with the use of Smart Contracts (SC) to ensure the reliability and trustworthiness of decisions. RA is also designed for controlling users' privacy and making them aware of the associated risks.

Control and Monitoring (CM). Three types of the user interfaces are forming this layer: Feedback Analytics (advanced professional-alike interfaces), Security Intervention (daily decision-making support tooling) and Configuration. The input data include historical and current packet flow behaviours, risk levels, device profiles, packet classification score, etc. The layer provides visual and intuitive presentations and reports of the smart home security status, including visualisations of packet features through time, visual monitoring and distinction of packet behaviours, and visual identification of potential anomalies and vulnerabilities. The appropriate visualisation and human-machine interaction mechanisms are put in place to allow users to effortlessly and effectively review security issues and take key decisions that affect their privacy and security.

3.4 Supplementary Layers

Blockchain Defense Infrastructure (BDI). GHOST uses blockchain technology and SC for ensuring data and code integrity. At this layer the decisions made by RA are verified according to commonly agreed SC, turning the decision making into a truly decentralised and resilient system against intrusions. The integrity of the code running on smart home gateways can be certified by the use of blockchain technology. Additionally valuable security related information can be stored at a blockchain infrastructure in order to be shared between smart home gateways.

Cross Layer Anomaly Detection Framework (CLADF). Cross layer anomaly detection framework integrates existing open source solutions for traditional cyber security features. The main purpose is to collect, correlate, combine, and provide a unified output to other components in terms of possible events that require further analysis.

Cyber Security Knowledge Base (CSKB). A common cloud based knowledge repository is integrated with GHOST to collect anonymised security intelligence and insights from external web-sources to enhance the automatic decision making and improve end-user visual experience within the CM layer. It will maintain list of malicious actors and properties (IP Addresses, Domains, URLs, File Hashes).

Shared Data Storage (SDS). The data structures defined by each of the components are normalised and unified within a single storage framework. A combination of relational and non-relational databases is used to satisfy the needs of all components. There is distinction between local and cloud based storage, as some components will perform off-site analytics.

3.5 GHOST Hardware Platforms

GHOST is based on the existence of a communication gateway with network monitoring capabilities, in which GHOST modules capture and analyse the different traffic patterns by devices and users. This gateway is a trustable and secure-by-design device as far as it is located inside the home network and it has two main responsibilities: (1) to provide connectivity capabilities for the devices inside the network, (2) to run the different algorithms and mechanisms for ensuring the security and privacy of the user data. Having these in mind, this element of the GHOST solution must accomplish market requirements related with size, weight and objective cost, among others. Therefore, it is needed to find a trade-off between the different features and capabilities of the gateway, resulting in a device that can be defined as constrained node [26]. The main restrictions that a constrained device can have are the following:

- maximum code complexity and size,
- size of the memory of the system,
- processing power that the device can offer in a certain period of time,
- allowed energy consumption or battery duration,
- communication methods and interfaces of the system,
- user interfaces and accessibility to the system in deployment.

Several techniques has been proposed in the literature to keep these set of constraints controlled in different environments and specific solutions [27–29], including the for security and privacy applications [30,31].

GHOST is being developed and tested using two resource-constrained platforms: a proprietary IoT gateway, and a Raspberry Pi (with some expansion modules for IoT networks). The use of both devices allows several different IoT protocols, such as 802.11, Bluetooth Low Energy, Z-Wave and 802.15.4 to run on GHOST. Differences do exist between these two devices, but there are also some similarities regarding their constraints as regards processing power; memory; communications; and energy efficiency. These constraints pose a number of research challenges.

4 GHOST Validation Process

The validation strategy defined for GHOST is based on a three-fold vision that combines a complete set of robustness and laboratory testing; the specific definition of realistic testbeds; and real-life trials or pilots. First, the laboratory testing will be done with the objectives of reducing the number of possible bugs and functional errors and of checking the stability of the hardware. Therefore, unit tests will be performed over each specific GHOST module and an acceptance test plan will be defined and tested, including both software and hardware stability testing. After this first stage, two already functional testbeds will be used to deeply test the functionality of the GHOST solution in a controlled environment. The testbeds designed for two specific smart home demonstrators include more than 15 different types of devices, involving up to 25 devices that will be simultaneously connected and monitored by the GHOST suite. In order to have a broad view of the possible services and solutions, devices like smart locks, biomedical devices, companion robots or smart lights based on several communication solutions (like 802.11, 802.15.4, Z-Wave or Bluetooth Low Energy) have been included in the testbeds. Potential threats against the smart home can be categorised into [32]: (i) Physical attacks, (ii) Unintentional damage (accidental), (iii) Disaster (natural/environmental), (iv) Damages or loss of IT assets, (v) Failures/malfunctions, (vi) Outages, (vii) Eavesdropping/interception/hijacking, (viii) Nefarious activity/abuse, and (ix) Legal. Of these, relevant to GHOST are groups (ii), (iv), (vii), and (viii). Each of these groups includes a number of threats that can exploit relevant vulnerabilities by launching different attacks. The response of GHOST when faced with those amongst the above attacks that lead to higher risks and/or are most prevalent will be assessed in the controlled environment of the GHOST testbeds.

In addition to the testbeds, a set of pilots in real scenarios (homes of end-users) in three different countries (Spain, Romania and Norway) and with complementary use cases related with telecare, eHealth, home security and home automation will be carried out. The real-life trials have been designed to cover a varied set of application and services. Four different use cases have been defined: Ambient assisted living in smart homes for older people in Galicia, Spain; Continuous health monitoring for adult people in Galicia, Spain; Regular private homes (smart-home solutions) in Norway and Regular private homes (smart-home solutions) in Romania.

Each use case has their own set of devices to be installed and a complete test plan is being developed to simulate the possible results of specific attacks (previously validated and performed in the testbeds) to capture the response of the users to the GHOST behaviour.

5 Conclusions

GHOST brings professional security tools down to regular home users. The strategic outcome of GHOST is threefold: increased resilience of existing cyber security solutions for smart homes and the IoT; a leap forward to usability and automation in cyber security; and a boost in the competitiveness of European ICT security industry in the advent of the IoT in the connected world. From a user perspective, GHOST will help end-users to increase their control over their smart-home IoT devices and it will provide an option for smart-living service providers to use its security services to ensure that they respect the security and privacy needs of their clients.

Future work includes the iterative implementation, testing and validation of GHOST in existing laboratory testbeds and in real-life and scale pilots in three European countries, using appropriately designed use case scenarios. Related work from the GHOST project can be also found in [33–35].

Acknowledgements. This work is partially funded by the European Union's Horizon 2020 Research and Innovation Programme through GHOST project (https://www.ghost-iot.eu/) under Grant Agreement No. 740923.

References

1. Chandrasekar, K., Cleary, G., Cox, O., Lau, H., Nahorney, B., Gorman, B.O., O'Brien, D., Wallace, S., Wood, P., Wueest, C.: ISTR April 2017. Internet Security Threat Report - Symantec **22**(April), 77 (2017)
2. Nurse, J.R., Creese, S., Goldsmith, M., Lamberts, K.: Guidelines for usable cybersecurity: past and present. In: Proceedings of the 2011 3rd International Workshop on Cyberspace Safety and Security, CSS 2011, pp. 21–26 (2011)
3. Realpe, P.C., Collazos, C.A., Hurtado, J., Granollers, A.: Towards an integration of usability and security for user authentication. In: Proceedings of the XVI International Conference on Human Computer Interaction, p. 43. ACM (2015)
4. August, T., August, R., Shin, H.: Designing user incentives for cybersecurity. Commun. ACM **57**(11), 43–46 (2014)
5. Roesch, M.: Snort: lightweight intrusion detection for networks. In: 13th Systems Administration Conference on LISA 1999, pp. 229–238 (1999)
6. (OISF), Open Information Security Foundation: Suricata. https://suricata-ids.org/
7. Paxson, V.: Bro: a system for detecting network intruders in real-time. Comput. Netw. **31**(23–24), 2435–2463 (1999)
8. Marchal, S., Jiang, X., State, R., Engel, T.: A big data architecture for large scale security monitoring. In: Proceedings of the 2014 IEEE International Congress on Big Data, BigDataCongress 2014, pp. 56–63 (2014)
9. Koike, H., Ohno, K., Koizumi, K.: Visualizing cyber attacks using IP matrix. In: 2005 Proceedings of the IEEE Workshop on Visualization for Computer Security, VizSEC 2005, pp. 91–98 (2005)
10. Xie, P., Li, J.H., Ou, X., Liu, P., Levy, R.: Using Bayesian networks for cyber security analysis. In: 2010 IEEE/IFIP International Conference on Dependable Systems and Networks DSN, pp. 211–220 (2010)
11. Jibao, L., Huiqiang, W., Liang, Z.: Study of network security situation awareness model based on simple additive weight and grey theory. In: 2006 International Conference on Computational Intelligence and Security, vol. 2, pp. 1545–1548 (2006)
12. Jakobson, G.: Mission cyber security situation assessment using impact dependency graphs. In: 14th International Conference on Information Fusion, pp. 1–8, July 2011
13. Tweneboah-Koduah, S., Skouby, K.E., Tadayoni, R.: Cyber security threats to IoT applications and service domains. Wirel. Pers. Commun. **95**(1), 169–185 (2017)
14. Pamukov, M.E.: Application of artificial immune systems for the creation of IoT intrusion detection systems. In: 2017 9th IEEE International Conference on Intelligent Data Acquisition and Advanced Computing Systems: Technology and Applications (IDAACS), pp. 564–568. IEEE, September 2017

15. Chen, C.Y., Hasan, M., Mohan, S.: Securing real-time internet-of-things. arXiv preprint arXiv:1705.08489, 1–10, May 2017
16. Zegzhda, P.: Safe integration of SIEM systems with internet of things: data aggregation, integrity control, and bioinspired safe routing. In: Proceedings of the 9th International Conference on Security of Information and Networks, SIN 2016, pp. 81–87 (2016)
17. Lin, H., Bergmann, N.W.: IoT privacy and security challenges for smart home environments. Information **7**(3), 44 (2016)
18. Pacheco, J., Hariri, S.: IoT security framework for smart cyber infrastructures. In: 2016 IEEE 1st International Workshops on Foundations and Applications of Self* Systems (FAS*W), pp. 242–247. IEEE, September 2017
19. Park, Y., Daftari, S., Inamdar, P., Salavi, S., Savanand, A., Kim, Y.: IoTGuard: scalable and agile safeguards for internet of things. In: Proceedings of the IEEE Military Communications Conference MILCOM, pp. 61–66 (2016)
20. F-Secure: F-secure sense router. https://www.f-secure.com/en/web/home_global/sense
21. Luma Home Inc. https://lumahome.com/
22. BullGuard: Dojo by bullguard. https://dojo.bullguard.com/
23. CUJO: Cujo llc. https://www.getcujo.com/
24. Bitdefender BOX 2. https://www.bitdefender.com/box/
25. Norton Core^{TM}: Symantec corporation. https://us.norton.com/core
26. Bormann, C., Ersue, M., Keranen, A.: Terminology for constrained-node networks. Technical report, Internet Engineering Task Force (IETF), May 2014
27. Mittal, S.: A survey of techniques for improving energy efficiency in embedded computing systems. Int. J. Comput. Aided Eng. Technol. **6**(4), 440 (2014)
28. Sheng, Z., Wang, H., Yin, C., Hu, X., Yang, S., Leung, V.C.M.: Lightweight management of resource-constrained sensor devices in internet of things. IEEE Internet Things J. **2**(5), 402–411 (2015)
29. Wang, H., Xiong, D., Wang, P., Liu, Y.: A lightweight XMPP publish/subscribe scheme for resource-constrained IoT devices. IEEE Access **5**, 16393–16405 (2017)
30. Sethi, M., Kortoci, P., Di Francesco, M., Aura, T.: Secure and low-power authentication for resource-constrained devices. In: 2015 5th International Conference on the Internet of Things (IOT), pp. 30–36. IEEE, October 2015
31. Porambage, P., Braeken, A., Gurtov, A., Ylianttila, M., Spinsante, S.: Secure end-to-end communication for constrained devices in IoT-enabled Ambient Assisted Living systems. In: 2015 IEEE 2nd World Forum on Internet of Things (WF-IoT), pp. 711–714. IEEE, December 2015
32. Barnard-Wills, D., Marinos, L., Portesi, S.: Threat landscape and good practice guide for smart home and converged media. Technical report, ENISA (2014)
33. Kouzinopoulos, C.S., Spathoulas, G., Giannoutakis, K.M., Votis, K., Pandey, P., Tzovaras, D., Katsikas, S.K., Collen, A., Nijdam, N.A.: Using blockchains to strengthen the security of internet of things. In: Gelenbe, E., Campegiani, P., Czachorski, T., Katsikas, S., Komnios, I., Romano, L., Tzovaras, D. (eds.) Euro-CYBERSEC 2018. CCIS, vol. 821, pp. 90–100. Springer, Cham (2018)
34. Gelenbe, E., Kadioglu, Y.M. : Energy life-time of wireless nodes with network attacks and mitigation. In: ICC 2018 Workshops. IEEE (2018)
35. Brun, O., Yin, Y., Gelenbe, E., Murat Kadioglu, Y., Augusto-Gonzalez, J., Ramos, M.: Deep learning with dense random neural networks for detecting attacks against IoT-connected home environments. In: Gelenbe, E., Campegiani, P., Czachorski, T., Katsikas, S., Komnios, I., Romano, L., Tzovaras, D. (eds.) Euro-CYBERSEC 2018. CCIS, vol. 821, pp. 79–89. Springer, Cham (2018)

Deep Learning with Dense Random Neural Networks for Detecting Attacks Against IoT-Connected Home Environments

Olivier Brun[1,2], Yonghua Yin[1], Erol Gelenbe[1(✉)], Y. Murat Kadioglu[1], Javier Augusto-Gonzalez[3], and Manuel Ramos[3]

[1] Imperial College, London SW7 2AZ, UK
e.gelenbe@imperial.ac.uk
[2] LAAS-CNRS, Université de Toulouse, CNRS, Toulouse, France
[3] TELEVES, 17 Rua B. de Conxo, 15706 Santiago de Compostela, Spain

Abstract. In this paper, we analyze the network attacks that can be launched against IoT gateways, identify the relevant metrics to detect them, and explain how they can be computed from packet captures. We also present the principles and design of a deep learning-based approach using dense random neural networks (RNN) for the online detection of network attacks. Empirical validation results on packet captures in which attacks were inserted show that the Dense RNN correctly detects attacks.

Keywords: Cybersecurity · IoT · Dense random neural network

1 Introduction

With the proliferation of network attacks aiming at accessing sensitive information without authorisation, or at rendering computer systems unreliable or unusable, cybersecurity has become one of the most vibrant of today research areas. Whereas most work has been done in the context of traditional TCP/IP networks, IoT systems have specific vulnerabilities which need to be addressed. In this paper, we analyze the cybersecurity threats against an IoT-connected home environment and present the principles and design of a learning-based approach for detecting network attacks.

The paper is organized as follows. In Sect. 2, we analyze the vulnerabilities of IoT gateways and identify the relevant metrics for detecting some of the attacks against them. In Sect. 3, we present the experiment performed in order to obtain some initial packet captures and explain how the previous metrics can be extracted from them. Section 4 is devoted to the description of the learning algorithm, whereas Sect. 5 presents empirical validation results.

E. Gelenbe et al. (Eds.): Euro-CYBERSEC 2018, CCIS 821, pp. 79–89, 2018.
https://doi.org/10.1007/978-3-319-95189-8_8

2 Network Attacks

In an IoT-connected home environment, there may be dozens or even hundreds of sensors with various functions, e.g., measuring temperature, light, noise, etc. These environments usually also include some actuators for controlling systems such as the heating, ventilation, and air conditioning system. Each of these devices may use different protocols to connect (Wi-Fi, Bluetooth, Ethernet, ZigBee and others) and most of them are not able to connect directly to the Internet. A crucial component is then the IoT gateway, which is a device capable of aggregating and processing sensor data before sending it to Internet servers.

IoT gateways sit at the intersection of edge devices (sensors and actuators) and the Internet, and are therefore vulnerable to both traditional IP attacks and to attacks against wireless sensor networks. In this section, we focus on the security of IoT gateways and consider both types of attacks. As there is a myriad of different computer and network attack methods, we focus on some of the most common and most damaging ones: Denial-of-Service attacks for TCP/IP networks, and Denial-of-Sleep attacks for wireless sensor networks.

2.1 Denial-of-Service Attacks

A denial-of-service attack (DoS attack) is typically accomplished by flooding the targeted machine or resource with superfluous requests in an attempt to overload systems and prevent some or all legitimate requests from being fulfilled. In a distributed denial-of-service attack (DDoS attack), the incoming traffic flooding the victim originates from many different sources, making it impossible to stop the attack simply by blocking a single source.

Some DoS attacks aim at remotely stopping a service on the victim host. The basic method for remotely stopping a service is to send a malformed packet. Below, are two standard examples of this type of attacks:

- **Ping-of-death attack:** the attacker tries to send an over-sized ping packet to the destination with the hope to bring down the destination system due to the system's lack of ability to handle huge ping packets.
- **Jolt2 attack:** the attacker sends a stream of packet fragments, none of which have a fragment offset of zero. The target host exhausts its processor capacity in trying to rebuild these bogus fragments.

Other well known examples of this type of attacks include *Land attacks*, *Latierra attacks* and *Rose attacks*, but there are many more.

Another form of DoS attack aims at remotely exhausting the resources of the victim host. This form of attacks involves flooding the remote victim with a huge number of packets. Below are some well-known examples:

- **TCP SYN attacks:** This type of attacks exploits a flaw in some implementations of the TCP three-way handshake. When an host receives the SYN request from another host, it must keep track of the partially opened connections in a "listening queue" for a given number of seconds. The attacker

exploits the small size of the listen queue by sending multiple SYN requests to the victim, never replying to the sent back SYN-ACK. The victim's listening queue is quickly filled up, and it stops accepting new connections.
- **UDP flood:** The attacker sends a large number of UDP packets to random ports on a remote host. The victims checks for the application listening on this port. After seeing that no application listens on the port, it replies with an ICMP "Destination Unreachable" packet. In this way, the victimized system is forced to send many ICMP packets, eventually leading it to be unreachable by other clients, or even to go down.

There are of course many other forms of flooding attacks, including *ICMP floods* and *HTTP POST DoS attacks*, and many more.

2.2 Denial-of-Sleep Attacks

In the context of the Internet of Things, low-rate wireless personal area networks are a prevalent solution for communication among devices. As discussed in [2], tights limitations on hardware cost, memory use and power consumption have given rise to a number of security vulnerabilities, including traffic eavesdropping, packet replay, and collision attacks, straightforward to conduct[1]. A simple form of attack is to deplete the energy available to operate the wireless sensor nodes [4,6,7]. For instance, vampire attacks are routing-layer resource exhaustion attacks aiming at draining the whole life (energy) from network nodes, hence their name [12]. In this section, we shall focus on another form of energy attacks, which are MAC-layer attacks known as Denial-of-Sleep attacks. Below are some examples of denial-of-sleep attacks:

- **Sleep Deprivation Attack:** the ability of sensor nodes to enter a low power sleep mode is very useful for extending network longevity. The attacker launches a sleep deprivation attack by interacting with the victim in a manner that appears to be legitimate; however, the purpose of the interactions is to keep the victim node out of its power conserving sleep mode, thereby dramatically reducing its lifetime [5,10,11].
- **Barrage Attack:** As in the sleep deprivation attack, the attacker seeks to keep the victim out of its sleep mode by sending seemingly legitimate requests. However, the requests are sent at a much higher rate and aim at making the victim performs energy intensive operations. Barrage attacks are more easily detected than sleep deprivation attacks, which are carried out solely through the use of seemingly innocent interactions.
- **Broadcast Attack:** malicious nodes can broadcast unauthenticated traffic and long messages which must be received by other nodes before being possibly discarded for lack of authentication [1]. Such attacks are hard to detect since they have no effect on system throughput, and nodes that receive them waste energy.

[1] For instance, these attacks can be conducted with KillerBee, a python-based framework for attacking ZigBee and other 802.15.4 networks.

Other forms of denial-of-sleep attacks include *Synchronization attacks* [9], *Replay attacks* [3], and *Collision attacks* [8].

2.3 Relevant Metrics to Detect Attacks

Table 1 presents the relevant metrics for detecting the attacks described above.

Table 1. Selected attacks and relevant metrics to detect them.

Attack	Metric
UDP flood	Number of destination UDP ports per second
	Number of outgoing ICMP "destination unreachable" packets
TCP SYN	Difference between the numbers of initiated and established connexions
Sleep deprivation attack	Number of data packets over a long time scale
Barrage attack	Number of data packets over a short time scale
Broadcast attack	Number of broadcast messages

3 Metering Cybersecurity Metrics from Packet Captures

In this section, we explain how the metrics identified in Sect. 2 can be obtained from packet capture files. We first present the experiment performed in order to obtain some initial packet captures. We then briefly describe Scapy, a python package for packet manipulation, which was used to analyse the packet capture files and extract the time-series of various metrics.

3.1 Packet Captures

A standard installation of the Carelife system was done to obtain packet captures. Several software modules were installed on the Televes gateway in order to capture and parse (in a PCAP format) the data packets exchanged with various sensors which were previously paired and registered by the gateway. The gateway was also connected to the Internet using a 3G SIM card. Packets were captured for a complete weekend on all the network interfaces of the gateway (see Fig. 1).

The packet captured during the experiment were analyzed using Scapy. Scapy is a packet manipulation tool for computer networks, written in Python by Philippe Biondi. It can forge or decode packets, send them on the wire, capture them, and match requests and replies. It can also handle tasks like scanning, tracerouting, probing, unit tests, attacks, and network discovery.

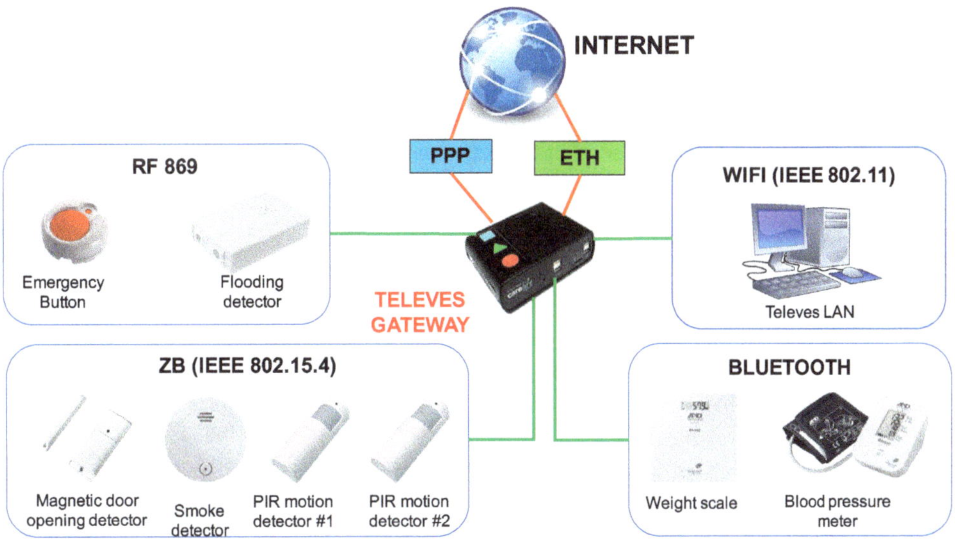

Fig. 1. Configuration used for the experiment.

3.2 Analysis of Packet Captures

In the following, we shall illustrate how some metrics are extracted from packet capture files. Instead of providing results for all network interfaces, we shall focus on the PPP interface, but we emphasize that the metering of metrics is similar for the other technologies. Scapy was used to extract some general packet-level characteristics from pcap files, in order to have a better understanding of what is "normal traffic", but also for computing the time-series associated to the various cybersecurity metrics.

General Packet-Level Characteristics. In total, 100,653 frames were captured during the experiment on the PPP interface. The total number of IP packets received by the gateway is 50,296, whereas it sent in total 41,938 packets. Analysis reveals that packets were sent to 158 distinct destination IP addresses, and that packets were received from 2,375 distinct origin IP addresses. Figure 2 shows the locations of packet origins and destinations. As a whole, the IP traffic exchanged with the gateway is composed of 93.8% of TCP packets, 4.1% of UDP packets and 2.1% of ICMP packets.

We have analysed several other packet-level characteristics of the traffic, distinguishing between the traffic sent by the gateway, and the traffic it receives, as well as between different protocols (ICMP, DNS, UDP, TCP):

- **Packet-size distributions:** The analysis of the packets emitted (resp. received) by the gateway reveals that there are 56 (resp. 130) different sizes. Small IP packets are the most frequent ones. Figure 3a shows the packet-size distribution of the incoming traffic.
- **Inter-arrival and inter-departure times:** Figure 3b shows the inter-arrival distribution of incoming packets at the gateway. The inter-departure

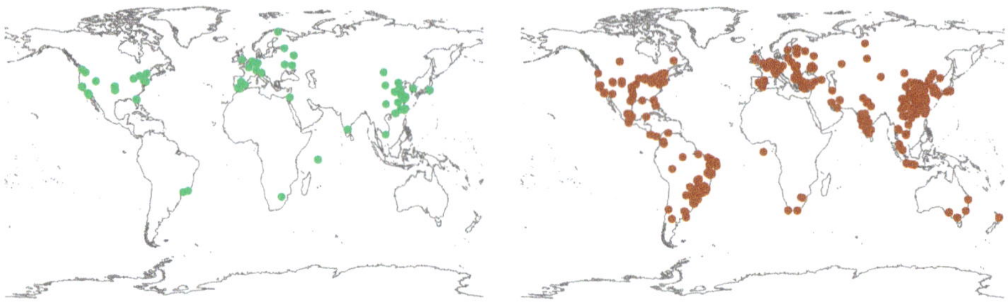

(a) Packet destinations (b) Packet origins

Fig. 2. Locations of packet origins and destinations.

time distribution of packets from the gateway is similar, but UDP and ICMP outgoing traffics follow an almost periodic pattern (one packet every 5 min).

- **Packet throughput:** Although there are some peaks, the non-TCP traffic exchanged with the gateway is usually in the order of a few hundred of Bytes per second. The throughput of TCP traffic is slightly higher, but does not exceed a few kilobytes per second.

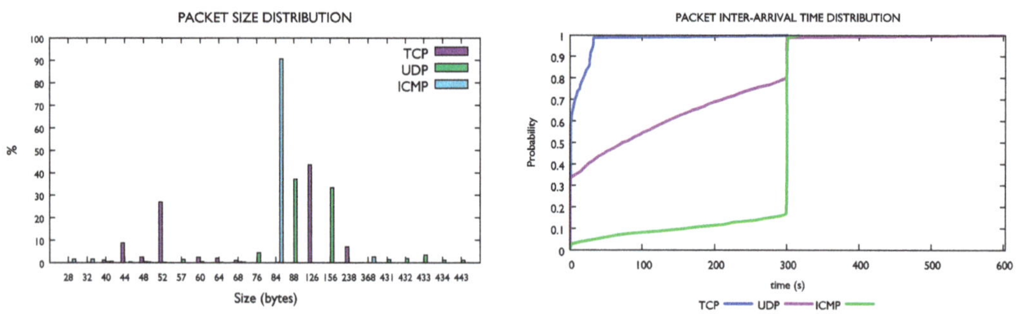

(a) Packet-size distribution of incoming traffic (b) Inter-arrival distribution of incoming traffic

Fig. 3. Packet-size distributions.

Cybersecurity Metrics

- **UDP flood attacks:** A UDP flood can be detected by looking either at the number of UDP destination ports or at the number of ICMP "Destination Unreachable" packet sent by the victim, or preferably at both metrics. Under an UDP flood, the "Destination Unreachable" messages sent by the victim will usually have their error code set to the value 3, to indicate a port unreachable error. Figure 4 shows the number of UDP destination ports opened per minute during the first 80 min of the experiment. Overall, the average number of UDP destination port opened on the gateway is 0.011, and the standard deviation is 0.065.

- **SYN flood attacks:** a SYN flood can be detected by looking at the difference between the numbers of initiated and established TCP connexions. A TCP connexion is initiated when the first SYN packet is received. It is established when the 3-way handshake is completed, that is, when the destination has sent a SYN-ACK packet which was acknowledged by the source with a ACK packet. Figure 5 shows the difference between the numbers of initiated and established TCP connexions per 10-min time slot. Except for a peak around 15:21 on 09/22/2017, this difference is usually quite low. Its average value is 4 and its standard deviation is 8.43.

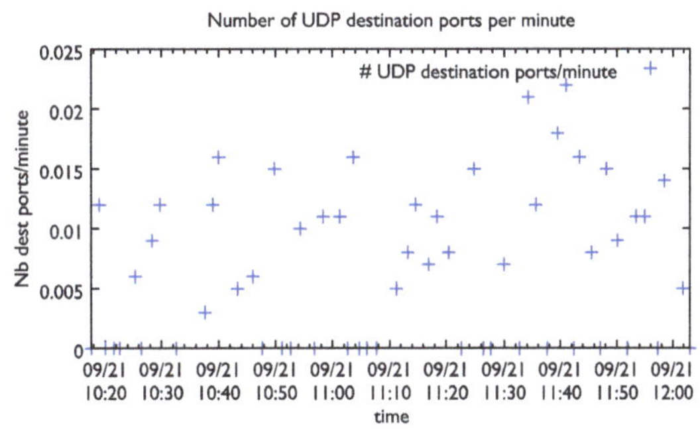

Fig. 4. Number of UDP destination ports opened per minute (first 80 min).

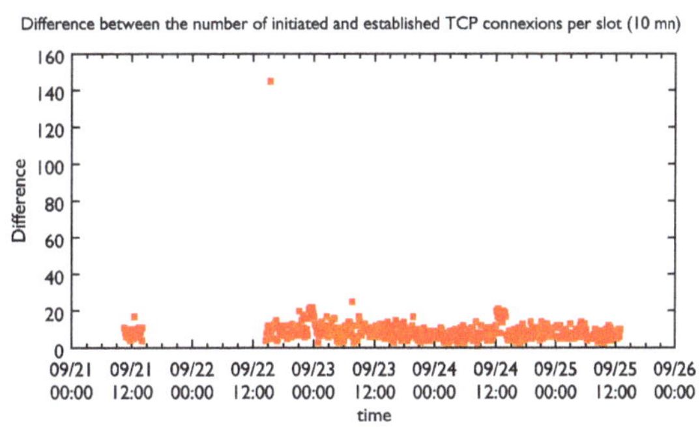

Fig. 5. Difference between the numbers of initiated and established TCP connexions per time slot (10 min)

4 Network-Attack Detection with Random Neural Network

This section describes the use of random neural networks (RNN) [17,18] developed for deep learning recently [13–16] to detect network attacks, which can be viewed as a binary classification problem. First, we show how to construct training datasets from captured packets. Then, the dense RNN is presented to learn given datasets so as to conduct classification.

4.1 Dataset Construction

Starting with the captured packets, statistical data (e.g., the number of UDP ports opened per time slot) in time series can be obtained as explained in Sect. 3. We extract samples from the time-series statistical data by setting a sliding window with length l. If a sample $X_n \in R^{l\times 1}$ is extracted in the non-attack case, then we assign the label of this sample denoted as y_n as 0; otherwise, if it is extracted in the attack case, the label of this sample is assigned as $y_n = 1$. Then, we have a dataset $\{(X_n, y_n)|n = 1, \cdots, N\}$, where the input is the statistical data extracted from captured packet data and the output is a binary value.

4.2 Dense Random Neural Network for Deep Learning

A dense cluster in a dense RNN [13,14,16] is composed of n statistically identical cells. Each cell receives inhibitory spike trains from external cells with rate x, whose spike behaviours follow the pattern of random selection of soma-to-soma interactions. Let q denote the probability of the activation state of a cell in the cluster in the steady state. Previous work shows that a numerical solution can be obtained for q such that

$$q = \zeta(x) = \frac{-(c - nx) - \sqrt{(c - nx)^2 - 4p(n-1)(\lambda^- + x)d}}{2p(n-1)(\lambda^- + x)},$$

with $d = n\lambda^+$ and $c = \lambda^+ p + rp - \lambda^- n - r - \lambda^+ pn - npr$, where p is the repeated-firing probability when a cell fires, r is the firing rate of a cell, and a cell receives excitatory and inhibitory spikes from external world with rates λ^+ and λ^- respectively. For notation ease, $\zeta(\cdot)$ is used as a term-by-term function for vectors and matrices.

Dense RNN in multi-layer architectures (DenseRNN) are constructed in the following manner.

The first layer (input layer) of the DenseRNN is made up of RNN cells that receives excitatory spike trains from external sources, resulting in a quasi-linear cell activation $q(x) = \min(x, 1)$ [19]. The successive L layers are hidden layers composed of dense clusters that receive inhibitory spike trains from cells in the previous layer, with a resultant activation function $q(x) = \zeta(x)$. The last layer is an RNN-ELM. Let us denote the connecting weight matrices between layers of a L-hidden-layer ($L \geq 2$) DenseRNN by $W_1, \cdots, W_L \geq 0$ and output weight matrix by W_{L+1}. Given input matrix X, a forward pass of X in the DenseRNN can be described as:

$$\begin{cases} Q_1 = \min(X, 1), \\ Q_l = \zeta(Q_{l-1}W_{l-1}) \text{ for } l = 2, \cdots, L+1, \\ O = Q_{L+1}W_{L+1}. \end{cases}$$

where Q_1 is the 1st layer output, Q_l is the lth layer output ($l = 2, \cdots, L+1$) and O is the final DenseRNN output.

Given a training dataset $\{(X_n, y_n) | n = 1, \cdots, N\}$, the works in [13,14,16] have developed an efficient training procedure for DenseRNN to determine the values of $W_1, \cdots, W_L, W_{L+1}$, which combines unsupervised and supervised learning techniques.

5 Experimental Results

In this section, we present the empirical results obtained for the detection of TCP SYN attacks. Using Scapy, we wrote a Python script for generating such attacks. The resulting pcap files can be used to train the learning algorithm, in addition to the "normal traffic" captured during the experiment described in Sect. 3. Moreover, using the utility tool *mergecap*, it is possible to insert a SYN attack into the files containing the packets captured during the experiment, thereby allowing to test the learning algorithm.

As an example, Fig. 6a plots the time-series for the difference between the numbers of initiated and established TCP connections per time slot (10 s) which was extracted from a pcap file obtained using the above procedure. As can be observed in Fig. 6b, the Dense RNN models correctly predicts that there was an attack.

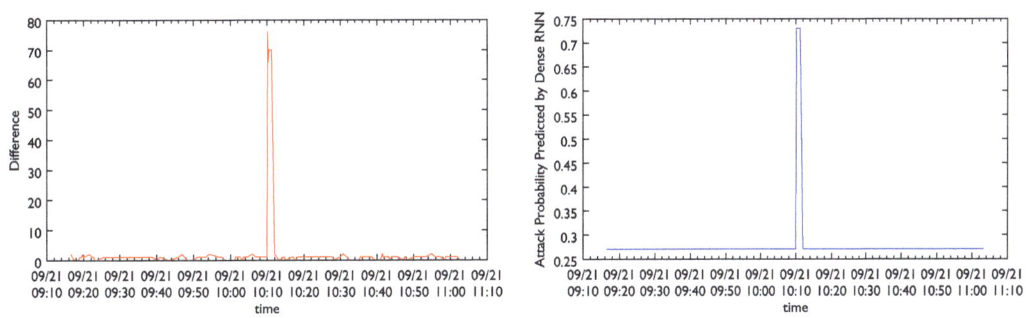

(a) (b)

Fig. 6. Scenario where a SYN attack was inserted into the normal traffic captured from 9:15 AM to 11:03 AM on Sep. 21st, 2017: (a) time-series of the difference between the numbers of initiated and established TCP connexions per time slot (10 s), and (b) attack probability predicted by the Dense RNN.

6 Conclusion

In this paper, we presented a methodology for the online detection of network attacks against IoT gateways. The methodology, which is based on a deep-learning approach with dense random neural networks, can predict the probability that a network attack is ongoing from a set of metrics extracted from packet captures. As future work, we intend to apply our methodology to a broad range of network attacks, including Denial-of-Sleep attacks against ZigBee and Bluetooth-connected devices, and to investigate the design of a one-class classification algorithm for network attack detection.

Acknowledgements. This work was partially funded by the European Union's Horizon 2020 Research and Innovation Programme through the GHOST project (https://www.ghost-iot.eu/) under Grant Agreement No. 740923.

References

1. Brownfield, M., Gupta, Y., Davis, N.: Wireless sensor network denial of sleep attack. In: Proceedings of the 2005 IEEE Workshop on Information Assurance and Security. United States Military Academy, West Point, NY (2005)
2. Dalrymple, S.D.: Comparison of ZigBee replay attacks using a universal software radio peripheral and USB radio. Master's thesis, AFIT, USAF (2014)
3. Di Mauro, A., Fafoutis, X., Mödersheim, S., Dragoni, N.: Detecting and preventing beacon replay attacks in receiver-initiated MAC protocols for energy efficient WSNs. In: Riis Nielson, H., Gollmann, D. (eds.) NordSec 2013. LNCS, vol. 8208, pp. 1–16. Springer, Heidelberg (2013). https://doi.org/10.1007/978-3-642-41488-6_1
4. Dubey, A., Jain, V., Kumar, A.: A survey in energy drain attacks and their countermeasures in wireless sensor networks. Int. J. Eng. Res. Technol. **3**(2), 1206–1210 (2014)
5. Falk, R., Hof, H.-J.: Fighting insomnia: a secure wake-up scheme for wireless sensor networks. In: 3rd International Conference on Emerging Security Information, Systems and Technologies, IEEE SECURWARE 2009, pp. 191–196 (2009)
6. Francois, F., Abdelrahman, O.H., Gelenbe, E.: Impact of signaling storms on energy consumption and latency of LTE user equipment. In: 2015 IEEE 7th International Symposium on Cyberspace Safety and Security, pp. 1248–1255, August 2015
7. Gelenbe, E., Murat Kadioglu, Y.: Energy life-time of wireless nodes with and without energy harvesting under network attacks. In: IEEE International Conference on Communications (ICC), Kansas City, MO, USA, 20–24 May 2018
8. Law, Y.-W., Palaniswami, M., Van Hoesel, L., Doumen, J., Hartel, P., Havinga, P.: Energy-efficient link-layer jamming attacks against wireless sensor network MAC protocols. ACM Trans. Sen. Netw. **5**(1), 6:1–6:38 (2009)
9. Lu, X., Spear, M., Levitt, K., Matloff, N.S., Wu, S.F.: A synchronization attack and defense in energy-efficient listen-sleepslotted MAC protocols. In: 2008 2nd International Conference on Emerging Security Information, Systems and Technologies (2008)
10. Pirretti, M., Zhu, S., Vijaykrishnan, N., McDaniel, P., Kandemir, M., Brooks, R.: The sleep deprivation attack in sensor networks: analysis and methods of defense. Int. J. Distrib. Sens. Netw. **2**(3), 267–287 (2006)
11. Stajano, F., Anderson, R.: The resurrecting duckling: security issues for ad-hoc wireless networks. In: Christianson, B., Crispo, B., Malcolm, J.A., Roe, M. (eds.) Security Protocols 1999. LNCS, vol. 1796, pp. 172–182. Springer, Heidelberg (2000). https://doi.org/10.1007/10720107_24
12. Vasserman, E.Y., Hopper, N.: Vampire attacks: draining life from wireless ad hoc sensor networks. IEEE Trans. Mob. Comput. **12**(2), 318–332 (2013)
13. Gelenbe, E., Yin, Y.: Deep learning with dense random neural networks. In: Gruca, A., Czachórski, T., Harezlak, K., Kozielski, S., Piotrowska, A. (eds.) ICMMI 2017. AISC, vol. 659, pp. 3–18. Springer, Cham (2018). https://doi.org/10.1007/978-3-319-67792-7_1

14. Yin, Y., Gelenbe, E.: Deep learning in multi-layer architectures of dense nuclei. arXiv preprint arXiv:1609.07160 (2016)
15. Yin, Y., Gelenbe, E.: Single-cell based random neural network for deep learning. In: 2017 International Joint Conference on Neural Networks (IJCNN), pp. 86–93. IEEE (2017)
16. Gelenbe, E., Yin, Y.: Deep learning with random neural networks. In: Bi, Y., Kapoor, S., Bhatia, R. (eds.) IntelliSys 2016. LNNS, vol. 16, pp. 450–462. Springer, Cham (2018). https://doi.org/10.1007/978-3-319-56991-8_34
17. Gelenbe, E.: Learning in the recurrent random neural network. Neural Comput. **5**(1), 154–164 (1993)
18. Gelenbe, E.: Random neural networks with negative and positive signals and product form solution. Neural Comput. **1**(4), 502–510 (1989)
19. Yin, Y., Gelenbe, E.: Nonnegative autoencoder with simplified random neural network. CoRR, abs/1609.08151 (2016). http://arxiv.org/abs/1609.08151

Using Blockchains to Strengthen the Security of Internet of Things

Charalampos S. Kouzinopoulos[1], Georgios Spathoulas[2], Konstantinos M. Giannoutakis[1(✉)], Konstantinos Votis[1], Pankaj Pandey[2], Dimitrios Tzovaras[1], Sokratis K. Katsikas[2], Anastasija Collen[3], and Niels A. Nijdam[3]

[1] Information Technologies Institute, Centre for Research and Technology Hellas, Thessaloniki, Greece
{kouzinopoulos,kgiannou,kvotis,Dimitrios.Tzovaras}@iti.gr

[2] Center for Cyber and Information Security, Norwegian University of Science and Technology, Gjøvik, Norway
gspathoulas@dib.uth.gr, {pankaj.pandey,sokratis.katsikas}@ntnu.no

[3] University of Geneva, Geneva, Switzerland
{Anastasija.Collen,Niels.Nijdam}@unige.ch

Abstract. Blockchain is a distributed ledger technology that became popular as the foundational block of the Bitcoin cryptocurrency. Over the past few years it has seen a rapid growth, both in terms of research and commercial usage. Due to its decentralized nature and its inherent use of cryptography, Blockchain provides an elegant solution to the Byzantine Generals Problem and is thus a good candidate for use in areas that require a decentralized consensus among untrusted peers, eliminating the need for a central authority. Internet of Things is a technology paradigm where a multitude of small devices, including sensors, actuators and RFID tags, are interconnected via a common communications medium to enable a whole new range of tasks and applications. However, existing IoT installations are often vulnerable and prone to security and privacy concerns. This paper studies the use of Blockchain to strengthen the security of IoT networks through a resilient, decentralized mechanism for the connected home that enhances the network self-defense by safeguarding critical security-related data. This mechanism is developed as part of the Safe-Guarding Home IoT Environments with Personalised Real-time Risk Control (GHOST) project.

Keywords: Internet of Things · Blockchain · Security · Cyber-security

1 Introduction

A Blockchain is a cryptographically-linked list of records that maintains a publicly verifiable ledger without the need for a central authority; as such, it is a new paradigm of trust between entities in various application domains. The technology behind Blockchains originated in cryptocurrency applications, while

E. Gelenbe et al. (Eds.): Euro-CYBERSEC 2018, CCIS 821, pp. 90–100, 2018.
https://doi.org/10.1007/978-3-319-95189-8_9

its advancements over existing architectures motivated researchers to apply it to domains that prioritize security. The main benefits of this new architecture are the decentralized nature, the inherent anonymity, resilience, trust, security, autonomy, integrity and the scalability. Some implementations support Smart Contracts for interactions between the Blockchain and third-party stakeholders.

A suitable application of the Blockchain technology is to the Internet of Things (IoT) which had a tremendous growth during the past few years, while their security mechanisms are often light-weight due to resource constraints, thus threatening user trust. As discussed in [1], IoT networks are vulnerable to external threats for a variety of reasons. It is easy to gain physical access to individual devices since they are often isolated and there is no administrator to manage them; They usually communicate with each other and with a gateway using different wireless communication protocols, making eavesdropping very easy; and finally, most devices have low processing capabilities and thus it is difficult to implement complex security schemes on a per device basis.

This paper discusses the main security-related benefits of integrating a Blockchain infrastructure in IoT ecosystems, and more specifically in smart homes installations. The inherent benefits of using a Blockchain in such systems are considered, while supplementary use cases are proposed to strengthen the security aspects of IoT installations. The proposed use cases are mainly focused on the interaction of data generated by IoT devices with external entities, while the relation with the Safe-Guarding Home IoT Environments with Personalised Real-time Risk Control (GHOST) project main architectural elements is defined.

The rest of the paper is organized as follows. Related work regarding the use of Blockchain in IoT environments is summarized in Sect. 2. Section 3 reviews security and privacy requirements in IoT environments, and it discusses the GHOST architecture and the use of Blockchain technology in GHOST. Security enhancements that the use of blockchain technology induces are discussed in Sect. 4. Concluding remarks and future work are discussed in Sect. 5.

2 Related Work

With the evolution of IoT networks and their strictly centralized architectures for manipulating device data, the new Blockchain distributed ledger technology inherently solves many fundamental security issues. The use of Blockchain technology in the IoT domain to facilitate the sharing of services and resources, and automate in a secure manner several time-consuming workflows, is studied in [2]. The authors concluded that the Blockchain-IoT combination is powerful and can pave the way for novel business models and distributed applications. Moreover, relative literature and work designed for Blockchain use in IoT was studied in [3]. The paper identified different research efforts, [4–6], that utilize the Blockchain infrastructure as a data storage management solution. In all cases, data exchanged between IoT devices are stored as unique transactions within the Blockchain and are subsequently distributed among the nodes, ensuring the integrity and security of the communication between them.

A decentralized peer-to-peer platform based on Blockchain networks for Industrial IoT was proposed in [7]. Their use cases focus on industrial and manufacturing applications, where Smart Contracts act as intermediaries between the Blockchain ecosystem and outside stakeholders. Dorri et al. proposed a private Blockchain infrastructure for Smart homes, [8]. They focus on security issues with respect to confidentiality, integrity and availability, while simulation results indicate that the overheads imposed by the use of such technology remain at low levels. Additionally, [9] discusses the security enhancements with the use of Blockchain in IoT. The role of Blockchain is examined through four challenges, namely: Costs and capacity constraints, Architecture, Unavailability of services and Susceptibility to manipulation. They conclude that with the decentralized and consensus-driven structures of Blockchain, more secure IoT ecosystems can be provided as the network size increases. Recently, FairAccess, a token-based access control model with the use of Blockchain, has been proposed in [10], that provides an access control mechanism for the transactions realized within a Blockchain infrastructure.

IT companies have also shown a great interest in applying Blockchain architectures in IoT ecosystems. The IBM Watson IoT platform supports private Blockchain ledgers for sharing IoT data via transactions. ADEPT (Autonomous Decentralized Peer-To-Peer Telemetry), a research project for Blockchain in IoT that uses the technology of Ethereum, Telehash and BitTorrent, was also announced [11]. Targeting an economy of Things, ADEPT focuses on Distributed Transaction Processing and Applications, Robust Security and Privacy By Design and Default. There are also other companies and start-ups that focus on transaction integrity, trust and security in the IoT domain.

Almost all relevant research work utilize the Blockchain technology as a data storage management solution, taking advantage of the underlying infrastructure that provides decentralization, resilience, trust, security, scalability, autonomy and integrity. This work proposes additional use cases for further enhancement of the security of IoT smart homes, especially regarding their interaction with external entities, such as caregivers.

3 Security in IoT Environments

An IoT installation consists of interconnected heterogeneous devices that collect sensitive user information and share it with other devices of the network, the gateway or third-party nodes connected via the Internet. Furthermore, modern IoT installations come in different configurations and modes of deployment. The decentralized deployment, high connectivity, diversity and heterogeneity results in a number of security and privacy challenges, that in turn induce requirements. These can be categorized in five groups, namely network security, identity management, privacy, trust and resilience. Network security requirements are split into confidentiality, integrity, authenticity and availability. Identity management requirements are separated into authentication, authorisation, accountability and revocation. Privacy requirements are split into data privacy, anonymity, pseudonymity and unlinkability. Trust requirements are divided into device, entity, and data trust. Finally, resilience requirements are split into robustness against attacks and resilience against failures [12].

3.1 The GHOST Approach

The H2020 European research project GHOST aims to develop a cyber-security layer on IoT smart homes installations. The proposed system analyses packet level data flows for building patterns of communications between IoT devices and external entities. The architecture of GHOST is detailed in [13]. GHOST includes the Data Interception and Inspection layer that is responsible to gather, aggregate and analyze data; the Contextual Profiling layer that builds behaviour trees for devices and data-flows and provides current state of data identification and related behaviour; the Risk Assessment layer that gathers information about the current risks and analyzes in real-time current network traffic flows; and the Control and Monitoring layer that presents a graphical interface to the end user.

Moreover different components are utilized, including the GHOST Blockchain Defence Infrastructure component that uses Blockchain and Smart Contracts to ensure data integrity in the process of distributed decision making, as well as additional security countermeasures; the Cross Layer Anomaly Detection Framework where traditional cyber security features are exploited, extended and adapted for the needs of the smart home environment; the Cyber Security Knowledge Base that consists of a cloud-based knowledge repository to collect anonymized security intelligence and insights to enhance the automatic decision making and improve end-user visual experience within the Control and Monitoring layer; and the Shared Data Storage, a single-storage framework.

3.2 IoT Blockchain Component

A Blockchain component can be incorporated, together with a Risk Assessment mechanism, at the core of IoT installations to offer an additional layer of security. It can ensure the integrity of such a mechanism through the decentralisation and replication of trusted decisions on the Blockchain network. Additionally, the Blockchain component can be used to capture data flows exchanged between IoT devices and the IoT gateway. The data flows captured, that represent part or all the messages exchanged, based on predetermined filtering settings, can be stored in the form of transactions that in turn can be subsequently published to the Blockchain distributed ledger.

A possible interaction between Blockchain nodes in smart homes is depicted in Fig. 1. As can be seen by the Figure, the IoT devices of each smart home communicate and exchange data flows with an IoT gateway, in this case the GHOST gateway. The gateway can function at the same time as Blockchain nodes if they possess adequate processing power or else perform the role of light Blockchain nodes. In this second scenario, additional, full Blockchain nodes must be used that can be installed either on a per smart home basis or centrally on an external location. These nodes can be used to serve as miners in order to achieve consensus in cases of validation of transactions and to publishing these transactions to the distributed Blockchain ecosystem of smart homes. Any external entities can interact with the Blockchain network through the use of the appropriate Smart Contracts.

4 Enhancing Security and Privacy in Smart Homes Using Blockchain

Section 3 identified security and privacy requirements of current smart home IoT installations. This Section details different ways an IoT device network can utilize the Blockchain technology to fulfil security and privacy requirements in a smart home context. Some of these cases will be modified and used appropriately as part of the operation of the GHOST network.

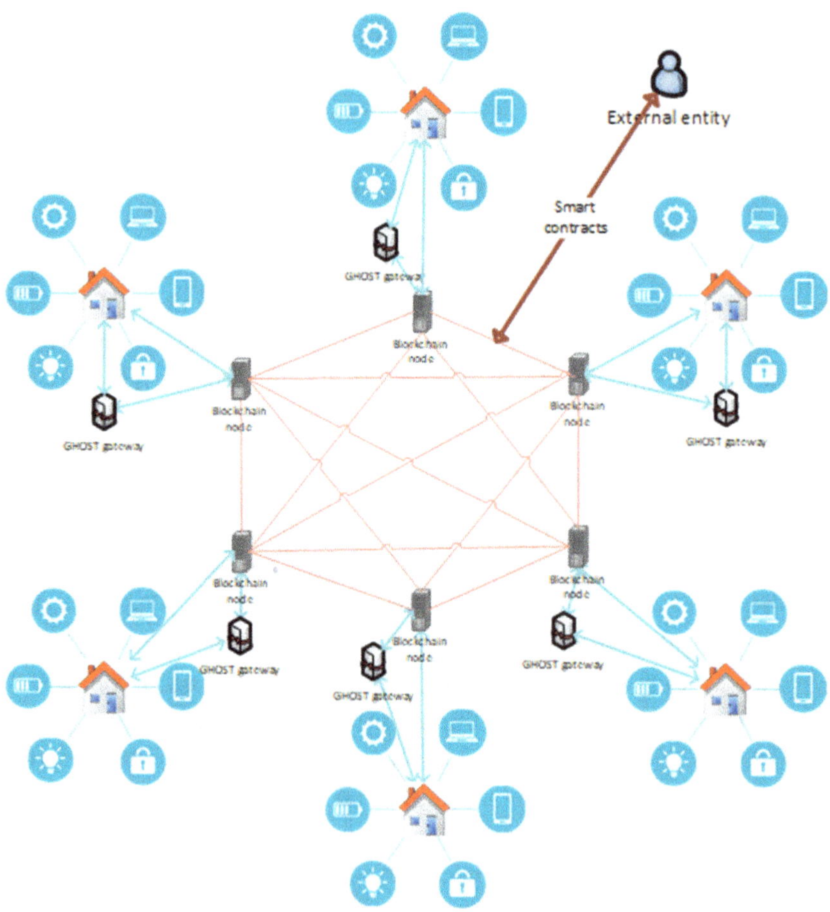

Fig. 1. GHOST Blockchain nodes interaction

4.1 Resilience

A widely used mechanism that can address part of the resilience requirement of IoT environments is intrusion detection, the monitoring and investigation of system events so that the attempts to access system resources in an unauthorized manner can be identified [14] and mitigated. There are two primary approaches to intrusion detection algorithms: signature based, where a collection of signatures that characterize known security threats is maintained as well as anomaly detection based, where network traffic is monitored continuously and compared against an established baseline of normal traffic profile [15]. However, both approaches are resource-intensive, making their execution by most low-powered and limited-processing IoT devices prohibitive.

The IoT network can use high-processing Blockchain nodes as the basis for its infrastructure. These nodes are using their computing power to verify and record transactions to a public ledger as per the standard Blockchain specification but also to execute intrusion detection algorithms. Since the public ledger contains a list of all transactions in the network in chronological order, and is synced across all the gateway nodes, the intrusion detection algorithms can be executed in parallel, speeding up their operation.

The use of high-processing Blockchain nodes to increase the resilience of IoT installations directly impacts the total energy consumption of the system. However, the energy increase can be kept at moderate levels if only a limited amount of Blockchain nodes is used and if a lower difficulty for the mining algorithm is selected. Both of these measures are valid for a private Blockchain network where access to unauthorized users is prohibited.

4.2 Identity Management

Device authentication is a mechanism to be used towards fulfilling the identity management requirement of IoT environments. It involves the connection of trusted devices to the IoT network excluding insecure devices or devices that an unauthorized user would try to add. Its enforcement is challenging though, due to the decentralized nature of IoT installations, in conjunction with the lack of secure authentication protocols in IoT gateways. The GHOST network maintains two lists of IP addresses, a whitelist and a blacklist. The initial whitelist is created by the Knowledge Base and contains a range of IP addresses marked as safe. This list consecutively is extended by the verified behaviour of the devices on the network by Risk Engine and direct end-user configurations through Control and Monitor layer.

The blacklist in turn consists of IP addresses that were flagged as unsafe by the Risk Engine, while correlating device activity on the network with profiles available from a Contextual Profiling layer. These lists are stored locally on the GHOST gateway with a limited corresponding information stored in a component called Shared Data storage. The Knowledge Base can also communicate with the Risk Engine to update the blacklist based on additional intelligence.

Both the whitelist and the blacklist are retrieved from the Risk Engine for any Smart Contract that requires them via the appropriate calls. If the lists cannot be sourced, a static list of IP addresses is hard-coded in a Smart Contract with its life limited to a fixed-time period. Once such a Contract expires, a new one is deployed with an updated list, for protection against any additional nodes that were flagged as unsafe. A similar mechanism based on Blockchain and Smart Contracts for collaborative DDoS mitigation strategy that is used to block suspicious IP addresses was detailed in [16].

4.3 Network Security

The firmware of IoT devices is a crucial part of their operation. Once a device is deployed, its firmware can be updated to address known bugs, increase its stability or add new functionality. At the same time though, its upgrade process can be easily hijacked by a malicious user [17] resulting to the compromise of the security of the network. Due to the always-on nature of many of these devices, their low processing capabilities and the reluctance of device manufacturers to improve their security for cost reasons, a successful attacker can intercept the updating firmware and replace it with a harmful version that makes the device operate in an unpredictable way.

The subject of firmware attacks in IoT devices has been extensively studied. In [18] it is shown that the firmware verification done by the Nest thermostat can be bypassed, due to the lack of protection by the device's hardware infrastructure. In [19], a security analysis of both consumer and industrial IoT devices is performed and is concluded that both types of devices are vulnerable to attacks. Moreover, in [20] was shown that it is trivial to intercept the firmware update process of Philips Hue lamps by plugging infected bulbs in the network and then exploiting bugs in the implementation of the Touchlink part of the ZigBee Light Link protocol and performing a side-channel attack to extract the global AES-CCM key that Philips uses to encrypt and authenticate new firmware.

IoT networks can utilize a new firmware update scheme, based on the Blockchain network. That way, the version of the firmware can be checked securely, its correctness can be validated and the installation of the most up-to-date firmware on all the devices of the network can be ensured.

4.4 Trust

Each IoT device can have a unique identification ID number assigned to it. The ID is created through a Smart Contract, by providing the "Entity ID" of the device and the "User ID" of the smart home user. The "Entity ID" depends on the underlying protocol of each device; it is the MAC address in case of a WiFi or Zigbee capable device, the Bluetooth Device Address in case of a Bluetooth capable device or the Network ID/Node ID pair in the case of a Z-Wave device. This procedure is performed centrally by an authorized user, such as the network administrator and is published as a Smart Contract in the Blockchain network.

Registering an IoT device creates an additional complexity layer to the IoT architecture but has the benefit of knowing the exact state of the IoT device infrastructure. Moreover, and since devices are uniquely identified, they can be managed both individually and in groups. Finally, by restricting connection to authorised devices, the network can be managed easier and with additional security.

Blockchain networks are built from the ground up based on a trustless proof mechanism of all recorded transactions [21], including all data circulated by the individual devices. In this type of network, all message exchanges between devices can be performed with the use of Smart Contracts and stored as records in a public ledger. The network cryptographically signs these records and verifies the signatures to ensure that they originate from each corresponding device, eliminating various potential threats including proxy or man-in-the-middle attacks and replay attacks [9].

On an already established IoT system, there is often a lack of motivation for individual users to enhance its security past its deployment, by updating the device firmware or substituting insecure and vulnerable devices with safer alternatives. For this reason, a virtual currency can be used. The concept behind the use of a virtual currency is to increase the safety of the network by assigning different costs to different devices based on risk assessment of previous tasks or on known vulnerabilities. Then, a higher virtual cost has to be paid by the users to access less secure devices. Furthermore, a virtual currency can be used not only at the device level but at the network level as well.

As part of the operation of an IoT device network, it is important to inform the participating users about its operating principles of the network as well as to request their acceptance by the users. This procedure can be performed by digital signing a Form of Consent. The signing is performed upon the users' first connection to the network as well as every time the principles are modified. The IoT devices of the users are only allowed to operate on the network after the user has signed the latest issued Form of Consent.

The digital signing of the Form of Consent is performed in the following steps:

- The Blockchain service receives the external connection request and asks the user to digitally sign/accept a Form of Consent using a Smart Contract
- The user signs the form and the transaction is added to the ledger
- The block containing the transaction will eventually be mined and received by the rest of the decentralized nodes.

4.5 Privacy

Often, IoT devices in a smart home capture sensitive private data for their users. It is imperative therefore that a permission handling mechanism is established. For this reason, the user must authorize access to exchange data between each of the IoT devices in their smart home and third-party entities. This access can be granted or revoked using a Smart Contract with the following inputs:

- Device ID number. This is a unique identification number for the devices in a users' smart home network, as discussed in Sect. 4.4
- Third party ID number. This is a unique identification number for a third party entity
- Status. Determines the status of the data access and can be set to either "grant" or "revoke"
- Time limit. This is an optional input and can be set to a specific time period that the access status change will take place. If the input is omitted, the status change is indefinite and can be only changed with a new call to the Smart Contract.

5 Conclusions

This paper presented a decentralized mechanism based on the Blockchain technology and Smart Contracts to improve the security of IoT in smart home installations. The mechanism is being developed as part of the GHOST project.

IoT installations in a smart home come with a number of security and privacy requirements, whose fulfilment is non-trivial, due to the unique structural and operational characteristics that such installations have. Blockchain technology can be used in such contexts to enhance security and privacy, by contributing to satisfying several of these requirements. Possible ways of doing so have been presented and discussed.

Further work will focus on the implementation details of the proposed Blockchain mechanism, as well as on its validation and performance evaluation within the GHOST environment.

Acknowledgments. This work is partially funded by the European Union's Horizon 2020 Research and Innovation Programme through the GHOST project (https://www.ghost-iot.eu/) under Grant Agreement No. 740923.

References

1. Atzori, L., Iera, A., Morabito, G.: The Internet of Things: a survey. Comput. Netw. **54**(15), 2787–2805 (2010)
2. Christidis, K., Devetsikiotis, M.: Blockchains and smart contracts for the Internet of Things. IEEE Access **4**, 2292–2303 (2016)
3. Conoscenti, M., Vetró, A., Martin, J.C.D.: Blockchain for the Internet of Things: a systematic literature review. In: 2016 IEEE/ACS 13th International Conference of Computer Systems and Applications (AICCSA), pp. 1–6, November 2016
4. Wörner, D., von Bomhard, T.: When your sensor earns money: exchanging data for cash with Bitcoin. In: Proceedings of the 2014 ACM International Joint Conference on Pervasive and Ubiquitous Computing: Adjunct Publication, UbiComp 2014 Adjunct, pp. 295–298. ACM, New York (2014)
5. Zhang, Y., Wen, J.: The IoT electric business model: using blockchain technology for the Internet of Things. Peer-to-Peer Netw. Appl. **10**(4), 983–994 (2017)

6. Zyskind, G., Nathan, O., Pentland, A.: Enigma: decentralized computation platform with guaranteed privacy. arXiv preprint arXiv:1506.03471 (2015)
7. Bahga, A., Madisetti, V.K.: Blockchain platform for industrial Internet of Things. J. Softw. Eng. Appl. **9**(10), 533 (2016)
8. Dorri, A., Kanhere, S.S., Jurdak, R., Gauravaram, P.: Blockchain for IoT security and privacy: the case study of a smart home. In: 2017 IEEE International Conference on Pervasive Computing and Communications Workshops (PerCom Workshops), pp. 618–623, March 2017
9. Kshetri, N.: Can blockchain strengthen the Internet of Things? IT Prof. **19**(4), 68–72 (2017)
10. Ouaddah, A., Elkalam, A.A., Ouahman, A.A.: Towards a novel privacy-preserving access control model based on blockchain technology in IoT. In: Rocha, Á., Serrhini, M., Felgueiras, C. (eds.) Europe and MENA Cooperation Advances in Information and Communication Technologies, pp. 523–533. Springer, Cham (2017). https://doi.org/10.1007/978-3-319-46568-5_53
11. Veena, P., Panikkar, S., Nair, S., Brody, P.: Empowering the edge-practical insights on a decentralized Internet of Things. IBM Institute for Business Value 17 (2015)
12. Vasilomanolakis, E., Daubert, J., Luthra, M., Gazis, V., Wiesmaier, A., Kikiras, P.: On the security and privacy of Internet of Things architectures and systems. In: 2015 International Workshop on Secure Internet of Things, pp. 49–57 (2015)
13. Collen, A., et al.: Ghost - safe-guarding home IoT environments with personalised real-time risk control. In: Gelenbe, E., et al. (eds.) Euro-CYBERSEC 2018. CCIS, vol. 821, pp. 68–78. Springer, Cham (2018)
14. William, S.: Computer Security: Principles and Practice. Pearson Education India, Delhi (2008)
15. Kumar, S.: Survey of current network intrusion detection techniques. Washington University in St. Louis (2007)
16. Rodrigues, B., et al.: A blockchain-based architecture for collaborative DDoS mitigation with smart contracts. In: Tuncer, D., Koch, R., Badonnel, R., Stiller, B. (eds.) AIMS 2017. LNCS, vol. 10356, pp. 16–29. Springer, Cham (2017). https://doi.org/10.1007/978-3-319-60774-0_2
17. Lee, B., Lee, J.H.: Blockchain-based secure firmware update for embedded devices in an Internet of Things environment. J. Supercomput. **73**(3), 1152–1167 (2017)
18. Hernandez, G., Arias, O., Buentello, D., Jin, Y.: Smart nest thermostat: a smart spy in your home. Black Hat USA (2014)
19. Wurm, J., Hoang, K., Arias, O., Sadeghi, A.R., Jin, Y.: Security analysis on consumer and industrial IoT devices. In: Design Automation Conference (ASP-DAC), 2016 21st Asia and South Pacific, pp. 519–524. IEEE (2016)
20. Ronen, E., Shamir, A., Weingarten, A.O., O'Flynn, C.: IoT goes nuclear: creating a ZigBee chain reaction. In: 2017 IEEE Symposium on Security and Privacy (SP), pp. 195–212. IEEE (2017)
21. Swan, M.: Blockchain: Blueprint for a New Economy. O'Reilly Media, Inc., Sebastopol (2015)

Research and Innovation Action for the Security of the Internet of Things: The SerIoT Project

Joanna Domanska[1], Erol Gelenbe[2](✉), Tadek Czachorski[1], Anastasis Drosou[3], and Dimitrios Tzovaras[3]

[1] IITIS Polish Academy of Science, Gliwice, Poland
[2] Department of Electrical and Electronics Engineering, Imperial College London, London, UK
e.gelenbe@imperial.ac.uk
[3] ITI-CERTH, Thessaloniki, Greece

Abstract. The Internet of Things (IoT) was born in the mid 2010's, when the threshold of connecting more objects than people to the Internet, was crossed. Thus, attacks and threats on the content and quality of service of the IoT platforms can have economic, energetic and physical security consequences that go way beyond the traditional Internet's lack of security, and way beyond the threats posed by attacks to mobile telephony. Thus, this paper describes the H2020 project "Secure and Safe Internet of Things" (SerIoT) which will optimize the information security in IoT platforms and networks in a holistic, cross-layered manner (i.e. IoT platforms and devices, honeypots, SDN routers and operator's controller) in order to offer a secure SerIoT platform that can be used to implement secure IoT platforms and networks anywhere and everywhere.

Keywords: Cybersecurity · IoT · Network attacks
Attack detection · Random Neural Network · Cognitive packet routing

1 Introduction

With roots in a globally connected continuum of RFID (Radio Frequency Identification and Detection)-based technology, the IoT[1] concept has been considerably extended to the current vision that envisages billions of physical things or objects, outfitted with different kinds of sensors and actuators, being connected to the Internet via the heterogeneous access networks enabled by current and future technologies [4]. Currently, IoT is emerging as the next big thing introducing the next wave of innovation with rather endless possibilities. For instance, it opens a huge window of opportunity for the creation of applications (e.g. automation, sensing, machine-to-machine communication, etc.), promises

[1] From now on, rather than write "the IoT" we shall simply say "IoT".

E. Gelenbe et al. (Eds.): Euro-CYBERSEC 2018, CCIS 821, pp. 101–118, 2018.
https://doi.org/10.1007/978-3-319-95189-8_10

to improve and to optimize our daily life and forms the infrastructure that allows intelligent sensors and smart objects to communicate and work together [11].

Contrary to the application layer of the World Wide Web that was developed on the infrastructure of the Internet (i.e. the physical layer or network made up of switches, routers and other equipment), IoT becomes immensely important because it is the first real evolution of the Internet - a leap that will lead to revolutionary applications that have the potential to dramatically improve the way people live, learn, work, and entertain themselves. Today the IoT is well under way, with the potential for changing people's lives for the better, especially with regard to human safety and security [27]. It has created new application domains and already infiltrated and dominated a wide range of existing ones (e.g. Consumer Automotive, Telecommunications, Home and Building Automation, Data Center and Cloud, Consumer Devices, Industrial, Medical, Commercial Transportation). So, as Personal Computers (PCs) start to show revenue declines, IoT is rising as the next big wave after PCs, networking and mobile systems. Moreover, based on the "cloud" trend that expects "everything to be connected" to Cloud services, we can also refer to the so-called Internet of Everything (IoE) [37], which represents the open access to data from one or more monitoring and control systems by third-party applications to provide unique, additional value to stakeholders.

In this context, it is a commonplace in the research community and the IoT related industry that challenges in future IoT and IoE will be affected by issues, such as the lack of a shared infrastructure and common standards, the management of (big) data, including control and sharing, security, flexibility, adaptability and scalability, and of course the maintenance and update of the IoT network. While analysts agree that security concerns and the effective management of produced data need to be worked out before the IoT can be fully developed, there is little doubt that the long-range impact will be substantial.

2 Security and the IoT

With IoT's arrival, EU industry, homes and society are catapulted into the huge arena of security risks that accompany an untested yet already universal technology that directly manages our cyber-physical reality on a daily, and indeed second by second, way beyond the security issues that are faced by mobile telephony [2,20,21], by the early machine to machine systems [1,42] or by software systems [15,16,22,25].

However by thinking in an innovative and positive manner, the security threats to the IoT are also a great opportunity for industry and business, and for all those who will know how to harness security science and technology in order to counter the emerging threats in a cost effective manner, and who will market products to support the development of a thriving business that assures the safety and security of the IoT [6].

While today security technologies can play a role in mitigating risks connected to IoT security [28], we foresee problems and potential threats that are not limited to what has been developed until now. In currently developed systems, the data is not delivered using uniform, consistent technology; often conflicting protocols are used with unverified designs. Moreover, we tend to think of the maintenance cycle in a short term span, which may mean that updates to IoT systems are not compliant. Lack of standards for authentication and authorization, as and security standards, as well as standards for platform configurations, means that every vendor creates its own ecosystem. On top of that comes prevention from attack all the way from information stealing, physical tempering to problems we have not encountered in the pre-IoT world, like denial-of-sleep, synchronization and energy attacks [24,35,41]. Since today the IoT infrastructure is centralized and focused on a client/server model, *in fine* all communication needs to go either through mobile networks or the Internet even when the devices are physically close to each other, it is vulnerable to standard Internet attacks as well [22,26]. Authentication relies on the central server that can be easily compromised. Thus, the model works well for small scale IoT but does not provide sufficient mechanisms for future, large scale IoT projects which incur very high costs.

In order to overcome these issues we will seek to provide an efficiently programmable approach for flexible network management [33] a decentralized approach with peer to peer communication, distributed file sharing and autonomous device coordination, using the latest Blockchain technology [46], a distributed ledger that provides information about data transfers between parties in a secure, publicly verifiable, and efficient way. The properties the technology brings to the system come from the features of the method. By design, a Blockchain is distributed in an anonymous peer to peer network. All transactions (or data transfers) are public, auditable and recorded in blocks that are added to the top of the chain. There is no way to remove anything from a Blockchain, one can only add a modified version of a block. As it is decentralized, there is no authority that can be easily compromised. We plan to use the properties offered by Blockchain technology to help improve the shortcomings of IoT: keep immutable record of the history of smart devices, as well as improve the security and trust of messaging by leveraging smart contracts and cryptocurrencies transactions. This cutting edge technology has been already introduced by some companies in the field of IoT [34], but we plan to seek to improve some of its shortcomings and explore how we can bring it to the standardization bodies.

3 Objectives of the Project

The SerIoT project will address all the aforementioned challenges under a common framework based on the cooperative efforts and prior expertise of a strong interdisciplinary consortium, including the most important European key players in the IoT domain. We bring together star European technology companies such as DT/T-Sys. And ATOS together with highly competent SMEs such as HIS, HOPU, GRUVENTA, HIT and ATECH and world-leading European research organisations such as CERTH, JRC, TUB, ICCS, IITIS-PAN and TECNALIA, and universities such as Essex and TU Berlin, with savvy users such as OASA, Austria Tech and DT/T-Systems.

SerIoT aims to conduct pioneering research for the delivery of an open, scalable, secure and trusted IoT architecture that operates across IoT platforms, which will pave the way for the market uptake of IoT applications across different domains. Key enabling technologies, including Software Defined Networks, Secure IoT routers, Fog Computing, Analytics for improving embedded intelligence of IoT platforms and devices, Design-driven features for improving both resource efficiency and self-monitoring of next generation of "Things", will be investigated in SerIoT, emanating from the market and industrial needs [36] for the delivery of safe and reliable IoT connected devices. SerIoT will consider a holistic approach in the formal definition of the end-to-end IoT network ecosystem, considering a multi-layered schema dealing with network, transport layer and perception layers. In this context, SerIoT technology will be installed, deployed and validated in emerging IoT-enabled application areas (i.e. Smart Transportation, Surveillance and Flexible Manufacturing/Industrie 4.0 as core business areas and Food, and Supply Chains) throughout its lifetime, enabling the conduction of pioneer R&D for the delivery of horizontal IoT end-to-end security platform in Europe.

With this overall ambition, the SerIoT project pursues a number of Technical Objectives which are listed below:

- To provide new means to understand the existing and emerging threats that are targeting the IoT based economy and the citizens' network. To research and analyse how Blockchain and distributed ledgers can contribute to improving IoT solutions. Moreover, to understand how to solve the know issues of IoT and blockchain.
- To introduce the concept and provide the prototype implementation of (virtualized) and self-cognitive, IoT oriented honeypots, easily configurable so as to meet the standards of and adapt to any IoT platform across domains (e.g. embedded mobile devices, smart homes/cities, security and surveillance, etc.) that will be both integrally connected with the core network components and centrally controlled, as well as that will have a transparent function within the network's total behaviour either it is active or passive.
- To deliver the design and implement the corresponding prototype of smart SDN routers [13] for the dynamic (i) detection of suspicious/high risk paths, (ii) re-planning and (iii) re-scheduling of the routing paths of the transmitted information in IoT networks over secure and (per user- or per case-) preferable connections, supporting among others the interference of the human (i.e. semi-supervised approach), when needed. Furthermore, this objective will design and implement a suitable substrate of fog nodes to support secure allocation of compute, storage and network resources for (i) localized processing of sensitive information, (ii) define the security requirements of a path coordinated by SDN, and (iii) enable secure communication with the core cloud.
- To introduce an extra, security dedicated, physical layer to the manufacturing of existing IoT platforms and devices so as to offer a secure-by-design

architecture and monitoring capabilities for the sake of the network. To explore introduction of Blockchain as a security and privacy preserving layer for IoT. Along with improving the shortcomings of the existing efforts devoted to it.
- To optimize the information security in IoT networks in a holistic, cross-layered manner (i.e. IoT platforms and devices, Honeypots, fog nodes, SDN routers and operator's controller) that will be based both on dynamic and distributed processing of variable complexity by single network components (i.e. IoT platforms, devices and honeypots will perform lightweight processes while fog/cloud nodes and SDN routers will be shouldered with more heavy processes), as well as on a centrally located server/controller that will have the main control of the network and will collect, aggregate and appropriately fuse the transmitted data and produced metadata.
- To utilize and develop the appropriate technologies, so as to implement an efficient and robust Decision Support System (DSS) on the controller's side, where all data and metadata will be collected, for (i) the detection of potential threats and abnormalities, (ii) including a competent package of comprehensive and intuitive (visual) analytics (i.e. put the human in the loop for reasoning, hypothesis testing and interference in the decision making), and (iii) the generation of escalating mitigation strategies according to the severity of the detected threat.
- To enhance the inter-connection of heterogeneous devices by speeding up the communication processes and by selecting the optimal routing path for the transmitted information in terms of both security and travel time.
- To introduce a methodology and to provide a tool-chain for automatic generation of design-driven security features, monitors and validators for IoT platforms and networks based on IoT architecture and behaviour model specifications.
- To validate these actions in both large- and small-scale representative real-case scenarios involving heterogeneous IoT platforms and devices in an EU wide testbed covering a wide variety of important areas.

SerIoT also aims to provide a useful open reference framework for real-time monitoring of the traffic exchanged through heterogeneous IoT platforms within the IoT network in order to recognize suspicious patterns, to evaluate them and finally to decide on the detection of a security leak, privacy threat and abnormal event detection, while offering parallel mitigation actions that are seamlessly exploited in the background. Furthermore, the project will also address the role of networking, and in particular transmission control, media access control, bandwidth allocation, and routing, for anomaly detection and mitigation in the IoT. Thus, the **SerIoT System Architecture** is based on the expected work-flow of the system, broken down into several core architectural elements (see Fig. 1).

3.1 IoT Data Acquisition Platform

This layer is comprised of low-level IoT-enabled components that constitute the distributed IoT infrastructure backbone ranging from IoT platforms and

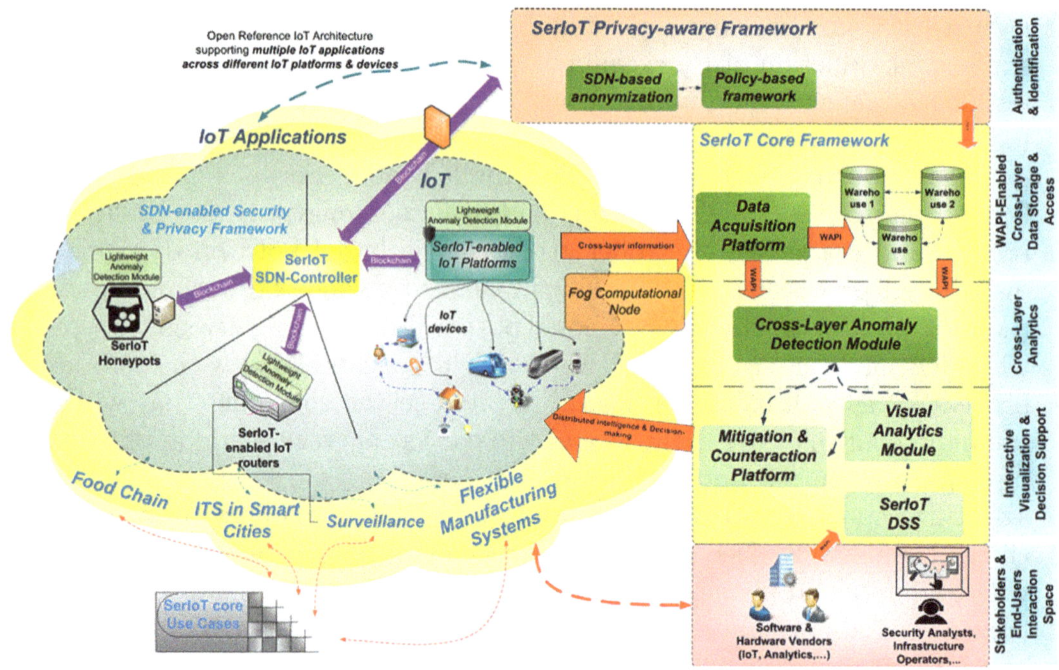

Fig. 1. Overview of SerIoT's planned architecture.

devices, foreseen SerIoT fog nodes including honeypots as well as normal computation engines and storage capabilities and the routers enriched with the Software Defined Network (SDN) framework of SerIoT.

The SDN framework will use an OpenFlow SDN-Controller that will specify and control routing paths for all given IoT applications. Similarly it will be possible to have specific SDN-Controller specialised to a single IoT application, or to groups of related IoT applications. The SDN-Controller will be a generic piece of software that may be incarnated for different IoT systems and it may be run on a given router for all routers in the SerIoT network, or it may be run remotely, as part of the core cloud or on a specific server. Thus, multiple SDN-Controllers may be running simultaneously for a complex set of IoT applications, even though some or all of the routers are common to some or all of the applications.

4 Smart Cognitive Packet Network (CPN) Flow Control and Data Acquisition

Smart network management of SDN [12,13] will be considered for anomaly detection and mitigation [32,39,40].

The smart flow controller will be based on the Cognitive Packet Network (CPN) [18] and its Random Neural Network [14,23] based learning algorithm. The CPN Goal Function in this case will consider security and attack activities over the network paths as a primary goal, but in the absence of attacks will follow paths that offer the best quality of service metrics, such as packet delay, packet desequencing which can significantly affect real-time applications, and end-to-end delay, which are important for IoT applications.

CPN routing, which is based on Reinforcement Learning using the specified Goal Function [5], that has also been used for managing the access to Cloud services [43] and Cloud networks [44] will be used by the SDN routing engine, but it will also be distributed over selected network routers for measurement, observation, and threat detection purposes. These additional CPN nodes will also feed information to the SDN routing engines, as well as to the visual analytics modules. Thus, these CPN enabled nodes, will continuously gather information in order to conduct the routing and flow function. However, the data gathered in this manner will also feed into the Analytics module (e.g. network activity, attack-related information) in a distributed manner.

In this context a modular middleware will be employed building upon previous successful paradigms, i.e. WAPI API [45], for the implementation of the SerIoT data collection framework. The framework has been initially developed in WOMBAT project and was further extended in Vis-SENSE and NEMESYS projects [3]. This layer will feed the necessary information needed by the other architectural elements of the distributed SerIoT framework, which will deal with the ad-hoc anomaly detection and the centralized decision support framework, supported by the core cloud. These components will be coupled with innovative visual analytics techniques to further support decision making to the respective operators [30,31]. In addition to the security monitoring, means for monitoring the energy consumption of the SerIoT network will also be introduced; indeed energy consumption has become an important issue in networks in general [19,29] since it is a significant component of the economic cost system operation, as well as significant from the point of view of CO2 impact.

4.1 Ad-Hoc Anomaly Detection Platform

This layer will deal with the design and implementation of a modular information network security component stack, which will support the provision of a number of security mechanisms that will be executed across IoT devices, honeypots and routers. Lightweight techniques fully exploiting the capabilities (single core versus multiple CPU cores) of each IoT device (accessed through the corresponding IoT platform) will be investigated for the identification and prediction of abnormal patterns [38]. Lightweight and robust anomaly detection techniques based on local traffic characteristics such as dynamic changes in queue lengths and second order properties of traffic will be regularly measured and probed by smart probe "cognitive packets" sent out by the SDN controller, feeding into the SDN-Controller's routing decisions. Analysis of wireless communication links based on research based evidence and performance data will also be used to feed the anomaly detection functions. These smart probe packets will bring back the information to the SDN-Controller's Cognitive Security Memory (CSM), which will be used for periodic or on-demand routing updates, to eliminate lack of security and points of failure (e.g. intelligently route traffic when an attack has been identified) and bottlenecks stemming from the network intrusion attempts.

This data will also be forwarded to the Analytics modules for confirmation (or the opposite), which will in turn come back to the SDN-Controller's CSM. Any alert at the CSM level that is clearly denied by the Analytics module will be removed, while alerts that are either confirmed or not denied clearly will be acted upon for greater security. Between updates from the Analytics module, the CSM will remain under the influence of the most recent information it has received, although it may not react to this immediately. This may lead to some reactions or re-routing under some false alarms, but the principle followed is that it is better to react than to discover a security breach after it has done its harm.

4.2 Interactive Visual Analytics and Decision Support Tools

This architectural layer will deal with the interactive decision support tool kits that will be delivered to the end-users (i.e. IoT network operators) of the SerIoT system. It will be composed of advanced information processing mechanisms, fully utilizing the raw measurements from the SerIoT IoT-enabled data collection infrastructure (i.e. devices, routers and honeypots), which will be able to effectively detect potential abnormalities at different levels of the IoT distributed network in the spatiotemporal domain. To support decision making in terms of analysing the root cause of attacks [10] in the IoT infrastructure, a novel visual analytics framework will be researched and developed dealing with the effective management and visualization of data.

4.3 Mitigation and Counteraction Platform

This component is responsible for orchestrating, synchronizing and implementing the decisions taken by the aforementioned DSS. Apart from a central processing unit, it will involve specific software on the network components (i.e. SDN routers, honeypots and IoT devices), remotely handled.

5 Overall Approach for SerIoT

SerIoT has adopted an agile, trans-disciplinary requirement engineering, modelling and design methodology, which includes the following aspects: (i) End-user and stakeholder requirements engineering and refinement, (ii) Architecture and system analysis and refinement [7–9,17], (iii) IoT-related research and innovation to implement the architecture, (iv) Prototype technical development and integration plus testing, (v) Creating pilot examples in large-scale business oriented applications (OASA and DT), (vi) Multi-level performance evaluation and end-user validation acceptance based on the fulfillment of Key Performance Indicators (KPI), and (vii) Lessons learned and concrete efforts towards standardization and market take-up of SerIoT results. It is therefore crucial for the successful outcome of the SerIoT project that a clear well-structured methodology be used. Thus, the overall methodology proposed involves five phases.

5.1 Phase One

Framework Design and Preparation (embodied in WP1 and WP2). This phase marks the beginning of the project and includes the identification of state-of-the-art technologies relevant to the project objectives, through existing knowhow of project partners and existing solutions. The output of this phase will be a comprehensive set of requirements, recommendations and guidelines covering all scientific and implementation aspects of the project. It also includes the conception of a business environment that can provide the framework for commercial exploitation of the envisioned framework along with its exploitable products. It involves market analysis, technology assessment, valorisation and business modelling for successful penetration in the emerging market around IoT.

5.2 Phase Two

Technical Development and Innovation (WP3 and WP6) will proceed in parallel with Phase One, where the definition of the SerIoT architectural framework takes place, this phase will involve the conceptual design and implementation of the envisioned IoT ecosystem. It includes the development of the architectural elements in accordance with their high-level functional, technical and interoperability specifications. The agile process followed in SerIoT will address in a unified way the whole reference chain, including end-users as well as business scenarios (defined in the previous phase) and system requirements, Thus, allowing for holistic implementation of the envisioned framework and tool sets (SDN-controller and secure router, design-driven self-monitoring of IoT devices, ad-hoc honeypots, cross-layer anomaly detection and analytics, mitigation engine, IoT reference malware warehouse infrastructure, etc.). The output of this phase is the effective definition of the SerIoT specifications to operational architectural elements by following a UML based approach and preparing the groundwork for the transfer of the SerIoT approach to real-world environments.

5.3 Phase Three

The Integration and Validation (WP7 and WP8) phase after the realisation of the SerIoT prototype components will include the following activities: (i) Individual Component/Module Configuration and Adaptation, will take place including experimental verification in the virtual testing environment towards integration int the SerIoT framework. (ii) Prototype integration and iterative testing, in with a specific integration methodology addressing interdependencies, hierarchy, software and hardware implementation, test-bed plans, etc., followed by system integration. Integration should assemble all architectural elements and iteratively deployed into real-life demonstration sites (DT, OASA, etc.).

5.4 Phase Four

This comprises Demonstration and Evaluation (WP8). Due to the agile approach we will adopt, this phase will be run almost in parallel with design, development and integration activities, and focus on fine-tuning and validation of the whole framework as well as on the assessment of the demonstration phase of the project. Thus, this phase is concerned with the iterative deployment of the end-to-end IoT framework in the business scenarios of SerIoT (OASA, DT) as well as the overall project evaluation (lessons learned). This should be followed by activities that address follow-up project achievements. Overall activities will include as (i) System Acceptance involving the execution tests, the recording of findings and the addressing of identified shortcomings. Furthermore, laboratory integration tests will be conducted in order to identify potential leaks and bugs of the prototype system prior its deployment and evaluation in realistic conditions. (ii) Validation of the whole system against the user requirement specifications and the developed business and exploitations plans. (iii) Evaluation of the entire project and its foreground along with tangible achievements compared to the initial project objectives, with adequate focus on technical evaluation (i.e. KPIs), user acceptance and impact assessment.

5.5 Horizontal Activities

These include Project Management, Dissemination/Exploitation and Standardization (WP9 and WP10). This work comprises all the horizontal activities of the project including (i) Overall Project Management (administrative, scientific and technical), (ii) Dissemination and Exploitation of SerIoT results by consortium partners during and after the end of the project, (iii) Standardization activities stimulating seamless connectivity with existing industrial bodies and initiatives in the domains addressed in the project and will be in line with the guidelines from the related standardization bodies and (iv) Sustainability of exploitable SerIoT products, based on a concrete strategy (IoT market analysis)" SWOT, CBA/CEA analysis stemming from Large-scale trials, detailed business plan, etc.).

5.6 Use Case 1: Surveillance

This Use Case will target the exploitation of the system on multimedia data streaming from surveillance networks and from proprietary sensor networks (e.g. cameras, registration points, etc.), that render valuable "loot" for fraudulent hackers or unauthorized companies or individuals. In this case, sensitive information related to personal data, and protected by privacy legislation, become available in the interconnected IoT and are obtained via unauthorized access and then are forwarded via the rerouting/bypassing of the information on secure paths. This Use Case will be combined with the next one regarding Intelligent Transport Systems in Smart Cities to demonstrate security scenarios in the context of Autonomic Sensor Systems. Examples of such autonomous systems related to SerIoT include critical infrastructures that can effectively monitor external facilities (Athens Pilot Concept I), and the case where embedded intelligence in IoT devices (e.g. placed on parts of a manufacturing system) can automatically notify storage areas and services to improve maintenance planning and worker safety. These are core impacts stemming from the Flexible Manufacturing domain, which SerIoT targets in particular by our partner DT/T-Sys. This Use Case will be also demonstrated through the infrastructure and public services offered by OASA, the largest transport authority in Greece.

5.7 Use Case 2: Intelligent Transport Systems in Smart Cities

This Use Case focuses on the analysis and definition of security solutions for Intelligent Transport Systems (ITS) integrated in a Smart City where ITS stations can be vehicles, but also mobile persons, other transportation infrastructures, etc. The term ITS refers to the application of Information and Communication Technologies (ICT) to road transportation to support and enhance various applications. The main concept is to integrate computers, electronics, wireless communications, sensors, and navigation systems such as Global Navigation Satellite Systems (GNSS), to enable the collection and distribution of information to and from the vehicles. One of the main standardization activities in ITS is specific to Vehicle to Vehicle communications where generic ITS stations (e.g. cars or a roadside platform) exchange information in a secure way through Dedicated Short Range Communication (DSRC), also called ITS G5 in Europe. A key aspect of such an example of Cooperative-ITS (C-ITS) is the establishment of "trust" between participating systems and devices. The C-ITS security framework (for cars and infrastructure stations) is mainly based on the Public Key Infrastructure (PKI) concept and is currently defined at the EU level in the C-ITS deployment platform.

While the use of PKI for a specific vehicle based ITS application like Collision Avoidance is well defined and described in specification documents, the secure and safe integration of ITS stations in the Smart City and transport systems is still a subject of investigation. We will explore the security framework for such applications beyond the ones prescribed at the EU level, through C-ITS deployment, namely the buses provided by OASA, and ATECH's contribution of roadside ITS stations. IoT security solutions will be integrated to ensure that the evolution of ITS will not generate security risks or vulnerabilities when different means of communication and devices are integrated. In addition, cyber-physical aspects are quite relevant in ITS and a security breach can generate not only loss of data but also risks to physical safety, including possible loss of life. Thus, the related security requirements will differ from generic IoT security requirements, as the reaction time of the cyber-physical components are very short and the related security solutions must react very quickly.

Two core aspects will have to be taken into consideration: (a) Vehicles and drivers will be connected through multiple wireless technologies such as Cellular Networks, Bluetooth, Wi-Fi, etc. (b) The security of the ITS station and the exchange of information (including personal data) will have to be protected in this heterogeneous context. (c) Beyond cars, people on the streets and other roadside nodes could also be connected to ITS stations Thus, widening the current concept of ITS station and its collaborative functionalities. This Use Case will also be coupled with the Surveillance Use Case (monitoring of an infrastructure) and will be instantiated in the large-scale IoT-enabled systems that are described below.

Bilbao Pre-demonstrator and Real World Scenarios. This pilot offers an intermediate step between early validation of algorithms in a laboratory environment, and the actual exploitation of the system in real world environments as in the next three use-case pilots. In particular, all applicable systems of the SerIoT solution will be tested in the controlled environment of the Bilbao park before being exploited on the streets of Athens so as to significantly facilitate the early detection of faults, bugs, etc., to minimize any risk to the public, and thoroughly and repeatedly check certain cases with no time restriction or environmental disturbances. The TECNALIA private test track is a fully instrumented permanent test site for Automated Vehicles composed of two Renault Twizzy automated vehicles, a private (dedicated) test track with central station (with I-to-V and Vehicle-to-Vehicle communication) and a driving platform simulator. This scenario will help validate some of the individual and cooperative manoeuvres in the vehicles: overtaking, intersection lane change and roundabouts. Dual mode services, such as control of automated functions and sharing techniques between vehicle and driver, can be tested. technology providers from the consortium will participate in this demonstrator.

Transport for Athens Pilot Concept I. Audio permanent sensors and cameras will be installed in public transport vehicles and depots to detect illegal or unwanted activities such as window scratch graffiti, graffiti, potential security incidents, and unsolicited activities (such as begging, in-vehicle music playing, etc.). This low-cost network of microphones and cameras, coupled with an "security incident control center", will have the capability to detect selected image frequencies for graffiti and scratch graffiti, and detecting and recognizing sound patterns that indicate security incidents or unsolicited activities. This in-vehicle and depot systems will have capabilities of audio feedback, in order to deter and avert unwanted and illegal actions. The central system will identify the vehicle in which an incident takes place and give the operators required information for incident management.

Transport for Athens Pilot Concept II. The installation of engine sensors in buses and trolleybuses (potential extensions to Metro will also be investigated during pilot designs), aims to enable the access to engineering data in order identify potential future breakdowns and create engineering log of required data, in order to plan maintenance activities, using the secure and safe IoT ecosystem of SerIoT. Both of the "Athens Pilot" Use Cases will be organized by OASA with ICCS and CERTH for the application development and integration in liaison with project partners ATOS, HOPU and DT/T-Sys.

C-ITS Stations Vienna Pilot Concept III. Use of existing and installed C-ITS stations in a living lab environment with additional security elements of SerIoT for the monitoring of security risk's and attacks form the connected sensors and external C-ITS dynamic communication links. Enable and support fast recognition of "insecure ITS stations" or other external users and contribute data reports and logs to the clarification of the "unclear situation" in terms of severity of the risk and the consequences for the extended and distributed C-ITS network (e.g. options could range from closing one network channel of the ITS station, temporarily close the receiving channel, temporarily shut down the C-ITS station, to report to central operators to close all "linked stations" down in "hibernation mode" till certain conditions are met again and operational capacity can be resolved). Generate for the operator additional recommendations and hints for regular network operation and propose improvements for regular and stable operations. ATECH has access to ITS stations in the Vienna Living lab environment and will offer the expertise and resources from there in order to set up the aforementioned scenario.

5.8 Use Case 3: Flexible Manufacturing Systems

This Use Case will deal with Flexible Manufacturing Systems (Industry 4.0), which concern a sophisticated approach for enabling connected industry to create value and novel business models. This Use Case will provide monitoring and detection of physical attacks to wireless sensor networks in the context of the Industry 4.0 and will be mainly supported by DT/T-Sys. and the testbed provided by UEssex. There will be two concrete scenarios, which will be instantiated in DT/T-Sys. infrastructure:

- Attack on an intelligent automatic warehouse such as those that are planned by Amazon. In this use case the warehouse is operated by wireless connected robots, which collect the purchase lists automatically and bring the goods to the packing stations. Since all data communication is wireless, many attack vectors may be used for breaking or jamming the communication line. Within SerIoT, techniques such as anomaly detection at SDN and device levels will be utilized for the early identification of such attacks.
- This use case is also an example of dealing with a critical infrastructure, where some of the components, actors or sensors are linked by wireless technology such as W-Lan or Bluetooth. Jamming attacks can disturb the communications, so that the supply of critical resources such as energy or water can be impacted seriously. The monitoring and detection system of SerIoT will be also utilized here to demonstrate the feasibility of mitigating such attacks, and tested in OASA pilots, in DT/T-Sys., and perhaps in other contexts.

5.9 Use Case 4: Food Chains

Food Chains can illustrate end-to-end security across communication channels, i.e. Transport Layer Security, Datagram TLS protocol, etc., by addressing device authentication mechanisms, the detection and avoidance of DoS and replication attacks, as well as early detection of the interruption of IoT devices (critical functionality), while the requirements related to the mobility of these devices will be explored, for instance when they are deployed in an environment where no protection is available by design. Since many food items are perishable and can only remain in shops for a certain time before they become unfit for consumption, replacing printed "deadlines" by IoT devices on packages will communicate to shop managers when a deadline is reached and flash a red LED indicator for the shop managers and customers, offering "on board sensing and communications" for food. This Use Case will be supported by third parties that will join the SerIoT consortium and interconnected to the project through the EU wide test-bed supported by UEssex.

6 Conclusions

As we move towards the IoT and the IoE, we are opening our most vital physical systems that support our daily life, to possible security and privacy breaches, and attacks that can impede and impair all of our common daily activities. Thus, in this paper we have outlined the EU H2020 SerIoT project which addresses the IoT Security Challenge by developing, implementing and testing a generic IoT framework based on a specific adaptation of the concept of smart Software Defined Networks, augmented with secure routers, advanced analytics and user friendly visual analytics. The SerIoT project will create a unique and portable software-based SerIoT network to spearhead Europe's success in IoT security. The SerIoT project has thus formulated major Scientific and Technological Objectives which will also help us monitor overall progress based on specific quantitative and qualitative indicators relevant to each objectives. These advances will also be evaluated in individual laboratory test-beds and in an integrated EU wide test-bed, which will be interconnected and demonstrated via significant use cases by our industry partners.

Acknowledgement. This research was partially supported by funding from the H2020-IOT-2016-2017 (H2020-IOT-2017) Program under Grant Agreement 780139 for the SerIoT Research and Innovation Action.

References

1. 3GPP: Study on machine-type communications (MTC) and other mobile data applications communications enhancements (release 12), December 2013. http://www.3gpp.org/DynaReport/23887.htm. 3GPP TR 23.887
2. Abdelrahman, O.H., Gelenbe, E.: Signalling storms in 3G mobile networks. In: IEEE International Conference on Communications (ICC 2014), Sydney, Australia, pp. 1017–1022, June 2014
3. Abdelrahman, O.H., Gelenbe, E., Gorbil, G., Oklander, B.: Mobile network anomaly detection and mitigation: the NEMESYS approach. In: Gelenbe, E., Lent, R. (eds.) ISCIS 2013. LNEE, vol. 264, pp. 429–438. Springer, Cham (2013). https://doi.org/10.1007/978-3-319-01604-7_42

4. Bera, S., Misra, S., Vasilakos, A.V.: Software-defined networking for internet of things: a survey. IEEE Internet Things J. **4**(6), 1994–2008 (2017)
5. Brun, O., Wang, L., Gelenbe, E.: Big data for autonomic intercontinental communications. IEEE Trans. Sel. Areas Commun. **34**(3), 575–583 (2016)
6. Collen, A., et al.: Ghost - safe-guarding home IoT environments with personalised real-time risk control. In: Gelenbe, E., et al. (eds.) Euro-CYBERSEC 2018, CCIS, vol. 821, pp. 68–78. Springer, Heidelberg (2018)
7. Czachórski, T., Domański, A., Domańska, J., Pagano, M., Rataj, A.: Delays in IP routers, a Markov model. In: Czachórski, T., Gelenbe, E., Grochla, K., Lent, R. (eds.) ISCIS 2016. CCIS, vol. 659, pp. 185–192. Springer, Cham (2016). https://doi.org/10.1007/978-3-319-47217-1_20
8. Czachórski, T., Grochla, K., Pekergin, F.: Diffusion approximation model for the distribution of packet travel time at sensor networks. In: Cerdà-Alabern, L. (ed.) EuroNGI 2008. LNCS, vol. 5122, pp. 10–25. Springer, Heidelberg (2008). https://doi.org/10.1007/978-3-540-89183-3_2
9. Domański, A., Domańska, J., Pagano, M., Czachórski, T.: The fluid flow approximation of the TCP Vegas and Reno congestion control mechanism. In: Czachórski, T., Gelenbe, E., Grochla, K., Lent, R. (eds.) ISCIS 2016. CCIS, vol. 659, pp. 193–200. Springer, Cham (2016). https://doi.org/10.1007/978-3-319-47217-1_21
10. Drosou, A., Kalamaras, I., Papadopoulos, S., Tzovaras, D.: An enhanced graph analytics platform (GAP) providing insight in big network data. J. Innov. Digit. Ecosyst. **3**(2), 83–97 (2016)
11. Elhammouti, H., Sabir, E., Benjillali, M., Echabbi, L., Tembine, H.: Self-organized connected objects: rethinking qos provisioning for IoT services. IEEE Commun. Mag. **55**(9), 41–47 (2017)
12. Francois, F., Gelenbe, E.: Optimizing secure SDN-enabled inter-data centre overlay networks through cognitive routing. In: 2016 IEEE 24th International Symposium on Modeling, Analysis and Simulation of Computer and Telecommunication Systems (MASCOTS), pp. 283–288. IEEE (2016)
13. Francois, F., Gelenbe, E.: Towards a cognitive routing engine for software defined networks. In: 2016 IEEE International Conference on Communications (ICC), pp. 1–6. IEEE (2016)
14. Gelenbe, E.: Learning in the recurrent random neural network. Neural Comput. **1**, 154–164 (1993)
15. Gelenbe, E.: Keeping viruses under control. In: Yolum, I., Güngör, T., Gürgen, F., Özturan, C. (eds.) ISCIS 2005. LNCS, vol. 3733, pp. 304–311. Springer, Heidelberg (2005). https://doi.org/10.1007/11569596_33
16. Gelenbe, E.: Dealing with software viruses: a biological paradigm. Inf. Secur. Tech. Rep. **12**(4), 242–250 (2007)
17. Gelenbe, E.: A diffusion model for packet travel time in a random multi-hop medium. ACM Trans. Sens. Netw. (TOSN) **3**(2), 10 (2007)
18. Gelenbe, E.: Steps towards self-aware networks. Commun. ACM **52**(7), 66–75 (2009)
19. Gelenbe, E., Caseau, Y.: The impact of information technology on energy consumption and carbon emissions. Ubiquity **2015**(June), 1:1–1:15 (2015)
20. Gelenbe, E., et al.: Nemesys: enhanced network security for seamless service provisioning in the smart mobile ecosystem. In: Gelenbe, E., Lent, R. (eds.) Information Sciences and Systems 2013. LNEE, vol. 264, pp. 369–378. Springer, Cham (2013). https://doi.org/10.1007/978-3-319-01604-7_36

21. Gelenbe, E., Gorbil, G., Tzovaras, D., Liebergeld, S., Garcia, D., Baltatu, M., Lyberopoulos, G.: Security for smart mobile networks: the NEMESYS approach. In: 2013 International Conference on Privacy and Security in Mobile Systems (PRISMS), pp. 1–8. IEEE (2013)
22. Gelenbe, E., Hernández, M.: Virus tests to maximize availability of software systems. Theoret. Comput. Sci. **125**(1), 131–147 (1994)
23. Gelenbe, E., Hussain, K.F.: Learning in the multiple class random neural network. IEEE Trans. Neural Netw. **13**(6), 1257–1267 (2002)
24. Gelenbe, E., Kadioglu, Y.M.: Energy life-time of wireless nodes with and without energy harvesting under network attacks. In: Advances in Cyber-Security: An ISCIS International Workshop. Springer, Heidelberg (2018)
25. Gelenbe, E., Kaptan, V., Wang, Y.: Biological metaphors for agent behavior. In: Aykanat, C., Dayar, T., Körpeoğlu, İ. (eds.) ISCIS 2004. LNCS, vol. 3280, pp. 667–675. Springer, Heidelberg (2004). https://doi.org/10.1007/978-3-540-30182-0_67
26. Görbil, G., Abdelrahman, O.H., Pavloski, M., Gelenbe, E.: Modeling and analysis of RRC-based signalling storms in 3G networks. IEEE Trans. Emerg. Top. Comput. **4**(1), 113–127 (2016)
27. Gorbil, G., Gelenbe, E.: Opportunistic communications for emergency support systems. Procedia Comput. Sci. **5**, 39–47 (2011)
28. He, D., Chan, S., Qiao, Y., Guizani, N.: Imminent communication security for smart communities. IEEE Commun. Mag. **56**(1), 99–103 (2018)
29. Jiang, H., Liu, F., Thulasiram, R.K., Gelenbe, E.: Guest editorial: special issue on green pervasive and ubiquitous systems. IEEE Syst. J. **11**(2), 806–812 (2017)
30. Kalamaras, I., Drosou, A., Polychronidou, E., Tzovaras, D.: A consistency-based multimodal graph embedding method for dimensionality reduction. In: 2017 IEEE International Conference on Data Science and Advanced Analytics (DSAA), pp. 351–360, October 2017
31. Kalamaras, I., Drosou, A., Tzovaras, D.: A multi-objective clustering approach for the detection of abnormal behaviors in mobile networks. In: 2015 IEEE International Conference on Communication Workshop (ICCW), pp. 1491–1496. IEEE (2015)
32. Kalkan, K., Gür, G., Alagöz, F.: Defense mechanisms against DDoS attacks in SDN environment. IEEE Commun. Mag. **55**(9), 175–179 (2017)
33. Kalkan, K., Zeadally, S.: Securing internet of things (IoT) with software defined networking (SDN). IEEE Commun. Mag. (2017)
34. Lei, A., Cruickshank, H., Cao, Y., Asuquo, P., Ogah, C.P.A., Sun, Z.: Blockchain-based dynamic key management for heterogeneous intelligent transportation systems. IEEE Internet Things J. **4**(6), 1832–1843 (2017)
35. Lu, X., Spear, M., Levitt, K., Matloff, N.S., Wu, S.F.: A synchronization attack and defense in energy-efficient listen-sleep slotted MAC protocols. In: Second International Conference on Emerging Security Information, Systems and Technologies, SECURWARE 2008, pp. 403–411. IEEE (2008)
36. Mehmood, Y., Ahmad, F., Yaqoob, I., Adnane, A., Imran, M., Guizani, S.: Internet-of-things-based smart cities: recent advances and challenges. IEEE Commun. Mag. **55**(9), 16–24 (2017)
37. Melcherts, H.E.: The internet of everything and beyond. In: Human Bond Communication: The Holy Grail of Holistic Communication and Immersive Experience, p. 173 (2017)

38. Papadopoulos, S., Drosou, A., Tzovaras, D.: A novel graph-based descriptor for the detection of billing-related anomalies in cellular mobile networks. IEEE Trans. Mob. Comput. **15**(11), 2655–2668 (2016)
39. Pavloski, M., Gelenbe, E.: Attacks on the signalling systems of mobile telephony. In: Gelenbe, E., et al. (eds.) Euro-CYBERSEC 2018, CCIS, vol. 821, pp. 130–141. Springer, Heidelberg (2018)
40. Pavloski, M., Görbil, G., Gelenbe, E.: Counter based detection and mitigation of signalling attacks. In: Proceedings of 12th International Conference on Security and Cryptography (SECRYPT 2015), Colmar, Alsace, France, pp. 413–418, July 2015
41. Pirretti, M., Zhu, S., Vijaykrishnan, N., McDaniel, P., Kandemir, M., Brooks, R.: The sleep deprivation attack in sensor networks: analysis and methods of defense. Int. J. Distrib. Sens. Netw. **2**(3), 267–287 (2006)
42. Ratasuk, R., Prasad, A., Li, Z., Ghosh, A., Uusitalo, M.A.: Recent advancements in M2M communications in 4G networks and evolution towards 5G. In: Proceedings of 18th IEEE International Conference Intelligence in Next Generation Networks (ICIN), Paris, France, pp. 52–57, February 2015
43. Wang, L., Brun, O., Gelenbe, E.: Adaptive workload distribution for local and remote clouds. In: 2016 IEEE International Conference on Systems, Man, and Cybernetics (SMC), pp. 003984–003988. IEEE (2016)
44. Wang, L., Gelenbe, E.: Adaptive dispatching of tasks in the cloud. IEEE Trans. Cloud Comput. **6**(1), 33–45 (2018)
45. Yan, L., Da, G.: Study of WAPI technology and security. In: 2010 IEEE 2nd Symposium on Web Society (SWS), pp. 716–719. IEEE (2010)
46. Zohar, A.: Bitcoin: under the hood. Commun. ACM **58**(9), 104–113 (2015)

Towards a Mobile Malware Detection Framework with the Support of Machine Learning

Dimitris Geneiatakis, Gianmarco Baldini(✉), Igor Nai Fovino, and Ioannis Vakalis

European Commission, Joint Research Centre (JRC), Cyber and Digital Citizens' Security Unit, Via Enrico Fermi 2749, 21027 Ispra, Italy
gianmarco.baldini@ec.europa.eu

Abstract. Several policies initiatives around the digital economy stress on one side the centrality of smartphones and mobile applications, and on the other call for attention on the threats to which this ecosystem is exposed to. Lately, a plethora of related works rely on machine learning algorithms to classify whether an application is malware or not, using data that can be extracted from the application itself with high accuracy. However, different parameters can influence machine learning effectiveness. Thus, in this paper we focus on validating the efficiency of such approaches in detecting malware for Android platform, and identifying the optimal characteristics that should be consolidated in any similar approach. To do so, we built a machine learning solution based on features that can be extracted by static analysis of any Android application, such as activities, services, broadcasts, receivers, intent categories, APIs, and permissions. The extracted features are analyzed using statistical analysis and machine learning algorithms. The performance of different sets of features are investigated and compared. The analysis shows that under an optimal configuration an accuracy up to 97% can be obtained.

1 Introduction

Digital Single Market (DSM) strategy[1], and other policy initiatives recognize the potentialities of digital business for innovation and growth. Smarthphones and mobile applications are considered a basic component in this ecosystem. This is not only because lately the 50% of web page traffic is generated by mobile devices as reported in [1], but also mobile networks enable users to interact with digital services at any time and almost at any place. Thus, service providers offer to users both web based applications and their mobile counterpart.

However, to exploit DSM capacities in mobile environments various challenges should be faced. Among them security, privacy and trust is of high concern. This is of especially importance for mobile applications that users can install either from trusted official sites (*i.e.,* Google Play) or through third

[1] https://ec.europa.eu/commission/priorities/digital-single-market_en.

E. Gelenbe et al. (Eds.): Euro-CYBERSEC 2018, CCIS 821, pp. 119–129, 2018.
https://doi.org/10.1007/978-3-319-95189-8_11

party applications stores. Note that even if mobile applications are inspected (*e.g.,* through Google bouncer), for security flaws before publishing, it is rather impossible to be completely sure about the quality of any given application from a security and privacy perspective as adversaries always find new ways and techniques to bypass the underlying protection mechanisms. Furthermore, third parties stores do not follow the same security policies as Google play and hence is most probable to be used as a vehicle for malware distribution.

However, lately systems' security have been highly enhanced by introducing different solutions [2,3] either at operating system or at application layer works, malware detection as a part of it is still an on-going and challenging research problem. Various research works [4,5] have shown that not only malicious software (malware) can get access to private information but also goodware might try to invade to users' digital space as it is considered the main asset for digital business in this new era, and consequently can threaten their private sphere. So a major question, considering the vast number of available mobile applications (apps), is whether users can be informed if a given app can act maliciously to a certain degree. To do so it is of high importance to:

1. understand mobile applications characteristics that can be used for such a classification
2. provide a solution capable of analyzing the large scale landscape and learn to identify potential problems and unknown patterns in the fly.

In this context, anomaly detection solutions with emphasis on machine learning (ML) have been considered as an alternative option, to traditional ones, recently. This is because (a) humans are incapable of identifying (common) patterns in a high frequency data, (b) cyber domain is currently supported by big data meaning that high volume of data can be used for developing the appropriate base line behaviours, and (c) ML assisted tools the last decades have been used successfully in diverse domains such as text processing, health-care, finance, *etc.*

We believe that a well-defined model relying on the advantages of ML can be a promising ally for improving and enhancing the current level of cyber security protection/identification solutions. Currently, related works *e.g.,* [6,7] demonstrate promising outcomes, however, additional analysis should be accomplished in order to identify the optimal parameters to achieve high accuracy and validate the outcomes of other related works. In this mind-set, we envision a ML assisted framework for mobile apps classification based on their intrinsic properties that is capable of (a) demonstrating ML based solutions capacities; currently it is not straight forward to compare different ML approaches and validate their outcomes, and (b) detecting malware with high accuracy.

In this work we set up the foundations for developing such a framework with emphasis on Android OS. More specifically, the proposed architecture relies on reverse engineering any given app for extracting through static analysis app's features such as activities, services, broadcasts, receivers, intent categories, APIs, and permissions that retrofit ML algorithms to characterize whether or not the examined app is malicious. We analyze the effectiveness of two well-known ML *i.e.,* k-NN and SVM to detect malware using different set of features over a data set of 2620 applications, equally divided among malware and goodware, and we provide a comparison with other related works. Further, we study the efficacy of applying a statistical analysis to the extracted features, which transform the initial set of features in a smaller dimensional space. We discuss the relevance of the different features using various selection approaches in order to identify the optimal parameters. Results indicate that we can reach accuracy up to 97%, by using optimal features with low overhead.

The rest of this paper is structured as follows. We briefly describe the related works in Sect. 2 and we introduce our ML based approach for malware detection in Sect. 3. We present the experimental evaluation and discuss our outcomes in Sect. 4. Finally, we conclude our work and we present possible future developments in Sect. 5.

2 Related Work

In this section we overview related works that rely on ML algorithms for detecting malware targeting the Android platform using as features data that can be extracted by static analysis of the app. We review, only the most relevant results to the approach proposed in this paper. This means that we consider only works that rely on features such as Application Programming Interfaces (APIs), system calls, permissions.

Applications Programming Interfaces and System Calls: A major group of Android malware detection techniques, are using systems calls or/and API calls. System calls have been used extensively for malware detection on personal computers [8–10]. So similar approaches have been introduced for detection malware in Android. More specifically, authors in [11] introduce a solution for detecting, among the others, polymorphic malware by monitoring system calls. Authors, assess the effectiveness of SVM algorithm over a dataset of 150 apps and and indicate accuracy up to 90%. Similarly, in [12] authors describe a malware detection tool called MALINE. In their solution they use as features system calls frequency as well as the corresponding call graphs. MALINE for the classification relied on SVM, Random Forest, LASSO and Ridge Regularization. Depending on the feature selection and the employed classifier accuracy results ranges between 85% to 97%. SafeDroid [13] provides another solution for Android malware detection that uses APIs as a feature, instead of relying on system calls, for retrofitting ML. It consists of the features extraction and the classification reporting services. SafeDroid considers in its analysis 743 APIs that are most frequent to malware apps, and demonstrates detection accuracy 99%, 98% and 97% for Random Forest, K-NN and SVM respectively. In a more coarse grained approach introduced in [14] authors make an analysis of ML classifiers efficiency for detecting malware using as a feature APIs packages. Authors have evaluated their idea using three well known algorithms *i.e.,* SVM, J48 and Random Forest, over 205 benign and 207 malware apps. Result indicate that detection accuracy can be as high as 92% for SVM and Random Forest, while for J48 reaches up to 89%.

Permissions: Permissions are an important factor for the proper operation of any given app, and reflect the access to sensitive resources as they have been defined by Android OS. For that reason, permissions have been considered as an alternative source of features for detecting malware in Android. Authors in [15] assess the accuracy of seven well known classifiers using as a feature app's permission on a data set consisted of 200 malicious and 200 benign Android apps. In this setup, authors demonstrate for SVM accuracy up to 95%, while for the remaining classifiers the accuracy levels are 88.6% for C4.5, 91,6% for JRip, 82.5 for Naive Bayes (NB). Permission risk rank solution introduced in [16] studies to what extend Android malware can be detected based on the permission they define in app's manifest. To do so authors first select the riskiest permission set (*i.e.,*, the most relevant from a statistical point of view) by employing statistical techniques such as T-test, and Principal Component Analysis (PCA) and secondly evaluate ML classifiers using the riskiest permission. Authors demonstrate accuracy as high as 99% for SVM, Decision Tree, and Random Forest under specific configuration using a high volume data set. In the same mind-set, the APK Auditor [17] relies on logistic regression, while evaluates its performance using a dataset of 6900 malware and 1850 benign apps. Results indicate accuracy up to 88%. Similarly, authors in [18] rely on different approaches (Gain Ratio Attribute Evaluator, Relief Attribute Evaluator) to select the optimal features to use for detecting malware with the support of machine learning algorithms. Authors evaluate their solution over a data set of 3784 apps, however, they do not report which of them was malware. The demonstrated results show accuracy up to 94%.

Other Features and Possible Combinations: One of the earliest works that combines APIs and permissions was introduce in a solution named DroidAPIMiner [7], in which well-known classifiers were assessed over on a dataset of 20000 and 3987 benign and malware apps. In this set-up authors demonstrate accuracy up to 99% in the case of K-NN, while other ML classifiers perform accuracy around 96%. In the same direction, authors in [19] combine also APIs and permissions assessing the performance of Random Forest, SVM, and Neural Networks. Authors evaluate their approach using a dataset of 5000 goodware and 1260 malware apps, and demonstrate accuracy up to 94% for all the classifiers depending on the setup. An extended set of features, such as intents, permissions, system commands, suspicious API calls, were used as input to ML in [20]. Authors accomplish an assessment different classifiers using an extended data set consisted of 18.677 malware and 11.187 benign apps correspondingly; their analysis indicates an F-score up to 0.96. In an earlier work Drebin [6] presents a holistic approach for malware detection based on SVM by using a the broadest set of features (Hardware components, Requested Permissions, App components, Filtered intents, Restricted API calls, Used permissions Suspicious API calls, Network addresses) in comparison with other related works. In the same mind set, as the other related works, Drebin evaluates its performance on the biggest public available dataset (consists of 123453 benign and 5560 malware apps). Drebin results shows accuracy 94% in the case of SVM.

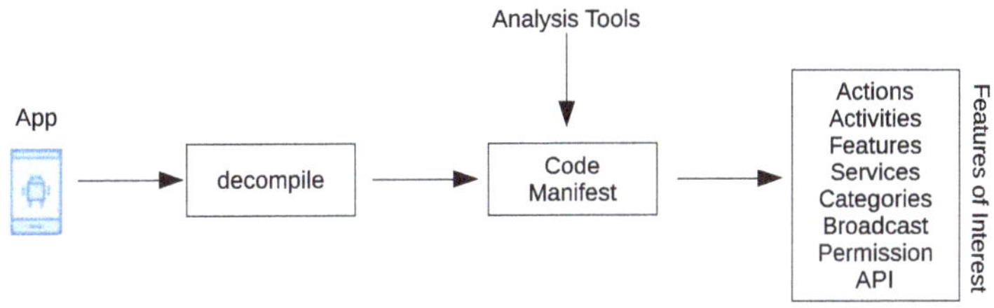

Fig. 1. High level architecture for feature extraction

3 Methodology

3.1 Overview

Any ML based approach for malware detection for Android platform consist of three phases: (a) apps collection, (b) feature extraction, and (c) apps' classification. This procedure is a standard textbook process [21] and is followed in any solution that builds on the advantages of ML.

So, similar to other ML approaches, to study the effectiveness of ML on malware detection for Android OS, firstly a collection of goodware and malware apps should be developed. To compile the appropriate datasets, we follow two different approaches. Briefly, we built a specific tool for downloading and getting access to a numerous of goodware from Google play, while for malware we made a literature research for public available data sets, as currently there is no central repository available that can be used to download them.

Secondly, towards a large scale analysis framework for ML based detection we develop the appropriate tools to automate and parellelize the experiments; especially for extracting the features of interest. Figure 1 illustrates the high level approach for extracting the features.

More specifically, we decompile any given app using the apktool[2] in order to get access to app's (original) resources, that is, among the others: (a) the manifest, (b) resources (images, fonts), (c) the source code, and (d) libs. In this work we focus on (a) app's manifest and (b) source code as they contain the core information for app's execution, however, we are planning to incorporate the remaining resources in our model in a future work. Our tools are able to distinguish the resources and analyze them in order to extract the features of interest and compile the corresponding vectors required in the third phase.

Thirdly, the classification phase takes place in order to identify whether a give app is a goodware or malware using the extracted features. In this last phase, apps' classification procedure relies on the data set of features extracted in the second phase to retrofit ML both for training and testing.

3.2 Feature Set

As various features can be used in classification, similar to other related work, we rely on features that can be extracted from any Android app namely actions, fea-

[2] https://ibotpeaches.github.io/Apktool/.

tures, services, categories, APIs, and permissions. However, based on the current related work analysis there is not any indication which of the available features are the optimal choices for Android malware detection. So at the classification phase we employ also a selection feature procedure to identify the optimal ones. In our approach for each and every feature (i) we assume that there is a vector F_i of n dimensions, where i is the type of feature. Each dimension of a vector corresponds to a binary variable which is set to 1 in case that the app contains an instance of the feature i, otherwise to 0. An app A(j) gain access a subset of these features sets F_i depending on its capabilities. In a formal way, each vector F_i is calculated using the formula 1. It should be mentioned that instead of applying the ML classification directly to raw features the statistical properties variance and sum are employed in the initial feature set. Table 1 overviews the features used to retrofit ML for the classification.

$$F_i = \{X_0, X_1, X_2 \ldots X_n\} \tag{1}$$

Since it is not known a priori which features are the most relevant feature, feature selection is a necessary step for any ML assisted detecting framework. Based on the related work there are not indications which are the dominant features for detecting malware on Android. The goal is to reduce the dimension of the data set to improve the classification time but without sacrificing the performance beyond a certain threshold. Most of the feature selection algorithms can be divided in two broad categories. The first one determines features significance using a ML algorithm that is to ultimately be applied to the data, while the second one estimates features dominance by using heuristics based on general characteristics of the data. The formers are referred to as wrappers and the latter as filters. In this paper, we assess both approaches for identifying the optimal features. For the wrapper approach we rely on the ML classifier SVM [21], and for filter we use the RELIEF algorithm proposed in [22].

Table 1. Used features for ML classification

ID	Feature description
1	Variance of actions
2	Variance of features
3	Variance of services
4	Variance of categories
5	Variance of API
6	Variance of permissions
7	Sum of actions
8	Sum of features
9	Variance of services
10	Variance of categories
11	Variance of API
12	Variance of permissions

3.3 Machine Learning Classification

Various ML algorithms are available in literature that can be used in binary classification. Recall that our goal is to provide ML based platform capable of determining whether an app is malware or not with a certain degree. So, in this preliminary work two well known ML algorithms have been used for assessing the effectiveness of ML in this domain; the K-Nearest Neighbour (K-NN) and the Support Vector Machine (SVM). We do not go into details about ML classifiers, and we refer the interested reader to relevant state-of-the-art sources such as [21].

K-NN: is probably among the most simple ML algorithms that classifies new instances based on a similarity function *e.g.,* Euclidean, Manhattan, in comparison with instances used in the training phase of classification. Considering a dataset of instances *i.e.,* the features of the goodware and malware apps in our case, each instance is classified to belong to a specific class by using the majority of votes from its neighbours, with the case being assigned to the class most common amongst its K nearest neighbour measured by the distance function.

SVM: is capable of defining a model, based on labeled data, for classifying a new instance to a specific class. To do so, SVM finds a linear separating hyperplane, that is the decision boundary, with an optimal margin among the different classes. A popular kernel, which used in this paper also, is the Radial Basis Function (RBF) kernel.

4 Evaluation

To test the accuracy and efficiency of the classifiers presented in the previous section, we performed a comparative analysis of different configurations and applied them on the collected datasets. There are two aspects to validate with regard to our work, namely the validity of (a) relevant features, and (b) the classification model and process itself.

4.1 Data Set Configuration

In our evaluation two data sets were used. The first data set (named Dataset-1) was balanced and composed by two subsets of 1300 goodware and malware apps respectively. We used this dataset to identify the optimal parameters *i.e.,* the most relevant features and evaluate ML accuracy. We assess also the effectiveness of K-NN and SVM classifiers using an unbalanced dataset (named Dataset-2) which consist of 31000 goodware and 1300 malware apps, and relying on optimal parameters that have been selected from the first dataset.

For classifiers evaluation we used a 10-fold approach where each collection of statistical features is divided into ten blocks. Nine blocks from each set of data are used for training and one block is held out for testing. The training and testing process is repeated ten times until each of the ten blocks has been held out and classified. Thus, each block of statistical features is used once for classification and nine times for training.

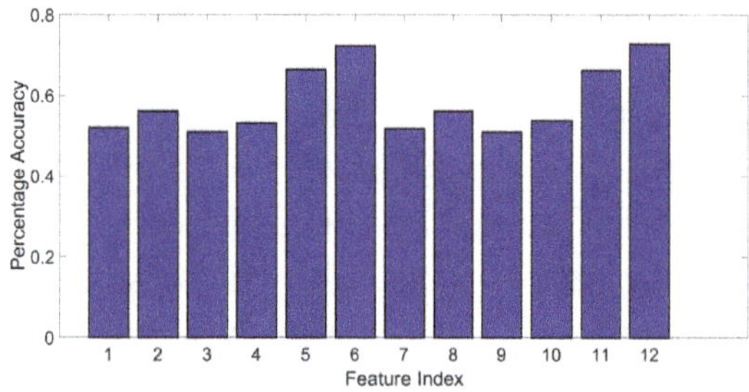

Fig. 2. Features relevance based on a wrapper approach using the SVM

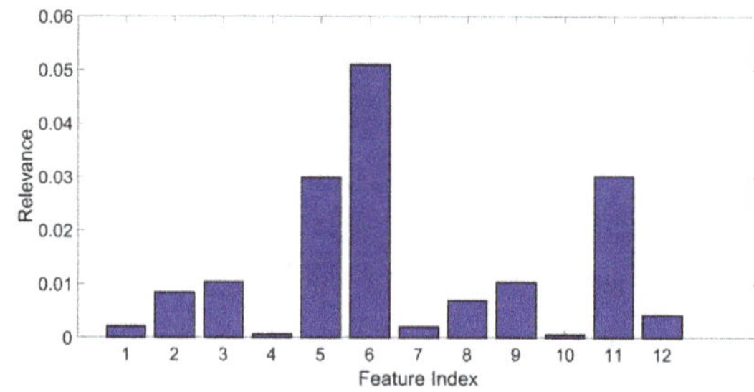

Fig. 3. Predictor relevance weight on the basis of the RELIEF algorithm

4.2 Classification Metrics

To evaluate the performance of a classifier one might use different types of metrics. For the needs of this paper we rely on accuracy that is defined as the percentage of correctly classified instances over the total instances, and is calculated according to the formula 2.

$$Accuracy = TP + TN/TP + TN + FP + FN \tag{2}$$

4.3 Results

At the first step of our approach we should select the dominant features following both a wrapper and a filter approaches as briefly described in Sect. 3). In the first case we use the SVM, while for the second we rely on RELIEFF algorithm. Figures 2 and 3 reports on the features with the highest relevance for both approaches respectively.

More specifically, we employ SVM over every single feature to identify their importance in malware detection. The values of the optimization parameters in this specific case are BoxConstraint = 5 and Scaling Factor = 5. According to this approach the dominant features are the variance and the sum of APIs and permissions in which accuracy ranges between 70% to 75%. To validate this outcome we employ also a filter selection approach by using the RELIEFF algorithm. In that case outcomes demonstrate that the variance of APIs and permissions, as well as the sum of APIs are the features with the highest relevance. In this point it should be noted that none of the related works identify the most relevant features that should be used as input to ML. The only work that select the dominant features is proposed in [16], nevertheless, they focus only on permissions.

So considering the outcomes of the two feature selection approaches we opt the variance and the sum of APIs and permissions as the features to be used for retrofitting ML classifiers, that are the $[5, 6, 11, 12]$ of the Table 1. Using this set of features we evaluate the performance of both the SVM and K-NN. Our preliminary results demonstrate (see Fig. 4) accuracy up to 95% for SVM and

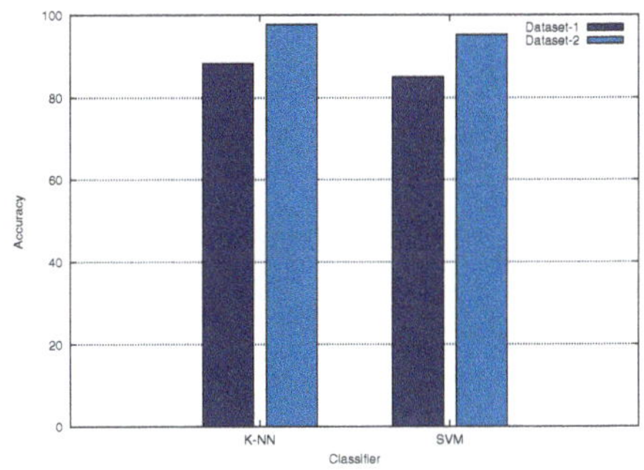

Fig. 4. K-NN and SVM accuracy for the dominant features [5, 6, 11, 12].

up to 97% for K-NN in the case of the extended dataset (Dataset-2). This means that the dataset size influence the detection accuracy. For both ML algorithms K-NN and SVM the performance is enhanced approximately to 10%. However, additional tests should be taken place for validating this outcome. For instance how the size of malware subset influence the accuracy.

Although some of the related works (*i.e.,* Safedroid [13, 16], *etc.*) report accuracy up to 99%, we believe that our approach, relying on statistical features, can be an alternative option for detecting malware on Android. This is because the related works use the initial data as input to ML classifiers instead of depending on statistical transformation, and thus they perform on higher dimensions that on one side offer higher accuracy. On the other side, such approaches introduce additional processing overhead for the classification. So as there is always a trade-off between security and performance our initial outcomes demonstrate a promising solution without sacrificing accuracy. We are planning to provide a detailed analysis with regard to processing overhead that ML classifiers face in a future work.

5 Conclusions and Future Work

Apps intrinsic properties can be a valuable ally, among the others, in order to identify apps that tend to have malicious behaviour. In this paper we have described the main components for evaluating ML classifiers accuracy for detecting malware on Android platform. In our approach, we rely on the statistical properties *i.e.,* variance, mean of the initial selected feature set, and we opt the most dominant features by using the outcomes of Relief algorithm and SVM classifier. This way, ML classifiers operates on a lower dimension space, and thus less overhead can be introduced. Our initial results show accuracy up to 97%.

Though our results are promising other related works demonstrate accuracy up to 99%. For that reason, we foresee additional tests and configurations in order to reach this level of accuracy without imposing high overhead. Furthermore, the current analysis should be supported with other features that might be critical for malware detection such as (a) Cryptographic libraries, (b) application source code update, and (c) dynamic code loading presence.

References

1. Statista: Mobile Internet Usage Worldwide. https://www.statista.com/topics/779/mobile-internet/
2. Abadi, M., Budiu, M., Erlingsson, Ú., Ligatti, J.: Control-flow Integrity. In: Proceedings of the 12th ACM Conference on Computer and Communications Security, CCS 2005, pp. 340–353. ACM, New York (2005)
3. Portokalidis, G., Keromytis, A.D.: Fast and practical instruction-set randomization for commodity systems. In: Proceedings of the 26th Annual Computer Security Applications Conference, ACSAC 2010, pp. 41–48. ACM, New York (2010)
4. Enck, W., Gilbert, P., Han, S., Tendulkar, V., Chun, B.G., Cox, L.P., Jung, J., McDaniel, P., Sheth, A.N.: TaintDroid: an information-flow tracking system for realtime privacy monitoring on smartphones. ACM Trans. Comput. Syst. **32**(2), 5:1–5:29 (2014)
5. Ma, K., Liu, M., Guo, S., Ban, T.: MonkeyDroid: detecting unreasonable privacy leakages of android applications. In: Arik, S., Huang, T., Lai, W.K., Liu, Q. (eds.) ICONIP 2015. LNCS, vol. 9491, pp. 384–391. Springer, Cham (2015). https://doi.org/10.1007/978-3-319-26555-1_43
6. Arp, D., Spreitzenbarth, M., Gascon, H., Rieck, K.: DREBIN: effective and explainable detection of android malware in your pocket (2014)
7. Aafer, Y., Du, W., Yin, H.: DroidAPIMiner: mining API-level features for robust malware detection in android. In: Zia, T., Zomaya, A., Varadharajan, V., Mao, M. (eds.) SecureComm 2013. LNICST, vol. 127, pp. 86–103. Springer, Cham (2013). https://doi.org/10.1007/978-3-319-04283-1_6
8. Madani, P., Vlajic, N.: Towards sequencing malicious system calls. In: 2016 IEEE Conference on Communications and Network Security (CNS), pp. 376–377, October 2016
9. Patanaik, C.K., Barbhuiya, F.A., Nandi, S.: Obfuscated malware detection using API call dependency. In: Proceedings of the First International Conference on Security of Internet of Things, SecurIT 2012, pp. 185–193. ACM, New York (2012)
10. Alazab, M., Venkatraman, S., Watters, P., Alazab, M.: Zero-day malware detection based on supervised learning algorithms of API call signatures. In: Proceedings of the Ninth Australasian Data Mining Conference - AusDM 2011, vol. 121, pp. 171–182. Australian Computer Society, Inc., Darlinghurst (2011)
11. Wahanggara, V., Prayudi, Y.: Malware detection through call system on android smartphone using vector machine method. In: 2015 Fourth International Conference on Cyber Security, Cyber Warfare, and Digital Forensic (CyberSec), pp. 62–67, October 2015
12. Dimjašević, M., Atzeni, S., Ugrina, I., Rakamaric, Z.: Evaluation of android malware detection based on system calls. In: Proceedings of the 2016 ACM on International Workshop on Security And Privacy Analytics, IWSPA 2016, pp. 1–8. ACM, New York (2016)
13. Goyal, R., Spognardi, A., Dragoni, N., Argyriou, M.: SafeDroid: a distributed malware detection service for android, pp. 59–66, November 2016
14. Westyarian, Rosmansyah, Y., Dabarsyah, B.: Malware detection on android smartphones using API class and machine learning. In: 2015 International Conference on Electrical Engineering and Informatics (ICEEI), pp. 294–297, August 2015
15. Milosevic, N., Dehghantanha, A., Choo, K.K.R.: Machine learning aided android malware classification. Comput. Electr. Eng. **61**(Suppl. C), 266–274 (2017)

16. Wang, W., Wang, X., Feng, D., Liu, J., Han, Z., Zhang, X.: Exploring permission-induced risk in android applications for malicious application detection. IEEE Trans. Inf. Forensics Secur. **9**(11), 1869–1882 (2014)
17. Talha, K.A., Alper, D.I., Aydin, C.: APK auditor: permission-based android malware detection system. Digit. Investig. **13**(Suppl. C), 1–14 (2015)
18. Pehlivan, U., Baltaci, N., Acartürk, C., Baykal, N.: The analysis of feature selection methods and classification algorithms in permission based Android malware detection. In: 2014 IEEE Symposium on Computational Intelligence in Cyber Security (CICS), pp. 1–8, December 2014
19. Qiao, M., Sung, A.H., Liu, Q.: Merging permission and API features for android malware detection. In: 2016 5th IIAI International Congress on Advanced Applied Informatics (IIAI-AAI), pp. 566–571, July 2016
20. Fereidooni, H., Conti, M., Yao, D., Sperduti, A.: ANASTASIA: ANdroid mAlware detection using STatic analySIs of Applications. In: 2016 8th IFIP International Conference on New Technologies, Mobility and Security (NTMS), pp. 1–5, November 2016
21. Witten, I.H., Frank, E.: Data Mining: Practical Machine Learning Tools and Techniques. Morgan Kaufmann Series in Data Management Systems, 2nd edn. Morgan Kaufmann Publishers Inc., San Francisco (2005)
22. Robnik-Šikonja, M., Kononenko, I.: Theoretical and empirical analysis of ReliefF and RReliefF. Mach. Learn. **53**(1), 23–69 (2003)

Signalling Attacks in Mobile Telephony

Mihajlo Pavloski(✉)

Department of Electrical and Electronic Engineering, Imperial College, London, UK
m.pavloski13@imperial.ac.uk

Abstract. Many emerging Internet of Things devices, gateways and networks, rely either on mobile networks or on Internet Protocols to support their connectivity. However it is known that both types of networks are susceptible to different types of attacks that can significantly disrupt their operations. In particular 3rd and 4th generation mobile networks experience signalling related attacks, such as signalling storms, that have been a common problem in the last decade. This paper presents a generic model of a mobile network that includes different end user behaviours, including possible attacks to the signalling system. We then suggest two attack detection mechanisms, and evaluate them by analysis and simulation based on the generic mobile network model. Our findings suggest that mobile networks can be modified to be able to automatically detect attacks. Our results also suggest that attack mitigation can be carriedout both via the signalling system and on a "per mobile terminal" basis.

Keywords: Signalling storms · Denial of Service
Mathematical modelling · Detection · Mitigation

1 Introduction

The security of computing systems is based on three basic principles: confidentiality, integrity and availability. System availability of networks and services can be significantly impaired by *Denial of Service* (DoS) attacks which can take various forms which differ according to the technology being considered. Thus DoS attacks for IP (Internet Protocol) networks differ significantly from DoS attacks against mobile networks.

Mobile networks are susceptible to DoS attacks, mostly because of the networks' openness to the Internet, the use of deterministic procedures, and the use of basic design principles based on "typical" user behaviour. In the last ten years, there were huge advances from an algorithmic, manufacturing 'and software perspective, pushing forward the innovation of mobile smart devices and applications, which operate over a mobile network - while the network itself did not keep up with the pace. One of the problems caused by these circumstances, is the appearance of DoS attacks known as *signalling storms*, which overload the control plane of the mobile network, unlike many previously known data plane flooding attacks [26,37].

E. Gelenbe et al. (Eds.): Euro-CYBERSEC 2018, CCIS 821, pp. 130–141, 2018.
https://doi.org/10.1007/978-3-319-95189-8_12

Network security is ranked as one of the top priorities for future self-aware networks [18], which is why there is well established research in the field. Furthermore, while work in [21,33] focuses on a general defensive approach against DoS attacks in future networks, signalling storm specific research can roughly be categorised in the following groups: problem definition and attacks classification [5,30,31,41]; measurements in real operating networks [11,40]; modelling and simulation [1,27]; impact of attacks on energy consumption [10,12]; attacks detection and mitigation, using counters [19,20,38], change-point detection techniques [32,42], IP packet analysis [28], randomisation in RRC's functions [45], software changes in the mobile terminal [8,34], monitoring terminal's bandwidth usage [39], and detection using techniques from Artificial Intelligence [2]. As we look to the future, such as the Internet of Things (IoT), various forms of attacks will also have to be considered [6,9].

The communication schemes may be opportunistic [25] and attacks may use similar opportunistic means to access IoT devices, viruses and worms will continue being important threats [16] and they can diffuse opportunistically through a network [17], video input is one of the uses of the IoT and video encoding [7] can also be specifically targeted by attacks. Furthermore, many network services are organised to flow over overlay networks [4] that cooperate with the Cloud [43,44] to offer easy deployable and flexible services for the mobile network control plane. Thus research needs to remain alert to such developments.

In this paper we mainly use stochastic modelling techniques, in order to represent complex communication protocols, such as the Radio Resource Control (RRC), in simplified mathematic terms. In particular we use open and closed queueing networks with multiple classes of calls. The analysis of these systems is first described by Jackson [29], Basket et al. [3], and Gelenbe [14,15,22–24], among others. A second approach is used through discrete event simulation, whose results in many cases are comparable to queueing network models. More precisely, we are using a specialised Mobile Networks Security Simulator (SECSIM) created by in research group [27].

The remainder of the paper is organised as follows. In Sect. 2 we present a queueing network model of a generic architecture of a mobile network, and model normal and attack behaviour in Sect. 2.2. In Sect. 3 we present two attack detection techniques, respectively in Sects. 3.1 and 3.2, and a mitigation technique in Sect. 3.3. Finally, Sect. 4 concludes the paper.

2 Network Model

The proposed model describes a general network architecture, focusing on its radio access part, from the perspective of both, the control and data (user) plane. It's envisioned to represent different mobile network technologies, which is achieved through representing the resource allocation in the data plane as a "black box" where different technologies' sub-models can be plugged in, while keeping the control plane unchanged. The core part of the model consists only the basic elements of the architecture, such as multiple Base Station (BS) nodes connected to a single network controller consisting one Signalling Server (SS) node, and the communication stage nodes.

2.1 Model Description

An example workflow captured by our model goes as follows. When a mobile terminal wants to communicate, it sends a connection setup request through the control plane of the network, which needs to be processed at the BS and the SS. If admitted, the mobile proceeds to communicate in the data plane of the network, in sessions (each comprising multiple data packets), which we denote as *calls* in the rest of the paper. If a call is blocked, then the mobile may either leave the network or attempt to reconnect with a probability that depends on the type of call. There are two types of calls or connection setup requests in the network: (i) normal calls representing traffic from legitimate users or applications, and (ii) attack traffic generated by malicious or malfunctioning applications that may overload the network. The network model is open with calls joining and leaving the network, representing for example the arrival and departure of mobiles to WiFi areas. Its parameters are defined in Table 1 where the superscript $r \in \{n, a\}$ denotes the class of a call (normal n or attack a) (Fig. 1).

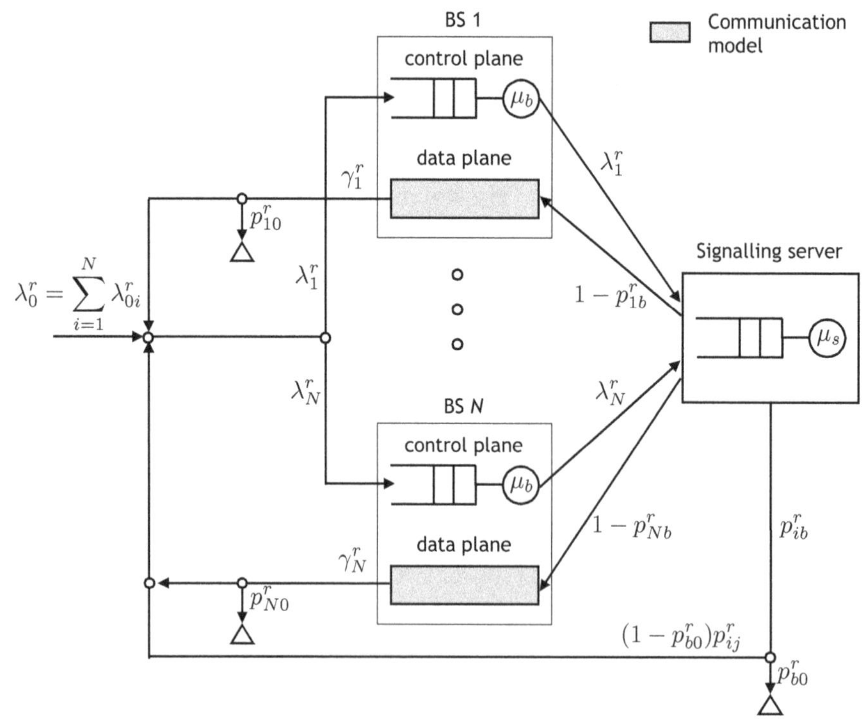

Fig. 1. A model of the radio access part of a mobile network.

We assume calls arrive from outside the network according to independent Poisson processes and the service times in each node are independent and exponentially distributed. Since calls may be blocked at the SS due to congestion,

Table 1. The main parameters of the model

N	Number of cells covered by one signalling server
λ_{0i}^r	Rate of new class-r calls joining cell $i \in \{1,\ldots,N\}$, which corresponds to mobile phone activations and handovers by roaming users
λ_i^r	Rate of class-r connection requests traversing the i-th BS. These include calls joining from outside the network, calls that have been successfully served and return as new calls, and calls that retry connecting after not being admitted at cell j due to insufficient data channels
λ_s^r	Total rate of class-r calls arriving at the SS, $\lambda_s^r = \sum_{i=1}^N \lambda_i^r$
γ_i^r	Rate of class-r calls that timed out after being admitted to cell i
p_{ib}^r	Proportion of class-r calls not admitted for communication at cell i
p_{b0}^r	Probability that a blocked class-r call leaves the network; p_{b0}^a represents attackers' stubbornness while p_{b0}^n reflects human persistence
p_{i0}^r	Proportion of class-r calls leaving the network after successful service at cell i
p_{ij}^r	Proportion of class-r calls joining cell j after being blocked at cell i given that they stay in the network, i.e. $\sum_{j=1}^N p_{ij} = 1$
μ_b	Class-independent service rate of connection requests in the BS, representing the *cell signalling capacity*
μ_s	Class-independent service rate of connection requests in the SS, representing the *SS capacity*
t_0^r	Inactivity timer

the aggregate arrival processes at different parts of the network are not Poisson. Nevertheless, to simplify matters so as to obtain analytical solutions, we make the approximation that all flows within the network are Poisson. The service time distribution for the BS and SS nodes in the signalling stage is same for both classes of calls, because the signalling procedure undertaken by the network does not distinguish call classes. On the other hand, in the communication stage, the service time distribution is distinct for different classes of calls because of the different bandwidth usage behaviour of the normal and malicious calls.

The flow of calls in the above model could be expressed in a closed form as follows. The total arrival rate of class-r connection requests at BS i is the sum of the rates of (i) new calls, (ii) returning calls that timed out, and (iii) calls that were blocked at a cell j by the SS and are attempting to connect at cell i:

$$\lambda_i^r = \underbrace{\lambda_{0i}^r}_{\text{new calls}} + \underbrace{\gamma_i^r(1-p_{i0}^r)}_{\text{reconnecting after timeout}} + \underbrace{\sum_{j=1}^N \lambda_j^r p_{jb}^r (1-p_{b0}^r) p_{ji}^r}_{\text{joining after being blocked at cell } j \text{ due to congestion}}, \tag{1}$$

where the proportion of blocked calls p_{ib}^r and the rate of admitted calls that has timed out γ_i^r depend on λ_j^r, $\forall j$. The model as presented is suitable for modelling different mobile technologies under an attack. More details, and a comparison of the attacks' influence on two groups of technologies, are presented in [36].

2.2 User Behaviour Model

An important part of the network model is the user behaviour model. In general, the two classes of calls have different service time distributions. A normal call, for example web browsing traffic, would usually happen in bursts which would occupy the channel for a longer period. Contrary, attack calls would usually transfer only a small portion of data in order to trigger quick bandwidth allocations and deallocations. The two patterns are depicted on Fig. 2 with T^n denoting the *normal session duration* and T^a the *attack session duration*, and s and q respectively denoting "service" and "quiet" periods. In this part we need to estimate the average session duration $E[T^r] = 1/\mu^r$.

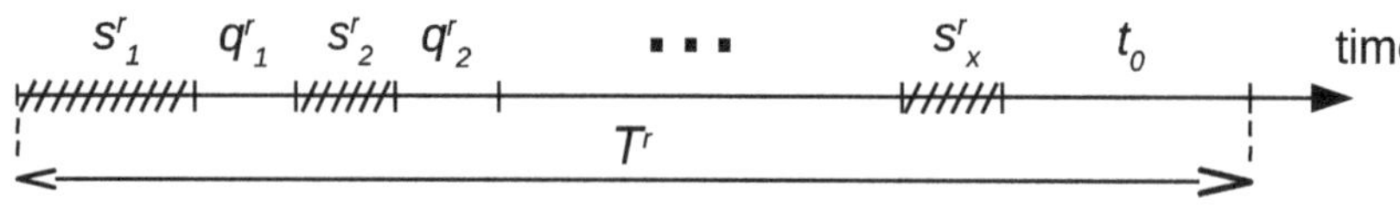

Fig. 2. The user behaviour model describing the duration of a single data session T^r of class r.

Figure 2 could be translated to a Markov Chain model as in Fig. 3, using the states: service (S), quiet (Q), and end of session (F). The transitions among S and Q states are controlled with α^r, and β^r, where $1/\alpha^r$ is the average communication time of a class-r burst, and $1/\beta^r$ is the average duration of a quiet (inactivity) period, regarding class-r calls. The timeout rate is given with $\tau = 1/t_0$.

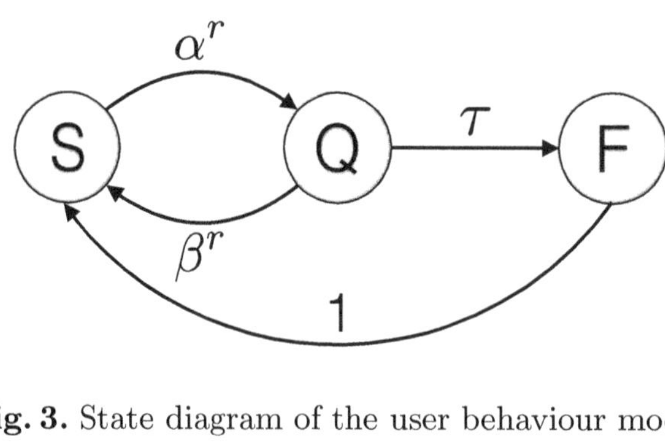

Fig. 3. State diagram of the user behaviour model.

Let us denote with Π_i the probability of the session being in one of the states $\{S, Q, F\}$. The average session duration could be found using the following ratio:

$$\frac{\Pi_S + \Pi_Q + \Pi_F}{1 + E[T^r]} = \Pi_F.$$

Solving the balance equations yields the state probabilities in equilibrium, and the above equation solves to:

$$(\mu^r)^{-1} = E[T^r] \equiv \frac{1}{\mu^r} = \frac{1}{\alpha^r} + \frac{1}{\tau} + \frac{\beta^r}{\alpha^r \tau}. \tag{2}$$

In the above expression, one can see that when the timeout is very short, with $\tau \to \infty$, the average session duration tends to the communication time of a single burst $1/\alpha^r$. Modifying the α^r and β^r parameters, this modelling approach can be used to investigate different traffic types, and different attack patterns.

3 Detection and Mitigation

In this Section, we first present two real-time storm detection mechanisms based on counting channel allocations and monitoring bandwidth usage. Both are tested in the SECSIM simulator. The mitigation mechanism employs an idea of using a adjustable inactivity timer, and is tested with the model in Sect. 2.

3.1 Counter Detection

Description. The *Counter detection mechanism* enables detection of signalling storms per mobile terminal in real-time. It is based on counting the repetitive bandwidth allocations of same channel type (eg. a shared FACH or dedicated DCH channel in a 3G UMTS network). It is envisioned as a lightweight mechanism that should not impose any processing, storage, and memory problems if implemented on a mobile terminal.

Decision Making. The mechanism requires two input parameters: the time instances of bandwidth allocation and the type of bandwidth allocation, which are stored in memory for the duration of a time window of length t_w. A decision of an attack being detected is simply taken when the number of repetitions reaches a predefined threshold called *counter threshold* - n. The length of the window t_w is chosen such that $t_w > n \cdot t_I$, where t_I the duration of the inactivity timer of the attacked state. The upper limit of t_w is set according the memory and storage capacities of the device on which it is implemented.

Evaluation. Figure 4 shows the performance of the described detection algorithm using a ROC curve, as calculated with the SECSIM simulator. A threshold of $n = 3$ could be a suitable choice resulting in around 40% true positive detection p_{tp} and less than 0.2% false positive detection p_{fp}.

3.2 Bandwidth Monitoring Detection

The *Bandwidth monitoring detection mechanism* uses a simple idea of tracking the bandwidth usage of each mobile terminal in a given sliding time window, and calculating a cost function to estimate the likelihood of a terminal performing a signalling attack. It's based on previous analyses which showed that signalling storms are inefficient bandwidth users. The mechanism monitors two input parameters: the total time that the terminal spends while allocated bandwidth within a given time window t_w (denoted with t_D, and t_F respectively for DCH and FACH states in 3G UMTs), and the time which the mobile terminal is allocated bandwidth but does not transfer any data in a time window t_w (denoted with t_{Di} and t_{Fi}). Whenever resources are de/allocated, the detector calculates the ratio $\frac{t_{Fi}+t_{Di}}{t_F+t_D}$, which is then rolled in time using the Exponential Weighted Moving Average (EWMA) algorithm as:

$$C[k] = \alpha \frac{t_{Fi}[k] + t_{Di}[k]}{t_F[k] + t_D[k]} + (1-\alpha)C[k-1], \tag{3}$$

where $k \in \mathbb{N} > 0$ is the index of the state change, $0 \leq \alpha \leq 1$ is a weight parameter and $C[0] = \frac{t_{Fi}[0]+t_{Di}[0]}{t_F[0]+t_D[0]}$ is the initial cost value. As defined, C is between 0 and 1 with values closer to 1 indicating higher probability of an attack.

Decision Making. For decision making, we define two thresholding rules, and a rule based on the cost function. Observing the cost C, and having calculated an average C_{avg} over all historical C values, a simple rule of $C \geq \beta C_{avg}$ can be used to detect an attack. A second rule is using an *upper threshold* θ^+ above which we make a decision of an attack. This rule helps in detecting attacks with very small attack rate, for which the cost function rule cannot be used, because $\beta C_{avg} > 1$. A second threshold is defined as *lower threshold* θ^- below which we assume a normal behaviour of the mobile terminal. The θ^- rule helps in protecting mobiles with normal behaviour of high activity, which are assigned a low value of C_{avg}. Setting up these thresholds should be based on offline traffic analysis by the mobile operators.

Evaluation. The performance of the Bandwidth monitoring detection algorithm is depicted with the ROC curve on Fig. 4, which combines the p_{fp} and p_{tp} metrics. Values in the top-left corner of the graph are most desirable, as it produces the highest true positive and lowest false positive detection probabilities. The simulation results suggest that $\alpha = 0.3$ is the most suitable value, producing 95% true positive and 0.04% false positive detection.

3.3 Dynamic Timer Mitigation

Mobile networks today use a fixed value for the inactivity timer with possible manual corrections for specific situations, which we consider to not be the optimal approach. While it plays an important role in controlling radio resource

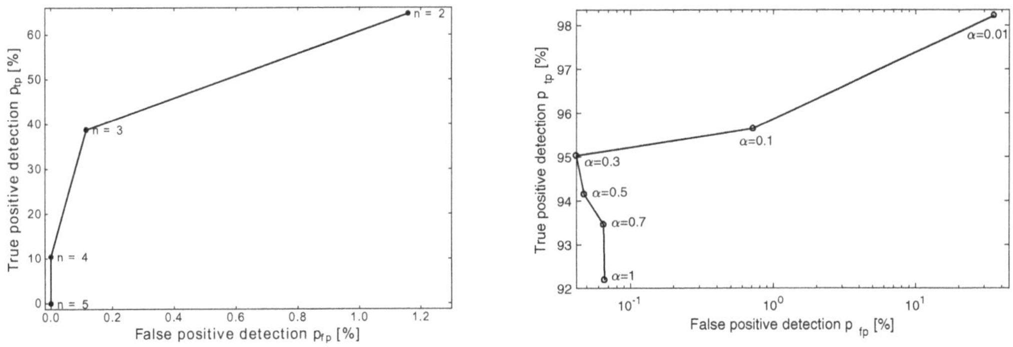

Fig. 4. ROC curves of the counter detector (left), and bandwidth detector (right).

allocation, being a trade-off parameter between the bandwidth reuse and number of connections, this section examines if it could possibly play a similar role controlling the impact of a signalling attack on the network. For this, we propose a *dynamic inactivity timer* which is set as a function of the network load, and use the model described in Sect. 2 to study its performance.

One possible approach is to increase the timer linearly with the load on the signalling server, after a signalling load threshold value θ is reached:

$$t_0(\lambda_s) = \begin{cases} t_0^{min} & \lambda_s \leq \theta, \\ \frac{(t_0^{max} - t_0^{min})}{\lambda_s^{max} - \theta} \cdot (\lambda_s - \theta) + t_0^{min} & \lambda_s > \theta, \end{cases}$$

where λ_s^{max} is the maximum allowed load on the signalling server, θ is a load threshold and t_0^{min} and t_0^{max} are the minimum and maximum values that the timer can take. In real operating network, these parameters need to be estimated from statistical observations.

Results. Using the model in Sect. 2 we select a data plane model with $m = 20$ non-sharing data channels, such as in 3G UMTS Rel. 99, modelled as M/M/m/m Markov chain [35]. The rest of the parameters are selected as follows: $\lambda_0^n = 1, p_0^n = 0.9, p_0^a = 0.1, p_{b0}^n = 0.9, p_{b0}^a = 0.3$, $\lambda_e = 0.05, t_0 = 2\,\text{s}$ (static), $t_0^{max} = 60\,\text{s}, t_0^{min} = 2\,\text{s}, \lambda_s^{max} = 5\,\text{calls/s}\theta = 3\,\text{calls/s}$.

Figure 5 shows the comparison of a static and dynamic inactivity timer for varying network load. The dynamic timer activates when the threshold load θ is reached and manages to lower the resulting network load, compared to the static approach. Although the timer can play a control role, it cannot completely mitigate a signalling storm. One downside of using this approach is increasing the portion of normal calls that don't get a service. Therefore, the timer controls the trade-off between the signalling load in the network and the number of unserviced normal calls.

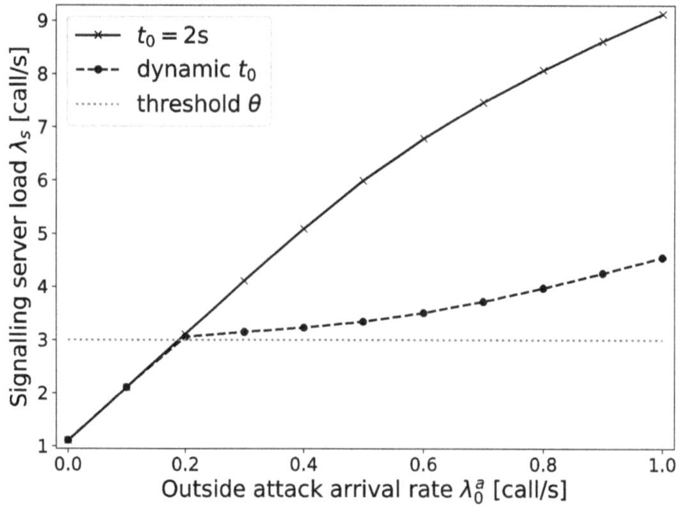

Fig. 5. Signalling server load for static and dynamic inactivity timer.

4 Conclusions

This paper has briefly explained the ongoing research in the field of mobile networks security, looking at in particular, signalling related attacks. It introduced a generic mathematical model of the radio access part of a network, which can be used to model different mobile technologies, and different user patterns. The model was afterwards used to examine an attack mitigation technique using a modified inactivity timer. The two proposed attack detection mechanisms were implemented in a simulation environment and their evaluation showed satisfactory results of 95% true positive and 0.04% false positive detection. Recent work has used the Random Neural Network [13] for attack detection [2] and we expect that further results will become available with similar machine learning techniques.

References

1. Abdelrahman, O.H., Gelenbe, E.: Signalling storms in 3G mobile networks. In: IEEE International Conference on Communications (ICC 2014), Communication and Information Systems Security Symposium, Sydney, Australia, June 2014, pp. 1023–1028 (2014)
2. Abdelrahman, O.H.: Detecting network-unfriendly mobiles with the random neural network. Prob. Eng. Inf. Sci. **30**, 514–531 (2016)
3. Baskett, F., Chandy, K.M., Muntz, R.R., Palacios, F.G.: Open, closed, and mixed networks of queues with different classes of customers. J. ACM **22**, 248–260 (1975)
4. Brun, O., Wang, L., Gelenbe, E.: Big data for autonomic intercontinental communications. IEEE Trans. Sel. Areas Commun. **34**(3), 575–583 (2016)
5. Choi, Y., Yoon, C., Kim, Y.S., Heo, S.W., Silvester, J.A.: The impact of application signaling traffic on public land mobile networks. IEEE Commun. Mag. **52**, 166–172 (2014)

6. Collen, A., et al.: Ghost - safe-guarding home IoT environments with personalised real-time risk control. In: Gelenbe, E., et al. (eds.) Euro-CYBERSEC 2018. CCIS, vol. 821, pp. 68–78. Springer, Cham (2018)
7. Cramer, C.E., Gelenbe, E.: Video quality and traffic QoS in learning-based subsampled and receiver-interpolated video sequences. IEEE J. Sel. Areas Commun. **18**, 150–167 (2000)
8. Delosières, L., Sánchez, A.: DroidCollector: a honeyclient for collecting and classifying android applications. In: Czachórski, T., Gelenbe, E., Lent, R. (eds.) Information Sciences and Systems 2014, pp. 175–183. Springer, Cham (2014). https://doi.org/10.1007/978-3-319-09465-6_19
9. Domanka, J., Gelenbe, E., Czachorski, T., Drosou, A., Tzovaras, D.: Research and innovation action for the security of the Internet of Things: the SerIoT project. In: Gelenbe, E., et al. (eds.) Euro-CYBERSEC 2018. CCIS, vol. 821, pp. 101–118. Springer, Cham (2018)
10. Francois, F., Abdelrahman, O.H., Gelenbe, E.: Impact of signaling storms on energy consumption and latency of LTE user equipment. In: Proceedings of the 7th IEEE International Symposium on Cyberspace safety and security (CSS 2015), New York, August 2015
11. Francois, F., Abdelrahman, O.H., Gelenbe, E.: Feasibility of signaling storms in 3G/UMTS operational networks. In: Mandler, B., et al. (eds.) IoT360 2015. LNICST, vol. 169, pp. 187–198. Springer, Cham (2016). https://doi.org/10.1007/978-3-319-47063-4_17
12. Francois, F., Abdelrahman, O.H., Gelenbe, E.: Towards assessment of energy consumption and latency of LTE UEs during signaling storms. In: Abdelrahman, O.H., Gelenbe, E., Gorbil, G., Lent, R. (eds.) Information Sciences and Systems 2015. LNEE, vol. 363, pp. 45–55. Springer, Cham (2016). https://doi.org/10.1007/978-3-319-22635-4_4
13. Gelenbe, E.: Reseaux neuronaux aleatoires stables. Comptes Rendus de l'Academie des Sciences Serie 2 **310**(3), 177–180 (1990)
14. Gelenbe, E.: Probabilistic models of computer systems. Acta Informatica **12**(4), 285–303 (1979)
15. Gelenbe, E.: Product-form queueing networks with negative and positive customers. J. Appl. Prob. **28**, 656–663 (1991)
16. Gelenbe, E.: Dealing with software viruses: a biological paradigm. Inf. Secur. Tech. Rep. **12**, 242–250 (2007)
17. Gelenbe, E.: A diffusion model for packet travel time in a random multi-hop medium. ACM Trans. Sens. Netw. (TOSN) **3**, 10 (2007)
18. Gelenbe, E.: Self-aware networks. In: 2011 Fifth IEEE International Conference on Self-Adaptive and Self-Organizing Systems (SASO), pp. 227–234. IEEE (2011)
19. Gelenbe, E., Abdelrahman, O.H.: Countering mobile signaling storms with counters. In: Mandler, B., et al. (eds.) IoT360 2015. LNICST, vol. 169, pp. 199–209. Springer, Cham (2016). https://doi.org/10.1007/978-3-319-47063-4_18
20. Gelenbe, E., Abdelrahman, O.H., Gorbil, G.: Detection and mitigation of signaling storms in mobile networks. In: 2016 International Conference on Computing, Networking and Communications (ICNC), pp. 1–5. IEEE (2016)
21. Gelenbe, E., Loukas, G.: A self-aware approach to Denial of service defence. Comput. Netw. **51**, 1299–1314 (2007)
22. Gelenbe, E., Mitrani, I.: Analysis and Synthesis of Computer Systems, vol. 4. World Scientific, Singapore (2010)
23. Gelenbe, E., Muntz, R.R.: Probabilistic models of computer systems-part I (exact results). Acta Informatica **7**(1), 35–60 (1976)

24. Gelenbe, E., Pujolle, G.: Introduction aux Réseaux de Files d'Attente. Edition Hommes et Techniques, Eyrolles (1982)
25. Gorbil, G., Gelenbe, E.: Opportunistic communications for emergency support systems. Procedia Comput. Sci. **5**, 39–47 (2011)
26. Gorbil, G., Abdelrahman, O.H., Gelenbe, E.: Storms in mobile networks. In: Proceedings of the 9th ACM Symposium on QoS and Security for Wireless and Mobile Networks (Q2SWinet 2014), pp. 119–126, September 2014
27. Gorbil, G., Abdelrahman, O.H., Pavloski, M., Gelenbe, E.: Modeling and analysis of RRC-based signaling storms in 3G networks. IEEE Trans. Emerg. Top. Comput. **4**, 1–14 (2015). Special Issue on Emerging Topics in Cyber Security
28. Gupta, A., Verma, T., Bali, S., Kaul, S.: Detecting MS initiated signaling DDoS attacks in 3G/4G wireless networks. In: 2013 Fifth International Conference on Communication Systems and Networks (COMSNETS), pp. 1–60, January 2013
29. Jackson, J.R.: Jobshop-like queueing systems. Manag. Sci. **10**, 131–142 (1963)
30. Kambourakis, G., Kolias, C., Gritzalis, S., Park, J.H.: Dos attacks exploiting signaling in UMTS and IMS. Comput. Commun. **34**, 226–235 (2011)
31. Kotapati, K., Liu, P., Sun, Y., LaPorta, T.F.: A taxonomy of cyber attacks on 3G networks. In: Kantor, P., et al. (eds.) ISI 2005. LNCS, vol. 3495, pp. 631–633. Springer, Heidelberg (2005). https://doi.org/10.1007/11427995_82
32. Lee, P.P.C., Bu, T., Woo, T.: On the detection of signaling DoS attacks on 3G wireless networks. In: Proceedings - IEEE INFOCOM, pp. 1289–1297 (2007)
33. Loukas, G., Oke, G., Gelenbe, E., et al.: Defending against Denial of service in a self-aware network: a practical approach. In: NATO Symposium on Information Assurance for Emerging and Future Military Systems. Ljubljana, Slovenia (2008)
34. Mulliner, C., Liebergeld, S., Lange, M., Seifert, J.P.: Taming Mr Hayes: mitigating signaling based attacks on smartphones. In: Proceedings of the International Conference on Dependable Systems and Networks (2012)
35. Pavloski, M.: A performance approach to mobile security. In: 2016 IEEE 24th International Symposium on Modeling, Analysis and Simulation of Computer and Telecommunication Systems (MASCOTS), pp. 325–330, September 2016
36. Pavloski, M.: Performance analysis of mobile networks under signalling storms. Ph.D. thesis, Imperial College London (2017)
37. Pavloski, M., Gelenbe, E.: Signaling attacks in mobile telephony. In: Proceedings of the 11th International Conference on Security and Cryptography (SECRYPT 2014), pp. 206–212, August 2014
38. Pavloski, M., Görbil, G., Gelenbe, E.: Counter based detection and mitigation of signalling attacks. In: Obaidat, M.S., Lorenz, P., Samarati, P. (eds.) SECRYPT 2015 - Proceedings of the 12th International Conference on Security and Cryptography, Colmar, Alsace, France, 20–22 July, 2015, pp. 413–418. SciTePress (2015)
39. Pavloski, M., Görbil, G., Gelenbe, E.: Bandwidth usage—based detection of signaling attacks. In: Abdelrahman, O.H., Gelenbe, E., Gorbil, G., Lent, R. (eds.) Information Sciences and Systems 2015. LNEE, vol. 363, pp. 105–114. Springer, Cham (2016). https://doi.org/10.1007/978-3-319-22635-4_9
40. Qian, F., Wang, Z., Gerber, A., Mao, Z.M., Sen, S., Spatscheck, O.: Characterizing radio resource allocation for 3G networks. In: Proceedings of the 10th ACM SIGCOMM Conference on Internet Measurement, IMC 2010, pp. 137–150. ACM, New York(2010)
41. Ricciato, F., Coluccia, A., D'Alconzo, A.: A review of DoS attack models for 3G cellular networks from a system-design perspective. Comput. Commun. **33**, 551–558 (2010)

42. Wang, H., Zhang, D., Shin, K.G.: Change-point monitoring for the detection of DoS attacks. IEEE Trans. Dependable Secur. Comput. **1**, 193–208 (2004)
43. Wang, L., Brun, O., Gelenbe, E.: Adaptive workload distribution for local and remote clouds. In: 2016 IEEE International Conference on Systems, Man, and Cybernetics (SMC), pp. 003984–003988. IEEE (2016)
44. Wang, L., Gelenbe, E.: Adaptive dispatching of tasks in the cloud. IEEE Trans. Cloud Comput. **6**(1), 33–45 (2018)
45. Wu, Z., Zhou, X., Yang, F.: Defending against DoS attacks on 3G cellular networks via randomization method. In: 2010 International Conference on Educational and Information Technology (ICEIT), pp. V1-504–V1-508 (2010)

Static Analysis-Based Approaches for Secure Software Development

Miltiadis Siavvas[1,2](✉), Erol Gelenbe[1], Dionysios Kehagias[2], and Dimitrios Tzovaras[2]

[1] Imperial College London, London SW7 2AZ, UK
{m.siavvas16,e.gelenbe}@imperial.ac.uk
[2] Centre for Research and Technology Hellas, Thessaloniki, Greece
{diok,dimitrios.tzovaras}@iti.gr

Abstract. Software security is a matter of major concern for software development enterprises that wish to deliver highly secure software products to their customers. Static analysis is considered one of the most effective mechanisms for adding security to software products. The multitude of static analysis tools that are available provide a large number of raw results that may contain security-relevant information, which may be useful for the production of secure software. Several mechanisms that can facilitate the production of both secure and reliable software applications have been proposed over the years. In this paper, two such mechanisms, particularly the vulnerability prediction models (VPMs) and the optimum checkpoint recommendation (OCR) mechanisms, are theoretically examined, while their potential improvement by using static analysis is also investigated. In particular, we review the most significant contributions regarding these mechanisms, identify their most important open issues, and propose directions for future research, emphasizing on the potential adoption of static analysis for addressing the identified open issues. Hence, this paper can act as a reference for researchers that wish to contribute in these subfields, in order to gain solid understanding of the existing solutions and their open issues that require further research.

Keywords: Software security · Reliability · Static analysis
Vulnerability prediction · Checkpoint and Restart

1 Introduction

Software security is usually considered an afterthought in the software development lifecycle (SDLC). It is normally added after the implementation of software products chiefly by using mechanisms aiming to prevent malicious individuals from exploiting existing vulnerabilities (e.g. intrusion detection systems). However, the increasing number of the security incidents reported annually indicates the inability of these mechanisms to fully protect the software products against

E. Gelenbe et al. (Eds.): Euro-CYBERSEC 2018, CCIS 821, pp. 142–157, 2018.
https://doi.org/10.1007/978-3-319-95189-8_13

attacks [1,2]. To this end, software houses have shifted their focus towards building software products that are highly secure (i.e. as vulnerability-free as possible) from the ground up.

A software vulnerability is a weakness in the specification, development, or configuration of software such that its exploitation can violate a security policy [3]. Most of the software vulnerabilities stem from a small number of common programming errors [4]. These errors are introduced by the developers during the coding phase, mainly due to their lack of security expertise [5], or due to the accelerated production cycles [6]. However, it is unrealistic to expect from them to remember thousands of security-related bug patterns and bad practices that they should avoid. As a result, efficient tools are required to help them avoid the introduction of such security bugs, and therefore write more secure code [7,8].

Automatic static analysis (ASA) tools have been proven effective in uncovering security-related bugs early enough in the software development process [4]. Their main characteristic is that they are applied directly to the source or compiled code of the system, without requiring its execution [5]. However, since their results comprise long lists of raw warnings (i.e. alerts) or absolute values of software metrics, they do not provide real insight to the stakeholders of the software products. In fact, a great number of ASA tools have been proposed over the years providing a huge volume of such raw data, which may contain security-relevant information that may be useful for secure software development. Hence, appropriate knowledge extraction tools are needed on top of the raw results produced by ASA tools for facilitating the production of secure software.

To this end, the outputs of ASA tools have recently started being used for vulnerability prediction. In fact, recent studies have highlighted the ability of ASA tools to predict software components that contain vulnerabilities (i.e. vulnerable components) [9,10]. The prediction outcome may provide useful insights to project managers about where to focus their testing efforts. However, none of the already proposed vulnerability prediction models (VPMs), especially those that are not based on static analysis, managed to achieve a satisfactory trade-off among accuracy, practicality and performance [10]. The accuracy of the existing VPMs in cross-project prediction is also observed to be poor. In addition to this, static analysis results can be used to facilitate the development of software products that are fault tolerant, and therefore reliable, from the beginning, since they can be used in order to highlight expensive loops and fault-prone components prior of which application-level checkpoints should be inserted. Although several mechanisms have been proposed for assisting developers in the selection and insertion of application-level checkpoints (e.g. [11,12])), they failed to provide complete recommendations, while the required development effort is high.

To sum up, we can state that the current trend in the field of Software Security is the development of knowledge-discovery mechanisms for the intelligent processing of the results produced by ASA tools to support the secure software development. A thorough literature review led us to the conclusion that the exploitation of the raw results produced by ASA tools in order to conduct (i) prediction of vulnerable software components, and (ii) optimum checkpoint recommendation constitute two interesting subfields with potential positive impact on the production of secure and reliable software products. To this end, the purpose of this paper is to review the most significant attempts in each one of the aforementioned subfields, identify existing open issues of high interest, and potentially propose direction for future research, emphasizing on how these mechanisms may leverage from static analysis. Hence, this paper can act as a reference for researchers that wish to contribute in these subfields, in order to gain a solid understanding of existing solutions and identify open issues that require further research. All these are presented in detail in the rest of the paper.

2 Literature Review

2.1 Vulnerability Prediction Modeling

Vulnerability prediction modeling is a subfield of software security, aiming to predict software components that are likely to contain vulnerabilities (i.e. vulnerable components). Vulnerability prediction models (VPMs) are normally built based on machine learning techniques that use software attributes as input, to discriminate between vulnerable and neutral components. These models can be used for prioritizing testing and inspection efforts, by allocating limited test resources to potentially vulnerable parts. Although it is a relatively new area of research, a great number of VPMs has already been proposed in the related literature. As stated in [9], the main VPMs that can be found in the literature utilize software metrics [13–22], text mining [23–28], and security-related static analysis alerts [10,29–32] to predict vulnerabilities. These types of VPMs are analyzed in the rest of this section.

Software Metrics. Shin and Williams [13,14] were the first to investigate the ability of software metrics, particularly complexity metrics, to predict vulnerabilities in software products. Several regression models were built based on different subsets of the studied metrics in order to discriminate between vulnerable and non-vulnerable (i.e. neutral) functions. The results of their analysis (which was based on Mozilla JavaScript Engine) suggest that complexity metrics can be used only as weak indicators of software vulnerabilities. Based on the same code base, Nguyen and Tran [15] evaluated the ability of semantic complexity in vulnerability prediction. The models which were built using semantic complexity demonstrated on average a better predictive performance compared to the best models of [14]. In [16] an empirical study conducted on Mozilla Firefox and Whiteshark revealed the ability of execution complexity metrics (i.e. complexity metrics that are collected during the code execution) to discriminate between vulnerable and neutral functions. In particular, VPMs built on these features were found to predict vulnerability-prone functions with similar prediction performance to commonly used statically collected complexity metrics, but with lower inspection effort.

The main purpose of the previous studies was to empirically evaluate the experts' opinion that software complexity is the enemy of software security. The weak relationship that was generally observed between complexity and vulnerabilities led to the need for incorporating additional metrics in vulnerability prediction. Towards this end, Chowdhury and Zulkernine [17], based on 52 releases of Mozilla Firefox, highlighted the ability of complexity, coupling, and cohesion (CCC) metrics to indicate the existence of vulnerabilities in software files. Based on this observation, the same authors proposed a framework for the automatic prediction of vulnerable files based on CCC metrics [18]. The VPMs that were built demonstrated a high accuracy and tolerable false positive rate. Shin et al. [19] examined the ability of complexity, code churn, and developer activity to discriminate between vulnerable and neutral files in two widely-used software products, namely Mozilla Firefox and Red Hat Linux Kernel. The results of the analysis suggest that the selected metrics may be used as sufficient indicators of vulnerabilities in software files, while those retrieved from software history may be stronger indicators than the commonly-used complexity measurements.

Moshtari et al. [20], contrary to previous studies, examined and highlighted the ability of software complexity to predict vulnerabilities between software products (i.e. cross-project prediction), based on 5 open-source software products, namely Mozilla Firefox, Linux Kernel, Apache Tomcat, Eclipse, and Open SCADA. Similarly, in a recent study [21], the predictive power of complexity and coupling in cross-project prediction was compared. The results revealed that complexity metrics had better predictive power than coupling metrics in cross-project prediction, while the combination of traditional complexity measurements with a newly proposed set of coupling metrics led to an improvement in the recall of the best complexity-based VPM that was built in this work.

Text Mining. Apart from software metrics that have received much attention in the field of vulnerability prediction, VPMs using text mining have also demonstrated highly promising results. In this approach, the source code of the software artifacts is parsed and represented as a set of tokens (i.e. keywords). Subsequently, these tokens are intuitively combined and used to train vulnerability predictors. Neuhaus et al. [23] were the first to adopt a form of text mining for vulnerability prediction. They proposed Vulture, a VPM that predicts vulnerabilities in software components based on their import statements and function calls, which are parsed from their source code. An empirical evaluation of the model on Mozilla Firefox and Thunderbird, revealed that the proposed VPM was able to predict half of all the existing vulnerable components, and about one third of all the predictions were correct. Vulture is also the first known VPM that can be found in the related literature.

A more complete text mining-based prediction approach was introduced by Hovsepyan et al. [24]. According to their technique, each software component is characterized as a series of text terms extracted from their source code along with their associated frequencies, which are then used to forecast whether each component is likely to contain vulnerabilities. An empirical evaluation on 19 versions of a large-scale Android application, revealed that their technique may be promising for vulnerability prediction, as the produced predictors achieved sufficient precision (85% on average) and recall (87% on average). Based on these preliminary results, the same authors conducted a more elaborate empirical study to investigate the validity of their approach [25]. In particular, several VPMs using Naïve Bayes and Random Forest algorithms were constructed and evaluated on a code base of 20 large-scale Android applications. The evaluation results revealed that the predictive power of the proposed models is equal or even superior to what is achieved by state-of-the-art VPMs, which indicates that text mining can be used for the construction of satisfactory VPMs. However, the produced models performed poorly in cross-project prediction, which can be explained by the fact that their predictions are based on text terms, which are highly project-specific features.

Pang et al. [26] proposed an improvement of the aforementioned technique [24,25], by employing N-Gram analysis. According to their proposal, continuous sequences of tokens should be used instead of raw text features for predicting vulnerable components. An empirical evaluation based on 4 android applications (retrieved from the same code base with [25]), revealed that SVM predictors built based on N-Gram technique were able to predict vulnerable components with high accuracy, precision and recall. In a recent replication of their study [27], the same authors observed that the adoption of deep neural networks instead of SVM, can also lead to VPMs with highly satisfactory predictive performance. Despite their promising results, these techniques are too expensive in terms of memory and execution time, due to the nature of their features (i.e. long sequences of text terms), which restricts their practicality.

In [28] a sophisticated two-tier composite approach called VULPREDICTOR was proposed to predict vulnerable files. VULPREDICTOR [28] analyzes text features along with software metrics and is built on top of an ensemble of classifiers. VULPREDICTOR outperforms the state-of-the-art approaches proposed by Walden et al. [33], which use either software metrics or text features for vulnerability prediction, but not both. This indicates that the combination of software metrics with text mining may be promising for vulnerability prediction.

Static Analysis. Limited attempts can be also found in the related literature regarding the ability of security-related static analysis alerts to predict the existence of vulnerabilities. The idea of using static analysis alerts for the identification of attack- or vulnerability-prone software components was inspired by Gegick and Williams [29]. Based on this concept Gegick et al. [30] constructed several VPMs using ASA alerts density, code churn, and lines of code as inputs, while different combinations of these features were also considered. Recursive partitioning and logistic regression was employed for the construction of these models. An empirical evaluation of the produced VPMs on a large commercial telecommunication software system revealed that the model based on ASA alerts density and code churn was the best predictor, being able to detect 100% of the attack-prone components, with 8% false positive rate (FPR). This indicates that ASA alerts can be used effectively for vulnerability prediction, while their combination with other vulnerability indicators (e.g. software metrics) may also be promising. In [31] a replication of the work presented in [30] on a different code base (i.e. a large Cisco software system) led to different observations. In fact, the FPR of the produced model was found to be higher, which suggests that the selection of the code base may influence the predictive performance of the produced models.

Moreover, several recent studies have highlighted the need for refining existing VPMs by using security-specific metrics and ASA alerts as inputs in order to improve their accuracy [32]. To this end, Yang et al. [10] proposed a novel VPM that uses security-specific warnings produced by an ASA tool to predict vulnerable components. The evaluation results revealed that the proposed approach may lead to an improvement of up to 5% in terms of accuracy compared to the state-of-the-art models proposed in [33]. This suggests that the adoption of security-specific warnings, and especially their combination with software metrics, may be beneficial for the production of accurate VPMs.

Comparison of Existing Models. Finally, different empirical studies have shown that text mining-based models exhibit better predictive performance in comparison to other state-of-the-art techniques [9,33,34]. However, they perform poorly in cross-project prediction, which indicates that they are highly project-specific [33], while excessive amount of time and memory is required for their construction and regular application [9,34]. Hence, VPMs that use software metrics (such as complexity, code churns etc.) and density of ASA alerts may be a more viable solution in practice [34], as they are less expensive to build and apply [34], and they perform slightly better in cross-project prediction [33]. This highly suggests that the adoption of security-related ASA alerts and statically collected software metrics may be a promising approach for the construction of more accurate, as well as practical VPMs. Hence, future research attempts should focus towards this direction.

Open Issues and Contributions. Despite the multitude of VPMs that have been already proposed over the years, there are still many open issues that require further investigation. First of all, none of the already proposed techniques managed to achieve a satisfactory trade-off among accuracy, practicality and performance [10]. Accurate VPMs usually provide predictions at the binary level (i.e. file or component level), which is impractical in terms of inspection time, as binaries normally contain hundreds of source files [32]. More practical VPMs that provide predictions at the source code level are usually inaccurate [10] or they produce a large number of false positives (i.e. clean files wrongly predicted to be vulnerable), which renders the inspection process time-consuming and effort-demanding. On the contrary, models that are both accurate and practical, such as text mining-based VPMs [25], are highly expensive to build and apply [25,34]. Thus, a model able to achieve a sufficient compensation among the previously mentioned factors is necessary.

Another issue is that the datasets used in the literature for the derivation of VPMs are constructed based chiefly on reported vulnerabilities of real products. However, not all of the vulnerabilities that a product contains are always reported, and therefore many components that are considered clean in the dataset may in fact be vulnerable. Moreover, the number of vulnerable files that a software product includes is often too small [35], leading to highly imbalanced datasets, which influence significantly the accuracy of the produced predictors [32]. The usage of a highly balanced and sound dataset is expected to improve the accuracy of the produced VPMs. For this purpose, well-known vulnerability code bases like the Juliet suite [36] can be used for the construction of such a dataset.

The last issue is that the existing VPMs perform poorly in cross-project prediction [10]. This is normally due to the fact that they are based on project-specific features for providing their predictions. For instance, as stated previously, text mining VPMs [25] base their prediction on the frequencies of specific text features (i.e. keywords) extracted from the source code of software products, which makes them highly project-specific [33,34]. The usage of security-related software metrics and alerts produced by ASA tools are expected to lead to more generic VPMs (i.e. models with sufficient cross-project performance), as these factors can catch more high-level and abstract attributes of software products.

To sum up, an interesting topic would be to investigate whether the combination of security-specific static analysis alerts and statically collected software metrics, along with the usage of a highly balanced and sound dataset, may lead to a VPM that achieves an acceptable trade-off among accuracy, practicality and performance. Another topic that worths examination is whether such a model demonstrates sufficient prediction performance in cross-project prediction.

2.2 Optimum Checkpoint Recommendation

As will be discussed in the present section, the application-level checkpoint and restart (ALCR) mechanism is the most effective mechanism for building software applications that are fault tolerant from the beginning [37–39]. However, since it is based on the deliberate insertion of checkpoints into the source code, it requires significant expertise and development effort. Early work has considered the start of an execution block in block-structured programs [40] as a natural point to insert checkpoints.

On the otherhand, the optimum checkpoint recommendation (OCR) corresponds to the selection of the optimum source code locations where application-level checkpoints should be inserted, as well as of the optimum checkpointing frequency in case of repetitive processes (e.g. loops). This mechanism is highly useful during the SDLC as it helps developers make informed decisions regarding the optimum placement of the checkpoints, leading to more fault-tolerant and, thus, reliable software applications. In addition, by allowing the automatic insertion of the recommended checkpoints the development effort associated with the ALCR mechanism is reduced, and the developers' productivity remains almost unaffected. In the following sections, the related literature along with the fundamental background concepts of the overall field is provided.

Transaction-Oriented Systems and Optimum Checkpoint Interval. Checkpoint and rollback/recovery is one of the most widely-used mechanisms for adding fault tolerance to software applications [37–39]. It was originally developed for enhancing the reliability of transaction-oriented computer systems (e.g. database or file systems), which are responsible for the sequential processing of incoming transactions [41]. If no fault tolerance mechanism is adopted by these systems, all the transactions need to be re-executed in case of a failure, leading to significant performance burden. According to the checkpoint and rollback/recovery scheme, at predetermined instants of times (i.e. intervals), a snapshot (i.e. a secure valid copy) of all the data that have been successfully processed so far is taken and stored in an area that cannot be affected by failures (e.g. a secondary file system) [41–43]. This stored snapshot is called checkpoint [41–43]. In case of a failure, a rollback/recovery is performed, during which the contents of the checkpoint are copied from the secondary memory to the main memory of the system [44] and all the transactions since the most recent checkpoint are re-executed [41–43]. By using this scheme, the number of transactions that need to be re-executed is significantly reduced.

The major challenge of such systems is the selection of the *optimum checkpoint interval (OCI)*, that is, the time interval between two successive checkpoints that maximizes the system availability [41,43,44]. The term availability corresponds to the probability that the system is available for processing transactions [44,45]. Hence, the vast majority of the research attempts in this field have focused chiefly on the selection of the optimum checkpoint interval (e.g. [44–46]), as well as on the impact that the checkpoint interval may have on other qualities of transaction-oriented systems (e.g. [41,43]). The first attempt for determining the OCI was conducted by Young [46], who attempted to compute the optimum time interval between two successive checkpoints so as to achieve a satisfactory trade-off between the time required for the establishment of a checkpoint, and the time required for the system to recover from a failure. The author proposed a simple yet practical formula for the calculation of the OCI, in which the optimum interval depends on the mean time to failures, as well as on the time required for the creation of a checkpoint.

The selection of the OCI is crucial, as the cost of checkpointing is observed to be high if the checkpoints are frequent [47]. Based on this observation, in [41] the author investigated the impact that the selection of the OCI may have on the system performance. The results of the analysis revealed that the optimum value of the interval between two successive checkpoints that maximizes the system availability, does not optimize its performance as well. Therefore, the OCI should be calculated in a way that a sufficient compensation between the contradictory factors of availability and performance is achieved. Another important parameter of transaction-oriented systems is their response time. Hence, in [43] the authors examined the impact that the selection of the checkpoint interval may have on the availability and the response time of transaction-oriented systems. The results of their analysis revealed that the average response time depends highly on the checkpoint interval, and that the interval that minimizes the average response time is considerably different from the one that maximizes the system availability (i.e. the OCI). The authors also proposed a mathematical model for representing transaction-oriented systems that utilize the checkpoint and rollback/recovery mechanism. This model can be used both for the calculation of the OCI and for the estimation of its impact on important performance measures.

In [44] Gelenbe et al. proved that the checkpoint interval should be deterministic in order to maximize the system availability, and that the OCI is a function of the system load. Based on these observations, the authors proposed a new formula for the calculation of the OCI that also considers the system load among other parameters. In [45] the same authors, in an attempt to further enhance the completeness of the OCI calculation, proposed a formula that takes time dependence into account. In particular, they showed that the OCI is a function of (i) the system load and (ii) the time-dependent failure rate. The results of their analysis also highlighted that the checkpoint interval should be deterministic in order to maximize the availability of the system, further supporting their previous observation [44].

Finally, Gelenbe et al. [47,48] proposed a new fault tolerant mechanism, called failure (or virus) tests, which can be used in conjunction to the traditional checkpoint rollback/recovery technique for further enhancing the reliability of transaction-oriented systems. According to their newly proposed approach, the data and the transaction trail of the system are periodically checked for errors and inconsistencies. If at least one error (or inconsistency) is detected, the system is forced to go through a recovery as if a failure occurred. The authors also proposed a method for the calculation of the OCI, as well as the optimum interval between two successive failure tests that maximizes the system availability.

Long-Running Software Applications. Although the idea of the checkpoint and rollback/recovery has been initially proposed for transaction-oriented systems, it has been also found promising for enhancing the reliability of long-running software applications [49,50]. Long-running software applications are considerably more complex compared to the transaction-oriented systems, since even the most simple software programs consist of a tremendous number of execution states [51]. Therefore, periodically saving only the successfully processed data of a software application is not enough for ensuring its reliability. On the contrary, a "safe copy" (i.e. a checkpoint) of the overall execution state of the application should be taken and saved in a secondary file system that cannot be tampered by failures [37,52]. This safe state can be used for recovering the execution of the program in case of a failure.

It should be noted that the majority of software failures are caused by design and implementation errors [51]. However, due to the high complexity of modern software products, it is impossible to guarantee their correctness, even with the most exhaustive validation and verification. Hence, since software applications are inevitably bundled with such issues, effective fault tolerance mechanisms are required to enhance their reliability [51,53]. Several rollback/recovery-based fault tolerance mechanisms have been proposed over the years for enhancing the reliability of long-running software applications, including: (i) the Recovery Block (RB) scheme [51], (ii) the N-Version Programming (NVP) [54], and (iii) the Checkpoint and Restart (CR) [50] technique.

Despite their benefits in enhancing the reliability of software applications, NVP and RB approaches are characterized by high development costs, since they require the division of the source code into individual blocks and the definition of alternative implementations for each one of these blocks. Therefore, due to these high development costs, as well as to the significant overheads they introduce, their adoption is restricted to very critical applications (e.g. safety-critical applications), in which the reliability is the most important factor [55].

Checkpoint and Restart (CR) is a fault tolerance mechanism widely used for enhancing the reliability of long-running software applications [38,39,50], since it introduces significantly less overheads and development costs, compared to the aforementioned rollback/recovery fault tolerance mechanisms (e.g. [51,54]). A CR mechanism is responsible for keeping a "safe copy" of the current execution state of the software application, and use this "safe copy" for restoring the application in case of a failure. According to [39], three types of CR exist, which are (i) the system-level CR, (ii) the library-level CR, and (iii) the application-level CR, each one of them having its own strengths and shortcomings.

Both system- and library-level CR techniques are reactive approaches for adding fault tolerance, since they allow checkpointing of software applications without requiring any modification to their source code. However, their major shortcoming is that they create checkpoints with large memory footprints, as the entire execution state of the application and the operating system processes is saved, which inevitably contains redundant information. Two representative examples of system- and library-level CR tools are BLCR [56] and DMTCP [57] respectively.

When the CR is built within the application itself, it is called application-level CR (ALCR) [39,58]. Unlike its counterparts, it necessitates changes to the source code of the applications in order to define (i) the locations of the checkpoints, (ii) the checkpointing frequency, and (iii) the data that should be checkpointed. Although it requires significant development effort, it is considered the most effective CR approach [37–39], as it allows the creation of checkpoints with smaller memory footprints, since the minimum amount of information required for restoring the application state is essentially saved. A great number of tools for implementing ALCR in software applications can be found in the related literature [58]. A more detailed description and comparison of these types of CR can be found in [50,58].

Several CR tools and libraries are available for ensuring the reliability of single-process software applications, including the well-known: BLCR [56], and Condor [11]. However, the CR approach has recently become an attractive area of research due to our increasing reliance on long-running multi-process HPC applications. Such applications are characterized by expensive and time-consuming computations, and therefore excessive re-computation should be avoided in case of a failure [37]. For these applications, a distributed CR scheme should be employed, in which the checkpoints of the individual processes that constitute the parallel job should be effectively combined in order to create consistent recovery states of the overall parallel application.

The most common approach for incorporating the CR mechanism into the HPC applications is by integrating it into libraries that are required for the implementation of such applications, like OpenMPI (e.g. [59]), OpenCL (e.g. [12]), and OpenMP (e.g. [37,52]). For instance, in [59] the authors extended the OpenMPI library, which is commonly used by HPC applications, in order to support the CR fault tolerance mechanism. Contrary to previous fault tolerant MPI implementations that were characterized by complicated and difficult to use interfaces [49], the proposed implementation manages to automate the process of constructing the global checkpoint of the parallel application, increasing in that way its usability. In [12], the authors proposed CheCL, a tool for incorporating CR into OpenCL applications, since common CR libraries fail to checkpoint processes that use OpenCL. The main advantage of CheCL is that it does not require the modification of the application source code. Instead, the proposed tool monitors the execution of the software application and all the API calls are forwarded to an API proxy, which stores all the information required for restoring OpenCL objects. The application, which is decoupled from OpenCL calls, is then checkpointed using the BLCR [56] CR library.

As already mentioned, ALCR is the most effective CR mechanism as it incurs minimum overhead compared to its counterparts, but it requires significant development effort, which hinders its adoption in practice. To this end, Rodríguez et al. [52] proposed CPPC, a tool for providing ALCR to message passing applications. The tool manages to reduce the manual effort required by the developers, as it identifies the safe points of the applications where checkpoints should be inserted (i.e. code locations with no inconsistencies), and automatically implements the checkpoints. In fact, it identifies long-running loops and automatically inserts checkpoints at the first safe point of each loop. Losada et al. [37] proposed an application-level checkpointing solution for hybrid MPI-OpenMP applications. In fact, the proposed solution is an extension of the CPPC [52] tool, which allows checkpointing of applications implemented using either MPI or OpenMP, in order to support hybrid MPI-OpenMP applications.

Shahzad et al. [38] proposed CRAFT, a library for incorporating the application level CR fault tolerance mechanism to software applications implemented in C++. Similarly to CPPC [52] and [37], the proposed library aims to reduce the development cost associated with the ALCR mechanism, by allowing the identification of expensive loops and the automatic insertion of the application-level checkpoints. In a recent research attempt, Arora [39] proposed ITALC, a tool that helps the developers in semi-automatically re-engineering their applications to insert the code for the implementation of ALCR mechanism, without compromising their productivity. ITALC identifies hotspots (i.e. expensive loops or suspicious commands) where checkpoints can be inserted, and prompts the user in order to select which of those hotspots should be checkpointed.

Open Issues and Contributions. As already mentioned, among the CR mechanisms, ALCR is considered the most effective, since it leaves the minimum memory footprint, but it requires significant development effort and expertise for its implementation [38,39]. Although several libraries for assisting and automating the insertion of application level checkpoints have already been proposed (e.g. [37–39,52]), they are hindered by a set of shortcomings. Firstly, existing approaches provide incomplete recommendations, since although they identify hotspots for the insertion of the checkpoints (e.g. [39,52]), these hotspots are restricted only to expensive loops. Apart from the expensive loops, failure-prone software artifacts (e.g. classes or methods) should be also identified and checkpoints should be inserted prior to their execution, in order to achieve quick recovery in case of failure. Moreover, in case of expensive loops, existing approaches do not provide recommendations regarding the optimum checkpointing frequency. Static analysis can be used to highlight existing failure-prone components and expensive loops that may require checkpointing. It can be also used to calculate both the logical complexity and the total cost of the application loops, information that can be used for the recommendation of a reasonable checkpointing frequency for the loops that may require checkpointing. Such features are expected to reduce the expertise required for the implementation of the checkpoints, as well as the checkpointing overhead, as both the locations and the frequency of the checkpoints will be optimally defined.

3 Conclusion and Future Work

In the present study, two commonly used mechanisms for enhancing the security and reliability of software products, namely the vulnerability prediction models (VPMs) and the optimum checkpoint recommendation (OCR) mechanisms were examined, by investigating their state-of-the-art. Through our study we identified some interesting open issues regarding the aforementioned mechanisms that can be potentially addressed through static analysis. In particular, none of the existing VPMs that have been proposed so far has managed to achieve a satisfactory trade-off among the contradictory factors of accuracy, practicality and performance, while their predictive performance in cross-project prediction is generally observed to be poor. In addition, although several libraries and tools for assisting developers in the selection and insertion of application-level checkpoints have been proposed, they have failed to provide complete recommendations, since they focus exclusively on expensive loops, while they do not provide any recommendation regarding their checkpointing frequency. Therefore, an interesting direction for future research is to investigate whether the results produced by static analysis tools, can be used in order to (i) construct better VPMs, and (ii) facilitate the optimum selection of application-level checkpoint locations and frequencies.

Acknowledgements. This work is partially funded by the European Union's Horizon 2020 Research and Innovation Programme through SDK4ED project under Grant Agreement No. 780572.

References

1. Salini, P., Kanmani, S.: Survey and analysis on security requirements engineering. Comput. Electr. Eng. **38**(6), 1785–1797 (2012)
2. McGraw, G.: On bricks and walls: why building secure software is hard. Comput. Secur. **21**(3), 229–238 (2002)
3. Krsul, I.: Software vulnerability analysis. Ph.D. thesis, Department of Computer Sciences, Purdue University (1998)
4. Chess, B., McGraw, G.: Static analysis for security. IEEE Secur. Priv. **2**, 76–79 (2004)
5. McGraw, G.: Software Security: Building Security. Addison-Wesley Professional, Boston (2006)
6. Boehm, B., Basili, V.R.: Software defect reduction top 10 list. Computer (2001)
7. Wurster, G., van Oorschot, P.C.: The developer is the enemy. In: Proceedings of the 2008 Workshop on New Security Paradigms, NSPW 2008, pp. 89–97 (2008)
8. Green, M., Smith, M.: Developers are not the enemy! The need for usable security APIs. IEEE Secur. Priv. **14**, 40–46 (2016)
9. Jimenez, M., Papadakis, M., Traon, Y.L.: Vulnerability prediction models: a case study on the linux kernel. In: 2016 IEEE 16th International Working Conference on Source Code Analysis and Manipulation (SCAM), pp. 1–10 (2016)
10. Yang, J., Ryu, D., Baik, J.: Improving vulnerability prediction accuracy with secure coding standard violation measures. In: 2016 International Conference on Big Data and Smart Computing, BigComp 2016, pp. 115–122 (2016)
11. Litzkow, M., Tannenbaum, T., Linvy, M.: Checkpoint and migration of UNIX processes in the condor distributed processing system. Technical report CS-TR-199701346, University of Wisconsin, Madison (1997)
12. Takizawa, H., Koyama, K., Sato, K., Komatsu, K., Kobayashi, H.: CheCL: transparent checkpointing and process migration of OpenCL applications. In: Proceedings of the 25th IEEE International Parallel and Distributed Processing Symposium (2011)
13. Shin, Y., Williams, L.: Is complexity really the enemy of software security? In: Proceedings of the ACM Conference on Computer and Communications Security (2008)
14. Shin, Y., Williams, L.: An empirical model to predict security vulnerabilities using code complexity metrics. In: Proceedings of the 2008 ACM-IEEE International Symposium on Empirical Software Engineering and Measurement (2008)
15. Nguyen, V.H., Tran, L.M.S.: Predicting vulnerable software components with dependency graphs. In: Proceedings of the 6th International Workshop on Security Measurements and Metrics - MetriSec 2010 (2010)
16. Shin, Y., Williams, L.: An initial study on the use of execution complexity metrics as indicators of software vulnerabilities. In: Proceedings of the International Conference on Software Engineering (2011)
17. Chowdhury, I., Zulkernine, M.: Can complexity, coupling, and cohesion metrics be used as early indicators of vulnerabilities? In: Proceedings of the 2010 ACM Symposium on Applied Computing (2010)
18. Chowdhury, I., Zulkernine, M.: Using complexity, coupling, and cohesion metrics as early indicators of vulnerabilities. J. Syst. Archit. **57**, 294–313 (2011)
19. Shin, Y., Meneely, A., Williams, L., Osborne, J.A.: Evaluating complexity, code churn, and developer activity metrics as indicators of software vulnerabilities. IEEE Trans. Softw. Eng. **37**(6), 772–787 (2011)

20. Moshtari, S., Sami, A., Azimi, M.: Using complexity metrics to improve software security. Comput. Fraud Secur. **2013**(5), 8–17 (2013)
21. Moshtari, S., Sami, A.: Evaluating and comparing complexity, coupling and a new proposed set of coupling metrics in cross-project vulnerability prediction. In: Proceedings of the 31st Annual ACM Symposium on Applied Computing, SAC 2016 (2016)
22. Alves, H., Fonseca, B., Antunes, N.: Software metrics and security vulnerabilities: dataset and exploratory study. In: Proceedings of the 2016 12th European Dependable Computing Conference, EDCC 2016 (2016)
23. Neuhaus, S., Zimmermann, T., Holler, C., Zeller, A.: Predicting vulnerable software components. In: Proceedings of the 14th ACM Conference on Computer and Communications Security, CCS 2007, p. 529 (2007)
24. Hovsepyan, A., Scandariato, R., Joosen, W., Walden, J.: Software vulnerability prediction using text analysis techniques. In: Proceedings of the 4th International Workshop on Security Measurements and Metrics, MetriSec 2012, p. 7 (2012)
25. Scandariato, R., Walden, J., Hovsepyan, A., Joosen, W.: Predicting vulnerable software components via text mining. IEEE Trans. Softw. Eng. **40**(10), 993–1006 (2014)
26. Pang, Y., Xue, X., Namin, A.S.: Predicting vulnerable software components through N-gram analysis and statistical feature selection. In: 2015 IEEE 14th International Conference on Machine Learning and Applications (2015)
27. Pang, Y., Xue, X., Wang, H.: Predicting vulnerable software components through deep neural network. In: Proceedings of the 2017 International Conference on Deep Learning Technologies, ICDLT 2017, pp. 6–10 (2017)
28. Zhang, Y., Lo, D., Xia, X., Xu, B., Sun, J., Li, S.: Combining software metrics and text features for vulnerable file prediction. In: Proceedings of the IEEE International Conference on Engineering of Complex Computer Systems, ICECCS 2016, pp. 40–49, January 2016
29. Gegick, M., Williams, L.: Toward the use of automated static analysis alerts for early identification of vulnerability-and attack-prone components. In: Second International Conference on Internet Monitoring and Protection, ICIMP 2007 (2007)
30. Gegick, M., Williams, L., Osborne, J., Vouk, M.: Prioritizing software security fortification through code-level metrics. In: Proceedings of the 4th ACM Workshop on Quality of Protection, pp. 31–38 (2008)
31. Gegick, M., Rotella, P., Williams, L.: Predicting attack-prone components. In: Proceedings of the 2nd International Conference on Software Testing, Verification, and Validation, ICST 2009, pp. 181–190 (2009)
32. Morrison, P., Herzig, K., Murphy, B., Williams, L.: Challenges with applying vulnerability prediction models. In: Proceedings of the 2015 Symposium and Bootcamp on the Science of Security, pp. 4:1–4:9 (2015)
33. Walden, J., Stuckman, J., Scandariato, R.: Predicting vulnerable components: software metrics vs text mining. In: Proceedings of the International Symposium on Software Reliability Engineering, ISSRE, pp. 23–33 (2014)
34. Tang, Y., Zhao, F., Yang, Y., Lu, H., Zhou, Y., Xu, B.: Predicting vulnerable components via text mining or software metrics? An effort-aware perspective. In: Proceedings of the 2015 IEEE International Conference on Software Quality, Reliability and Security, QRS 2015, pp. 27–36 (2015)
35. Shin, Y., Williams, L.: Can traditional fault prediction models be used for vulnerability prediction? Empir. Softw. Eng. **18**(1), 25–59 (2013)
36. Boland, T., Black, P.E.: Juliet 1.1 C/C++ and Java test suite. Computer (Long. Beach. Calif.) **45**(10), 88–90 (2012)

37. Losada, N., Martín, M.J., Rodríguez, G., Gonzalez, P.: Portable application-level checkpointing for hybrid MPI-OpenMP applications. Procedia Comput. Sci. **80**, 19–29 (2016)
38. Shahzad, F., Thies, J., Kreutzer, M., Zeiser, T., Hager, G., Wellein, G.: CRAFT: a library for easier application-level checkpoint/restart and automatic fault tolerance. CoRR (2017)
39. Arora, R.: ITALC: interactive tool for application - level checkpointing. In: Proceedings of the Fourth International Workshop on HPC User Support Tools (2017)
40. Gelenbe, E., Mitrani, I.: Modelling the behaviour of block structured processes with hardware and software failures. In: Iazeolla, G., et al. (eds.) Mathematical Computer Performance and Reliability, pp. 329–339. Elsevier Science Publishers, New York City (1984)
41. Gelenbe, E.: A model of roll-back recovery with multiple checkpoints. In: Proceedings of the 2nd International Conference on Software Engineering, ICSE 1976, Los Alamitos, CA, USA, pp. 251–255. IEEE Computer Society Press (1976)
42. Gelenbe, E.: Model of information recovery using the method of multiple checkpoints. Autom. Remote Control **40**(4), 598–605 (1979)
43. Gelenbe, E., Derochette, D.: Performance of rollback recovery systems under intermittent failures. Commun. ACM **21**(6), 493–499 (1978)
44. Gelenbe, E.: On the optimum checkpoint interval. J. ACM **26**(2), 259–270 (1979)
45. Gelenbe, E., Hernàndez, M.: Optimum checkpoints with age-dependent failures. Acta Informatica **531**, 519–531 (1990)
46. Young, J.W.: A first order approximation to the optimum checkpoint interval. Commun. ACM **17**(9), 530–531 (1974)
47. Gelenbe, E., Hernàndez, M.: Enhanced availability of transaction oriented systems using failure tests. In: 1992 Proceedings of the Third International Symposium on Software Reliability Engineering, pp. 342–350 (1992)
48. Gelenbe, E., Hernández, M.: Virus tests to maximize availability of software systems. Theor. Comput. Sci. **125**(1), 131–147 (1994)
49. Elnozahy, E.N., Alvisi, L., Wang, Y.M., Johnson, D.B.: A survey of rollback-recovery protocols in message-passing systems. ACM Comput, Surv. **34**(1), 375–408 (2002)
50. Egwutuoha, I.P., Levy, D., Selic, B., Chen, S.: A survey of fault tolerance mechanisms and checkpoint/restart implementations for high performance computing systems. J. Supercomput. **65**(3), 1302–1326 (2013)
51. Randell, B.: System structure for software fault tolerance. Science (2) (1975)
52. Rodríguez, G., Martín, M.J., González, P., Touriño, J., Doallo, R.: CPPC: a compiler-assisted tool for portable checkpointing of message-passing applications. Concurr. Comput. Pract. Exp. **22**(6), 749–766 (2010)
53. Carzaniga, A., Gorla, A., Perino, N., Pezzè, M.: Automatic workarounds: exploiting the intrinsic redundancy of web applications. ACM Trans. Softw. Eng. Methodol. **24**(3), 1–42 (2015)
54. Chen, L., Avizienis, A.: N-version programming: a fault-tolerance approach to reliability of software operation. In: Proceedings of the 8th IEEE International Symposium on Fault-Tolerant Computing (FTCS 1978), vol. 1, pp. 3–9 (1978)
55. Armoush, A., Salewski, F., Kowalewski, S.: A hybrid fault tolerance method for recovery block with a weak acceptance test. In: Proceedings of the 5th International Conference on Embedded and Ubiquitous Computing, EUC 2008, vol. 1, pp. 484–491 (2008)
56. Duell, J., Hangrove, P., Roman, E.: The design and implementation of berkeley lab's linux checkpoint/restart. Berkeley Lab Technical report (2002)

57. Ansel, J., Arya, K., Cooperman, G.: DMTCP: transparent checkpointing for cluster computations and the desktop. In: Proceedings of the 2009 IEEE International Parallel and Distributed Processing Symposium, IPDPS 2009 (2009)
58. Walters, J.P., Chaudhary, V.: Application-level checkpointing techniques for parallel programs. In: Madria, S.K., Claypool, K.T., Kannan, R., Uppuluri, P., Gore, M.M. (eds.) ICDCIT 2006. LNCS, vol. 4317, pp. 221–234. Springer, Heidelberg (2006). https://doi.org/10.1007/11951957_21
59. Hursey, J., Squyres, J.M., Mattox, T.I., Lumsdaine, A.: The design and implementation of checkpoint/restart process fault tolerance for open MPI. Architecture (2007)

Author Index

www.ingramcontent.com/pod-product-compliance
Lightning Source LLC
LaVergne TN
LVHW082236200926
848484LV00008B/2360